IMMIGRANT CALIFORNIA

IMMIGRANT CALIFORNIA

*Understanding the Past, Present,
and Future of U.S. Policy*

Edited by David Scott FitzGerald
and John D. Skrentny

Stanford University Press
Stanford, California

Stanford University Press
Stanford, California

Printed in the United States of America on acid-free, archival-quality paper

Library of Congress Cataloging-in-Publication Data

Names: FitzGerald, David, 1972– editor. | Skrentny, John David, editor.
Title: Immigrant California : understanding the past, present, and future of U.S. policy / edited by David Scott FitzGerald and John D. Skrentny.
Description: Stanford, California : Stanford University Press, 2021. | Includes bibliographical references and index.
Identifiers: LCCN 2020020706 (print) | LCCN 2020020707 (ebook) | ISBN 9781503613485 (cloth) | ISBN 9781503614390 (paperback) | ISBN 9781503614406 (ebook)
Subjects: LCSH: Immigrants—California. | California—Emigration and immigration. | California—Emigration and immigration—Government policy. | United States—Emigration and immigration—Government policy.
Classification: LCC JV6920 .I55 2021 (print) | LCC JV6920 (ebook) | DDC 325.794—dc23
LC record available at https://lccn.loc.gov/2020020706
LC ebook record available at https://lccn.loc.gov/2020020707

Cover design: Rob Ehle
Cover imagery: flag—DreiKubik, via pexels.com; paper texture—iStock

Contents

Acknowledgments

This volume is the capstone project of the California Immigration Research Initiative, a four-year project funded by the University of California Office of the President. Faculty and graduate students from across the University of California system came together to better understand one of the most important phenomena affecting not only the state of California but all states in the U.S. and most countries of the world.

We shared those findings through a series of conferences, sixteen policy briefs, and this anthology. The Center for Comparative Immigration Studies (CCIS) at UC San Diego hosted the initiative in coordination with the Center for the Study of International Migration at UCLA, the Center for Research on International Migration at UC Irvine, the Center for Latino Policy Research at UC Berkeley, and the Immigration Research Group at UC Riverside.

We are grateful to the staff at CCIS, especially Ana Minvielle and Warren Tam, who coordinated the many moving parts of the project and kept everything running smoothly and on time. UC San Diego graduate students Gustavo López, Angela McClean, and Karina Shklyan provided invaluable research and editing in preparing the manuscript. The Yankelovich Center for Social Science Research provided financial support.

At Stanford University Press, Marcela Cristina Maxfield was a steadfast champion of the book. She and two anonymous reviewers gave valuable suggestions on the draft. Sunna Juhn stayed on top of the many details.

As this book goes to press, COVID-19 is posing unprecedented challenges to Californians, regardless of whether they were born here, in other states, or abroad. The pandemic is a reminder that our collective well-being depends on finding solutions to our problems together.

Contributors

Marisa Abrajano is a professor in the Department of Political Science at UC San Diego. Her research addresses the racial inequities that exist in the U.S. political system and the ways in which such discrepancies can be rectified. She is the author of four books, numerous peer-reviewed articles, review/invited articles, and book chapters. Her research has been supported by the NSF, the James Irvine Foundation, UCOP, and other funding agencies.

Frank D. Bean is Distinguished Professor of Sociology, Economics, and Education and the founding director of the Center for Research on Immigration, Population, and Public Policy at UC Irvine. Previously, he was director of the Center for Research on Immigration Policy at the Urban Institute, codirector of the RAND/Urban Institute's Ford Foundation–sponsored implementation and evaluation assessment of the 1986 Immigration Reform and Control Act, and Ashbel Smith Professor of Sociology and director of the Population Research Center at the University of Texas, Austin.

Susan K. Brown, professor of sociology at UC Irvine, focuses her research on population, immigrant integration, and urban studies. She is coauthor, with Frank D. Bean and James D. Bachmeier, of *Parents without Papers: Progress and Pitfalls of Mexican American Integration*, winner of the 2016 Otis Dudley Duncan Book Award from the Population Section of the American Sociological Association.

Allan Colbern is an assistant professor of political science at Arizona State University. He is a Presidential Award recipient from the Russell Sage Foundation and Carnegie Corporation (2018–2020) and coauthor of *Citizenship Reimagined: A New Framework for State Rights in the United States* (Cambridge University Press, 2020). His research has been featured in the *Washington Post* and the *Los Angeles Times*.

David Scott FitzGerald is Theodore E. Gildred Chair in U.S.-Mexican Relations, professor of sociology, and codirector of the Center for Comparative Immigration Studies at the University of California, San Diego. FitzGerald's books include *Refuge beyond Reach: How Rich Democracies Repel Asylum Seekers* (Oxford University Press 2019), winner of the American Sociological Association International Migration Section Best Book Award; and *Culling the Masses: The Democratic Origins of Racist Immigration Policy in the Americas* (Harvard University Press 2014), whose awards include the ASA Distinguished Scholarly Book Award.

Lisa García Bedolla is vice provost for graduate studies and dean of the Graduate Division at UC Berkeley. She is also a professor in Berkeley's Graduate School of Education. Her research focuses on understanding the causes of educational and political inequalities in the United States, using cross-disciplinary approaches to examine disparities that cut across the lines of ethnicity, race, gender, class, nativity, and sexuality. She has written five books, earning five national book awards for her work exploring why people choose to engage politically, and has consulted for presidential campaigns and statewide ballot efforts.

Zoltan Hajnal is a professor of political science at UC San Diego. A scholar of racial and ethnic politics, urban politics, immigration, and political behavior, Hajnal is the author of several award-winning books, has published in all of the top political science journals, and has been featured in the *New York Times*, *Washington Post*, and a range of other media outlets.

Taeku Lee is George Johnson Professor of Law and Political Science at UC Berkeley. His interests are in racial and ethnic politics, immigrant political incorporation, public opinion and survey research, identity and inequality, and deliberative and participatory democracy. His past appointments include assistant professor at Harvard, Robert Wood Johnson Scholar at Yale, Fernand

Braudel Senior Fellow at the European University Institute, and Non-Resident Senior Fellow at the Brookings Institution.

Hiroshi Motomura is the Susan Westerberg Prager Distinguished Professor of Law at UCLA. He is the author of two general-audience books, *Americans in Waiting* and *Immigration Outside the Law*, and the coauthor of two law school casebooks, *Immigration and Citizenship* and *Forced Migration*. He is the recipient of many teaching honors, including the UCLA Distinguished Teaching Award in 2014, and was selected as a Guggenheim Fellow for 2018.

Natalie Novick is a PhD candidate in sociology at UC San Diego. Natalie's research focuses on the social practice of entrepreneurship within start-up ecosystems. Her research has taken her to nearly thirty different countries to conduct fieldwork with early-stage start-up founders, investors, and community builders. In addition to her academic work, Natalie serves as an independent expert on small and medium enterprises for the European Commission and leads community outreach at Startup Boost, a global start-up accelerator program based in Los Angeles.

Kristy M. Pathakis is a PhD candidate in American politics at UC San Diego. She studies the effects of social disadvantage on political engagement for underrepresented groups. She is particularly interested in how social roles and cultural norms can create psychological barriers that undermine engagement with, and suppress participation in, politics for many Americans, including women, people of color, and people from disadvantaged socioeconomic backgrounds.

Ninez A. Ponce, MPP, PhD, is a professor in the UCLA Fielding School of Public Health and director of its Center for Health Policy Research. She leads the California Health Interview Survey, the nation's largest state health survey, recognized as a national model for data collection on immigrant health. In 2019, Ponce and her team received the Academy Health Impact award for their contributions to population health measurement to inform public policies.

Stephanie A. Pullés is a doctoral candidate in sociology at UC Irvine. In her work, Pullés integrates theories of immigrant incorporation and economic sociology to investigate the mechanisms that enable or constrain the economic mobility opportunities available to immigrants in the United States, especially for Mexican migrants and later generations.

Riti Shimkhada, MPH, PhD, is a senior research scientist at the Center for Health Policy Research, UCLA Fielding School of Public Health. She has been involved in research in the areas of immigrant health, disaggregated race/ethnicity data, state-level health mandates and policies, health care quality, and impacts of the physical and social environments on health.

John D. Skrentny is professor of sociology at the University of California, San Diego and a former Guggenheim Fellow. His most recent research focuses on workforce development of scientists and engineers, especially the immigration of PhDs to the U.S. His work on this topic has appeared in the *Proceedings of the National Academy of Sciences* as well as in popular media, such as the *Wall Street Journal*. Other work on immigration has focused on comparative policy, especially in East Asia and Europe, where his research has appeared in *International Migration Review* and *Ethnicities*, among others. He is the author or editor of several books related to ethnicity, race, and law, including *After Civil Rights* (Princeton University Press 2014), *The Minority Rights Revolution* (Harvard University Press 2002), and *The Ironies of Affirmative Action* (University of Chicago Press 1996).

Liesel I. Spangler is a PhD candidate at UC San Diego researching the politics of race and ethnicity, elite political behavior, and immigration.

Roger Waldinger is a Distinguished Professor of Sociology, UCLA. He is the author of *The Cross-Border Connection: Immigrants, Emigrants, and Their Homelands* (Harvard University Press, 2015) and, with Renee Luthra and Thomas Soehl, *Origins and Destinations: The Making of the Second Generation* (Russell Sage Foundation, 2018).

IMMIGRANT CALIFORNIA

1   Lessons from California

David Scott FitzGerald and John D. Skrentny

If California were its own country, it would have the world's fifth-largest immigrant population. There are more immigrants in California than there are in several countries where immigration has been exhaustively studied and debated, including the United Kingdom, United Arab Emirates, France, and Canada.[1] California has the most immigrants in the United States (almost eleven million) and the highest share in its population (27%).[2] The state is one of the most important immigrant destinations in the world.

The way these newcomers are integrated into the nation's most populous state will shape its schools, workforce, businesses, public health, politics, and culture for generations to come. Public policies in each of these areas affect integration. Understanding the incorporation of immigrants, defined here as all resident foreign-born individuals, and their descendants is essential for the state's future well-being. Given that immigration is one of the defining political, social, and economic issue of our times—both in the United States as a whole and across the developed world—the lessons of California are essential for anyone interested in human rights, social stability, and economic vitality.

We argue here that although California is unique in several respects, including its large and diverse demography, its powerful economy, and its progressive politics, it is nevertheless a bellwether for other states. Immigration may have slowed during the Trump administration, but demographic change and increased diversity are coming to most states. California provides important lessons for what to expect, and how to manage this new diversity.

Viewing California's history of demographic change shows evidence of, on the one hand, political backlash against rapid immigration and demographic change and, on the other, more accommodating immigration policies enacted once the size of an immigrant population reaches a tipping point. It is important to note that although correlated with demographic shifts, these policies are strongly moderated by partisan politics.

The California experience demonstrates the capacity of a state to absorb very high numbers of newcomers—much higher than the United States as a whole, though the record is not consistent, and the politics and policy have not always been harmonious or effective. High levels of immigration have occurred at the same time as economic growth and appear to have been a locomotive of expansion—nowhere more than in the world-leading technology sector of Silicon Valley. In other sectors, however, there is a more mixed record. The design of education systems to integrate children who arrive speaking languages other than English became highly politicized in the 1990s. The result has been suboptimal policies that track some children into programs that unintentionally downgrade their academic potential. In health care, the state has shown the possibilities of innovating to create new mechanisms guaranteeing access to basic care. However, the federal system also creates serious constraints, particularly given the hostility between the Trump administration and California's elected policymakers. The unsettled legal framework around public health care has generated uncertainties for both immigrants and the native-born seeking medical services. Finally, the state has promoted some areas of immigrant integration, such as allowing unauthorized immigrants to obtain driver's licenses, while doing relatively little to promote naturalization. As a result, as in the rest of the country, many of California's immigrants have not naturalized even though they are eligible, which creates a drag on the full political integration of the state's residents.

By examining the past and present of immigration policy in California, we show how a state that was the national leader in anti-immigrant policies quickly became a standard-bearer for greater accommodation. We argue that by reading these important cases together, other jurisdictions can see the importance of avoiding California's failed policies, its divisiveness, and its highly politicized provision of public services. At the same time, they may see what has worked in the Golden State. For example, the chapters that follow highlight the sometimes-successful leveraging of immigrant skills for technological innovation and the pragmatic adaptation to the realities of a multicultural population and a socially embedded group of long-term residents who lack legal immigration status. The book as a whole thus provides a road map for future prosperity for immigrants and natives alike in California and the rest of the nation.

Demographic Profile of California's Immigrants

Before exploring how California is a bellwether, model, or antimodel, we sketch a portrait of immigrant California and how it came to be where it is now. First, if we look back at the composition of the states since the time of the earliest immigration restrictions in the nineteenth century, we see that California has always been a leader in immigrant reception, hosting a greater percentage of foreign-born residents than the United States as a whole. Figure 1.1 shows that in 1870, 38% of its population was born abroad, compared to 14% in the United States as a whole. From 1960 to 1970, the share of Californians born abroad dipped to a low of 9%, but that figure was still nearly twice as high as in the entire United States. Immigration rapidly increased in the following three decades, to California in particular, and by the 2010s, 27% of Californians were born abroad, twice as high as in the United States as a whole. As sociologist Manuel Pastor (2018, 72) argues, "it is little wonder that anti-immigrant politics made a special debut in California, foreshadowing what would happen to the rest of America in the 2000s and 2010s."

Although California has always had a large immigrant population, the origins of California's immigrants have changed dramatically over time. Figure 1.2 shows that early migration was dominated by Europeans and Asians. Following restrictions on Chinese immigration in 1882, the Gentlemen's Agreement between Japan and the United States in 1907, the imposition of an "Asiatic Barred Zone" in 1917, and the quota acts beginning in 1921, Asian immigration fell sharply and did not return to a large share of the population until after 1965, when the national-origins quotas were dismantled. The Asian share of the total has been slowly increasing ever since. The Latin American share reached around half of all immigrants in 1980, and continued to increase until around 2000, before slowly falling. However, the political debates about immigration continue to focus on Latinos as public awareness lags actual demographic changes.

The United States captured Alta California from Mexico in the 1846–1848 war. The Treaty of Guadalupe gave residents the option of staying and becoming U.S. citizens. They didn't cross the border; the border crossed them. Since

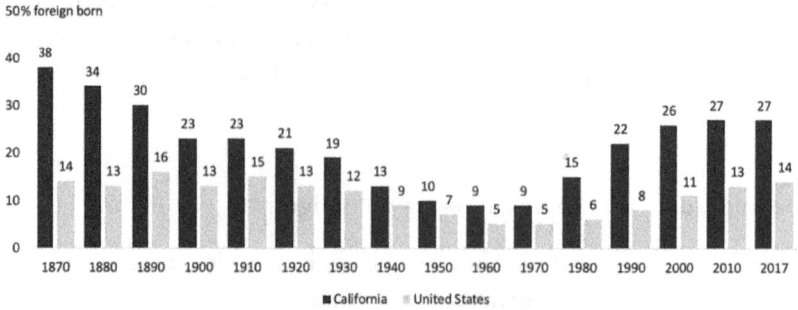

Figure 1.1. Foreign-born share of California and U.S. populations, 1870–2017
Sources: 1870–2010 Decennial Census; 2017 American Community Survey (IPUMS).

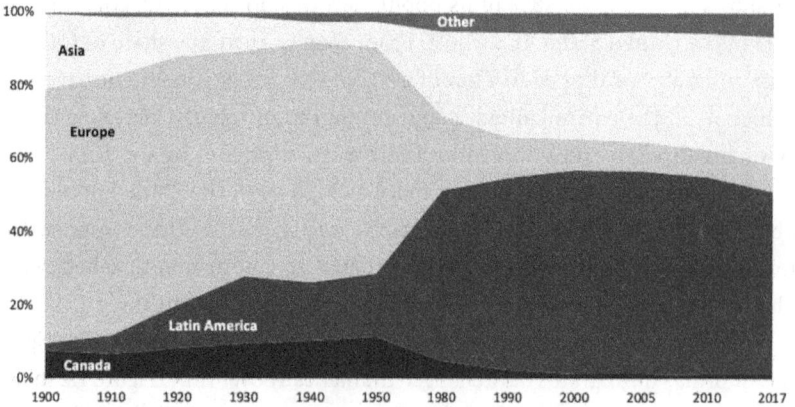

Figure 1.2. California's immigrants by region of origin, 1900–2017
Source: Analysis of 1900–2017 Decennial Census and American Community Survey data (1% IPUMS).

then, Mexico has been a consistently large source of immigration. Mexico continued to be the primary source of the state's immigrants in 2017, accounting for 38% of the foreign born. The four next-largest countries of origin were all in Asia—the Philippines, China, Vietnam, and India. Table 1.1 shows the twenty principal immigrant nationalities. The list shows the extreme diversity of origins, which includes countries such as Thailand, Germany, Armenia, and Peru. New flows are increasingly Asian. Of the immigrants who arrived in California between 2012 and 2016, 58% came from Asia. Just 28% came from Latin

Table 1.1. Twenty principal immigrant countries of origin in California, 2017

Country	Total	Percentage
Mexico	4,079,000	38
Philippines	860,000	8
China	683,000	6
Vietnam	526,000	5
India	509,000	5
El Salvador	434,000	4
Korea	324,000	3
Guatemala	270,000	3
Iran	213,000	2
Taiwan	188,000	2
Canada	129,000	1
Hong Kong	109,000	1
Japan	105,000	1
Armenia	79,000	1
Germany	77,000	1
Peru	73,000	1
Russia	71,000	1
Thailand	71,000	1
Nicaragua	69,000	1
Honduras	63,000	1

Source: Analysis of 2017 American Community Survey data (1% IPUMS).

America.[3] By comparison, in the rest of the United States, 38% came from Asia and 40% from Latin America. The origins of immigration to California have become increasingly diversified, making the state more like other major states that have immigration with diverse origins, such as New York.

Immigrants live throughout California's fifty-eight counties, but are concentrated in a few major metropolitan areas. The largest populations are in metropolitan Los Angeles–Long Beach–Anaheim, where 42% of the state's immigrants reside, followed by metropolitan San Francisco–Oakland (14%), Riverside–San Bernardino (9%), San Diego (7%), and San Jose (7%). These five metropolitan areas account for 78.9% of the foreign-born population, compared to just 67.6% of the native-born population. Map 1.1 shows the number of immigrants in each county in California.

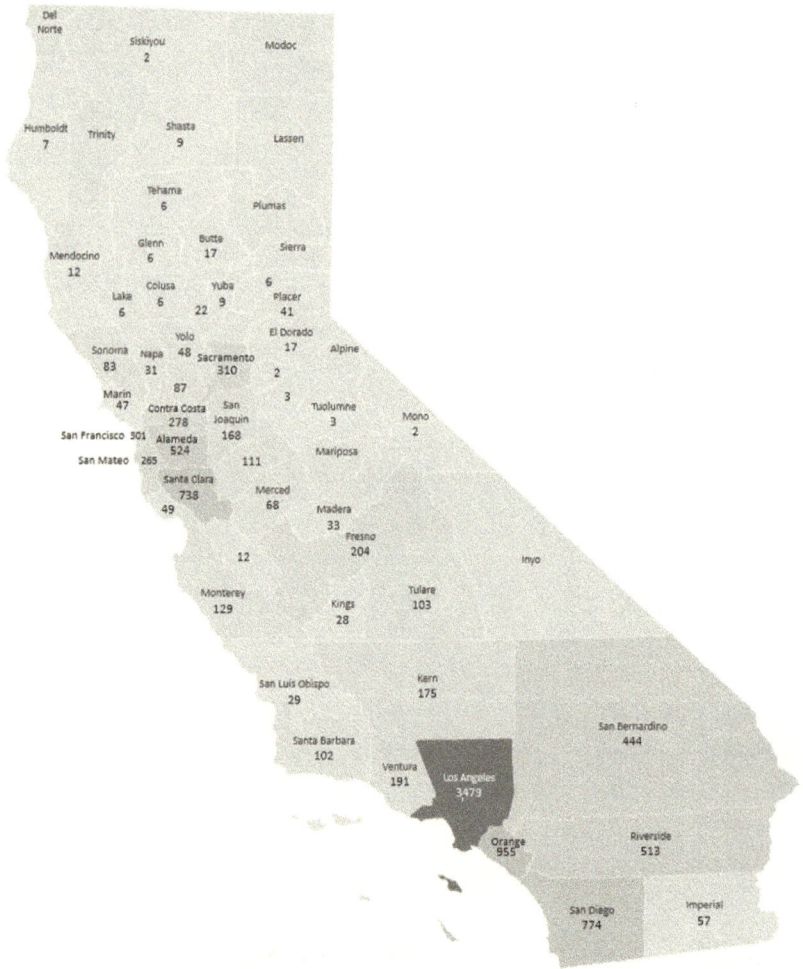

Map 1.1. Number of immigrants in California, by county (in thousands), 2017
Source: 2013–2017 American Community Survey data provided by Migration Policy Institute.

Fourteen percent of California's population are naturalized U.S. citizens. An estimated 7.6% are noncitizens with some kind of authorized status, such as legal permanent residency.[4] An estimated 5.6% of the population (20% of immigrants) are unauthorized.[5] Once again, there is a mismatch between the group that attracts the most heated political debate—unauthorized immigrants—and the dominant demographic pattern.

Although immigration can lead to major impacts on host states' school

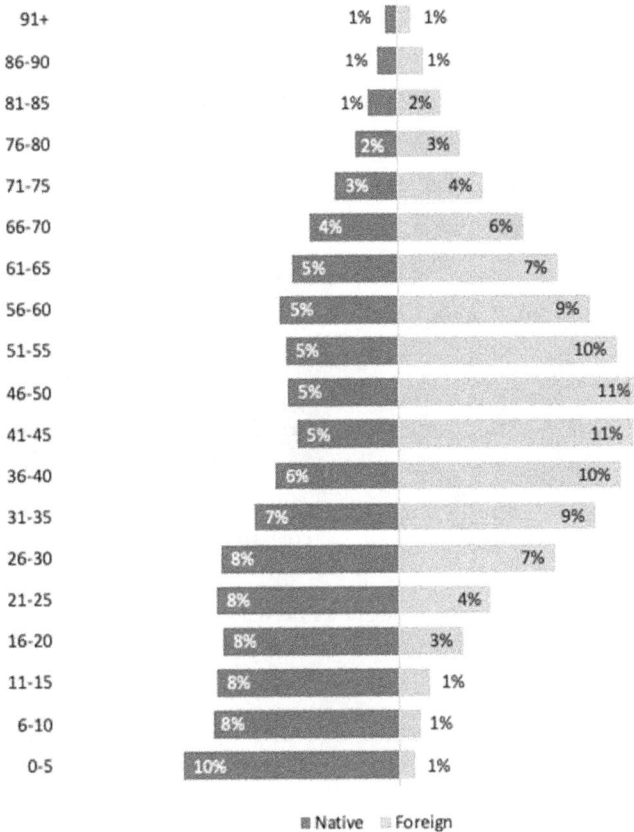

Age	Native	Foreign
91+	1%	1%
86-90	1%	1%
81-85	1%	2%
76-80	2%	3%
71-75	3%	4%
66-70	4%	6%
61-65	5%	7%
56-60	5%	9%
51-55	5%	10%
46-50	5%	11%
41-45	5%	11%
36-40	6%	10%
31-35	7%	9%
26-30	8%	7%
21-25	8%	4%
16-20	8%	3%
11-15	8%	1%
6-10	8%	1%
0-5	10%	1%

■ Native   ▦ Foreign

Figure 1.3. Age distribution of California's population, by nativity, 2017
Source: Analysis of 2017 American Community Survey data (1% IPUMS).

systems, California's immigrants are older on average than its native-born
population, highlighting the importance of immigrants in the labor force.
The median age for its immigrants is 47.4 years, compared to just 30.2 years
for natives. Figure 1.3 shows that the major difference in the populations is
that immigrants are much more concentrated in the working ages of the thir-
ties to sixties than those born in California. Only 6% of the immigrant population is age zero to twenty, compared to 34% of natives. California's immigrants skew slightly female, representing 52.1% of the immigrant population.
By contrast, females are only 49.7% of the native-born population.[6]

As in the United States as a whole, California's immigrants include people

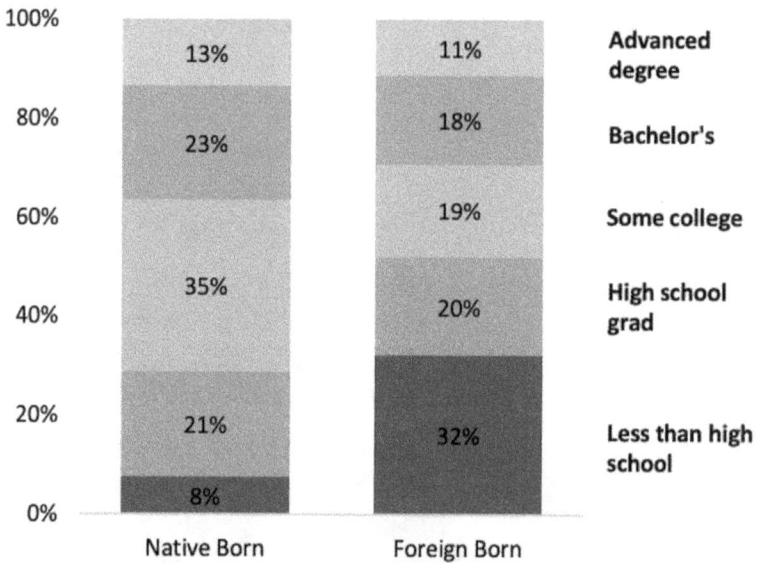

Figure 1.4. Educational composition of California's population, 2017
Source: Analysis of 2017 American Community Survey data (1% IPUMS).

with the highest and lowest levels of education. Figure 1.4 shows that among immigrants, 18% have a bachelor's degree, and 11% have an advanced degree. The biggest difference between the native and foreign-born populations is that 32% of immigrants have less than a high school education, compared to 8% of the native-born.

California has always been much more of an immigrant society than the United States as a whole. The nearly eleven million immigrants defy simple categorization, but several major patterns appear. The immigrant population tends to be older and more urbanized, and have either very high or very low levels of formal education. The origins of the foreign born have shifted through three major phases in response to racist policies and changes in the economy. From primarily European and Asian sources in the nineteenth century, immigration shifted to a pattern dominated by Latin Americans during the mid-twentieth century. By the turn of the twenty-first century, the origins had become increasingly global. Asian immigration grew as a consequence of policy reforms in 1965 that ended the national-origins quota system. Political debates in the state have often lagged these new realities or focused on small parts of the immigrant population. Controversies in recent decades

Table 1.2. Immigrant share of population by state, 2017

1%–5%		5%–10%		10%–15%		15%–30%	
WV	1.64	PA	5.00	VA	10.63	HI	16.09
MT	2.03	KS	5.01	RI	11.10	NV	17.77
MS	2.18	AK	5.53	IL	11.37	FL	18.69
SD	2.38	MI	5.58	AZ	11.85	NY	19.61
ND	2.65	NH	5.81	WA	12.37	NJ	20.07
WY	2.66	NC	6.63	CT	12.89	CA	26.12
AL	2.92	UT	6.66	MD	13.61		
WI	3.05	NM	7.71	DC	13.71		
IA	3.08	OR	8.08	MA	14.51		
ME	3.18	CO	8.21	TX	14.89		
KY	3.20	DE	8.41				
MO	3.51	GA	8.69				
AR	3.68						
OH	3.80						
LA	3.80						
VT	3.94						
IN	4.01						
TN	4.17						
SC	4.30						
OK	4.46						
ID	4.50						
NE	4.88						
MN	4.93						

Source: American Community Survey (downloaded from IPUMS).

(explained in Chapter 3) have focused on unauthorized Latino immigrants and the schooling of children. In reality, most immigrants have legal status and are working-age adults, and new flows are mostly Asian.

The "Next Californias"

California is not the only state receiving or having received large numbers of immigrants. Although it is the leader, other states have long been major destinations for immigrants, and the 1990s and 2000s saw the emergence of "new gateways" of immigration, especially in the South, but in other states as well

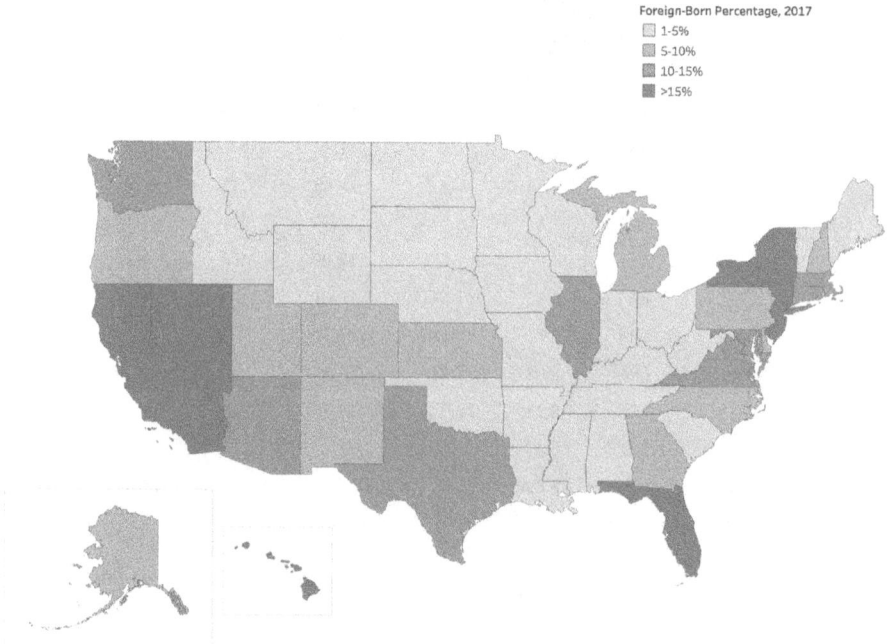

Figure 1.5. Map of immigrant share of population by state, 2017
Source: American Community Survey (downloaded from IPUMS).

(Waters and Jiménez 2005). Table 1.2 and figure 1.5 provide some insight into which states are furthest along the road to being a "Next California"—with comparable diversity created from immigration—showing four tiers based on the percentage in each state who are foreign born. The top tier, where the foreign born make up 15%–30% of the population, is mostly coastal, with New Jersey, New York, Florida, and Hawaii joining California, with the one non-coastal exception being Nevada. The next tier, where immigrants make up 10%–15% of the population, is also coastal, with the exception of Illinois and Arizona. As figure 1.5 shows, the states in the two lower tiers, where immigrants make up less than 10% of the population, are concentrated in the Rust Belt, South, and Northern Plains.

Another way to assess which states are likely to be the Next Californias is to examine where immigration is increasing at the fastest rates (see table 1.3 and figure 1.6). Here we have five tiers to take into account the fact that in some states, immigrants' share of the population is declining. This rate-of-change portrait, which focuses on change from 2009 to 2017,

Table 1.3. States by growth in immigrant population, 2009–2017

Decline		0%–10%		10%–20%		20%–30%		30+%	
NM	−9.16	HI	0.87	MS	10.84	LA	20.87	VT	31.58
ID	−4.49	AL	1.17	GA	10.89	PA	21.72	SD	31.88
WI	−2.86	OR	6.56	IN	11.39	TN	21.99	NH	36.77
RI	−1.77	OK	6.84	AR	12.87	MA	22.14	NE	40.35
AK	−0.53	KS	7.29	CT	13.07	MN	22.44	DC	41.29
		CA	8.01	NC	13.45	VA	22.45	ND	68.55
		ME	8.11	WY	13.77	IA	22.55		
		IL	8.72	NJ	14.00	WV	23.21		
		NV	9.21	MI	14.07	DE	23.89		
		AZ	9.29	OH	14.32	MO	24.13		
		SC	9.37	CO	14.67	WA	26.84		
				NY	16.15	KY	27.51		
				FL	16.37				
				MT	17.61				
				TX	17.89				
				MD	18.37				
				UT	19.52				

Source: American Community Survey (downloaded from IPUMS).

has some striking differences from the existing population percentages, and highlights some states where immigrants make up a small but rapidly growing part of the population, suggesting likely political or economic impacts.

One fact that jumps out is that although California has a large and growing immigrant population, it is in the slowest-growth tier, with only about 8% growth in this time period. Much more dramatic are several states with historically low levels of immigration that are experiencing rapid growth in their immigrant populations, such as North Dakota (nearly 69%), Nebraska (about 40%), and Vermont (almost 32%). These states, though far from being Next Californias, may be experiencing enriching but possibly disruptive diversification in particular towns or regions, with local politics, economies, schools, and health systems affected. On the other end of the growth spectrum, several states have seen a decline in their immigrant populations, and these states are not known for being distinctively hostile to immigrants. New Mexico (9%

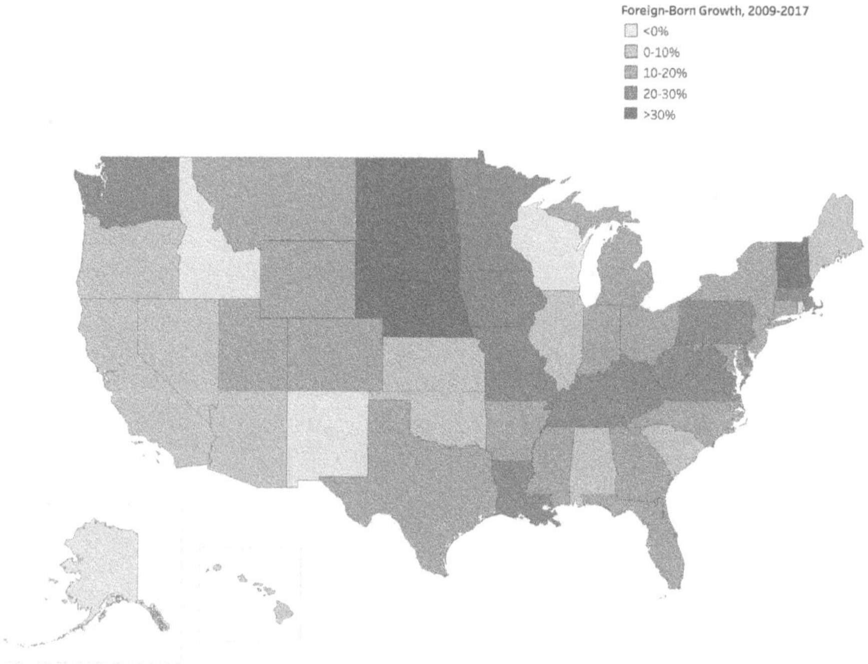

Figure 1.6. Map of states by growth in immigrant population, 2009–2017
Source: American Community Survey (downloaded from IPUMS).

decline), Idaho (a bit more than 4%), and Wisconsin lead the states where immigrants are leaving, and a California-like future is becoming less likely.

Lessons for the Next Californias

The California Dream and the Innovation Economy

Both foreign-born and domestic migrants to California have long played key roles in the state's booming economy. Although the state's exact path of economic development is unique and will not be replicated in all of its details, the current situation provides a model as well as a cautionary tale. As Chapter 2 demonstrates, California's recent history shows transitions through three distinct stages of development—"Early Development," when growth was similar to the nation as a whole (1900–1940); an "Industrial Boom" when manufacturing (defense, aerospace, autos) and agriculture attracted internal and domestic migrants throughout the state, and light manufacturing in Los Angeles attracted many undocumented migrants (1940–1990); and then the current stage, which is another boom, but one that has not attracted domestic migration except for those coming to work in the state's tech sector. This current stage of economic development, focusing on computer technologies and life sciences, is unique to California only in its massive scale. These tech firms tend to attract highly skilled international immigrants, but also low-skilled immigrants who work in the growing personal services sector that develops to satisfy demand from the high-salaried tech workers. Low-skilled migrants come to California to work in growing jobs in food service, construction, health care, and elder care. Other states with growing tech sectors can expect similar growth in immigration—and growing intermarriage and growing numbers of children of mixed backgrounds—as California has experienced.

Bean, Brown, and Pullés (Chapter 2) show that the growth of highly paid tech jobs has other effects besides the attraction of immigrants at all skill levels. Another outcome is a rapid increase in the cost of housing. The problem is so severe in California that it is driving out natives with less than a college education. The housing problem, currently unsolved by California and approaching a crisis situation, will likely vex any states or regions that develop strong tech economies that attract highly paid workers who can afford high rents and home prices but price out others.

Yet California has done some things right and is a model for other states, Chapter 2 argues, in how it has treated immigrants in recent years. After decades of exclusionary policies, Californians switched course, and began in the 2000s to welcome and protect immigrants, celebrate diversity, promote tolerance, temper gerrymandering (which in turn reduced partisan extremism), and reinvest in education and health care. States that do little or nothing for immigrant integration, the authors argue, risk creating conflict and a zero-sum attitude toward economic well-being.

Immigrants constitute nearly 37% of California's labor force. In 2008, their estimated economic output to the state's economy in goods and services was $900 billion, including $288 billion from unauthorized immigrant workers (Hinojosa-Ojeda 2012, 185–86). Immigrants incur both costs and benefits for state and local government budgets. The National Academies of Sciences, Engineering, and Medicine (Blau and Mackie 2017) estimated that first-generation immigrants on average cost California $2,050 in revenue. Their children, the second generation, produced an average net fiscal benefit of $1,550.

The third generation produced an average net fiscal benefit of $3,100, resulting in a net positive of $1,050 averaged over three generations.

Immigrants in California are slightly less likely to be unemployed than natives, but on average they earn a quarter less than natives.[7] Most research has found that immigration causes small benefits for native workers as a whole. Economist Giovanni Peri (2007) estimated that between 1900 and 2004, immigration caused a 3%–5% increase in the real wages of the average U.S.-born worker in California. The effect was nearly zero for native workers who did not finish high school. The greatest gains were enjoyed by the highest-skilled natives; those with at least some college earned 6%–7% more. The only group that suffered a notable wage loss was previous immigrants, who lost between 17% and 20% of their wages. The explanation for this pattern is that most immigrants have skills that complement, rather than substitute for, those of natives. Immigrants tend to raise the productivity and wages of natives, even as earlier waves of immigrants sometimes compete with new arrivals.

Another area where we see California as a model and also a cautionary tale is related to immigration of highly skilled workers. Chapter 6 explores the relationship between demand for skilled international migrants (technically not *immigrants* because they are on temporary H-1B visas) and innovation in California's several tech centers. The authors show that although Silicon Valley deservedly gets the most attention for being an innovation juggernaut, data on patents show that it is not the only tech center in California. The San Francisco–Oakland–Fremont area is third in the nation in patents; Los Angeles–Long Beach–Santa Ana is fourth, and San Diego–Carlsbad–San Marcos is sixth. Novick and Skrentny show that there is a strong correlation between firms filing for H-1Bs and patenting. Although not telling a causal story, these results are suggestive that skilled migrants are playing large roles in the innovation economy. States and regions seeking to develop their tech economies should be prepared for an increase in international residents and increased cultural diversity.

But Novick and Skrentny also uncover a darker side to the reliance of the tech sector on H-1B visa workers. Many of the firms that file the most applications for H-1Bs (Labor Condition Applications, or LCAs) do not patent at all. This highlights the H-1B's role as a dual-use visa. On the one hand, it can be essential for hiring highly skilled workers, such as foreign PhDs from top U.S. universities, and a bridge to permanent residence and integration into mainstream society. On the other, it can be a vehicle to import cheap labor and eventually outsource American jobs abroad. As Novick and Skrentny show, the H-1B visa program has been the subject of claims of abuse and even fraud. California is a lesson for other states, especially the Next Californias, regarding immigration of the highly skilled. Its experience shows that technology companies, and the staffing firms that serve them, are likely to use the visa for both permanent integration with high salaries *and* for temporary labor with lower pay. Until Congress acts, this is likely to remain the case.

Politics and Policy

Next Californias can learn much from how the Golden State has responded politically to its immigration, both legal and undocumented. Chapter 3 shows that a state that was the leading edge of anti-Asian policies in the nineteenth century and was prominent in policies targeting unauthorized Mexican immigrants in the 1990s became a national model of accommodation by the early 2000s. Other states adopted versions of California's earlier restrictive moves beginning in the 2000s. In the contemporary accommodating phase, provision of in-state tuition and access to financial aid for undocumented students, a ban on landlords discriminating against undocumented tenants, access to driver's licenses and professional licenses, and sanctuary jurisdictions provide models for other states. At the same time, Colbern shows that some of the Next Californias have provided models for California on some of these issues: Illinois was the first state to ban use of the E-Verify system of workplace regulation, meant to prevent employment of undocumented workers but known to produce false positives; and Connecticut passed the Trust Act, which made it harder to deport undocumented immigrants in that state. It is clear that there are now several states at the vanguard of immigrant—and undocumented immigrant—integration policies.

Of course, the policies enacted in California and in other states will be shaped in part by the preferences of voters. As Chapter 8 shows, Californians, like the residents in other states, are divided and ambivalent about immigration and its effects. However, public opinion surveys show that Californians are more likely to favor immigration and think that it has positive effects on balance. There has been a shift toward this position in both the United States and California, but the shift has taken place faster and is deeper in California so that California is 5 to 10 percentage points more welcoming and positive toward immigrants than other states on almost all issues. Will other states follow this pattern? Hajnal, Lee, and Pathakis find that several factors are related to the California pattern, including partisanship and religion, but the key shift appears to be related to changes in the ethnoracial makeup of the population. As immigrants and their children have become a larger share of the state's population, overall attitudes toward immigration have become more welcoming. The attitudes of non-Latino white Californians, who are overwhelmingly U.S. born, have not changed much on the aggregate and more closely mirror the views of whites in other parts of the country. The lesson for other states is clear: Without clear leadership, public preferences on immigration and thus also state policies are not likely to shift greatly until immigrants make up a large percentage of a state's population, with the exact tipping point likely to vary depending on the state, as well as on the presence of undocumented immigrants.

Public preferences are translated into policy through voting—and voting is restricted to citizens. The political clout of a state's immigrant population will depend critically on the naturalization rates of immigrants, who, even if eligible, are often deterred by the long, cumbersome, and expensive ($725) legal process of naturalization. What's especially fascinating about the preferences–policy connection uncovered by Hajnal and colleagues is that California's immigrants are punching far below their weight due to strikingly low naturalization rates. What accounts for this pattern, and will it translate to other states with large and growing immigrant populations? Chapter 5 provides some answers. Waldinger analyzes data from Los Angeles County, home to almost one-third of the state's adults who are eligible to naturalize. The rate of naturalization among Latinos lags far behind the rates for other immigrant groups. In his data, two-thirds of eligible immigrants are becoming citizens, a number that masks as much as it reveals. It turns out that Latinos drag this average significantly downward, with only 53% of Latinos who are eligible to become citizens actually doing so, whereas 86% of other immigrants naturalized. Part of this national-origin effect is related to the fact that many Latinos came to the United States as undocumented immigrants and adjusted their status later, but the lesson for other states is that the political participation of their immigrants will likely be higher or lower depending on the percentage of Latinos in their immigrant population. Demography is not destiny, however, as the experience of the Citizenship 2000 drive suggests that active promotion of naturalization could drive rates higher by disseminating better information about the process, offering classes, and subsidizing application costs.

Education and Health

Every state managing the well-being of its population will confront the issues of education and health. What does the California experience have for them as a model—or antimodel? California certainly has a large and growing amount of experience in this area, especially regarding schooling, as fully half of the children in California have at least one immigrant parent.

Unfortunately, California's experience in educating immigrant children, or the children of immigrants, is not one of stellar success. In Chapter 7, Abrajano, García Bedolla, and Spangler reveal how the process of classifying which of those children are English language learners varies across the state's school districts. In many districts, classification is based on a single test. Truly bilingual children may be misclassified as deficient in English as a matter of policy simply because a foreign language is spoken by someone in their home. Misclassification of immigrant children is a serious problem in many districts because it tracks children who may not need remedial English instruction into programs where the type of education does not match the students' aptitudes. The result is often reduced access to postsecondary education, leading to self-esteem issues and potentially slower progress and lower graduation rates. The politicization of bilingual education interferes with holding the best interests of the child as the guiding principle of efforts to manage the education of English learners and other students.

Since the 2000s, California has emerged as a national leader in attempting to increase access to health care for immigrants. Shimkhada and Ponce (Chapter 4) show the possibilities and constraints of state policymaking around immigration in a federal system. The state has passed laws to increase access to interpreters in health care settings and to limit cooperation with federal immigration authorities seeking information about patients in state hospitals. The 2010 Affordable Care Act (ACA) left states considerable discretion in the implementation of health care insurance programs. The state of California expanded coverage to residents who had been lawful permanent residents for at least five years, and to subpopulations of recently arrived lawful permanent residents. California was the fifth state in the country, along with other high-immigration states—Washington, New York, Massachusetts, Illinois, and the District of Columbia—to expand health care insurance to include children of unauthorized immigration status. As a result of these and other reforms, the rate of uninsured Californians fell from 15% in 2013 to 8% in 2018. Despite these innovations, attempts to expand eligibility to purchase insurance to all of California's two million unauthorized immigrants foundered in the face of the Trump administration's hostility in 2017, as well as the ACA itself, under which unauthorized immigrants were ineligible to buy insurance on the state exchanges. Survey evidence shows that unauthorized immigrants in California are less likely to visit the doctor, emergency room, or preventive health providers compared to the rest of the population.

Changes in federal law announced in 2019 that make those likely to become a public charge inadmissible for permanent immigration are likely to worsen public health. Past experience suggests there is a serious risk of a chilling effect in which even many people eligible for health care resources do not use them for fear of running afoul of poorly understood changes in the law. Shimkhada and Ponce's analysis of the public charge rule suggests that if adopted, it could cause more than 740,000 Californians to drop out of the Medi-Cal program and 300,000 Californians to drop out of the state nutrition assistance program. Nearly 70% of those disenrolling would be children. The effects on the health and educational attainment of these children are likely to be negative, in addition to triggering the loss to the state of an estimated $1.67 billion in federal benefits, economic output of $2.8 billion, and 17,700 jobs.

The National Context

This volume begins with the thought experiment of considering California as if it were its own country of immigration—the fifth largest in the world. In reality, of course, California is one of fifty states in a federal republic. How do state-level policies around immigration articulate with the national level? In his afterword, Hiroshi Motomura reminds us that law creates a context in which immigrant integration can occur through two different kinds of interaction. First, there are interactions between the federal laws and the state or local laws, and second, there are interactions between enforcement and integration. Crucially for California's recent moves toward immigrant accommodation and integration, turns toward restriction and enforcement can limit what the state and local laws are intended to achieve. In a perceptive analysis, Motomura reminds us that any U.S. states (or provinces of other countries) intent on learning from the California experience must always consider the changing stances and direction of laws at the national level. A critical lesson from Motomura, a leading expert on the law of immigration and immigrant integration, is that although citizenship is legally a function of national governments, different forms of local integration are consistent with national citizenship.

This volume provides other lessons for governments or civil society leaders intent on smoothing the path for immigrant integration so that all members of society can participate in the full experience and opportunities available. Although no other place will share the exact mix of immigrant diversity, local history, governmental configurations, and economic dynamism of California, the chapters here reveal that immigration provides challenges as well as opportunities, and that periods of relative peace—and openness—can follow even some of the most conflict-ridden periods. It also shows that immigrant integration requires all hands on deck—educators, health professionals, employers, and political leaders to attend to the shifting demographics and socioeconomic diversity that large-scale immigration can bring. Although we make no claims here that California has done everything right—and the continuing resistance of native white populations as well as persistent indices of immigrant inequality suggest that California has *not* done everything right, or certainly not optimally—it does seem safe to say that policy choices can improve outcomes, including the great benefits that well-managed immigration can bring.

Notes

1. United Nations, Department of Economic and Social Affairs, Population Division, *International Migration Report 2017: Highlights,* 2017, https://www.un.org/en/development/desa/population/migration/publications/migrationreport/docs/MigrationReport2017_Highlights.pdf.

2. *Source:* Analysis of 2017 American Community Survey data (1% IPUMS).

3. Public Policy Institute of California, "Immigrants in California," 2019, https://www.ppic.org/publication/immigrants-in-california/.

4. *Source:* Analysis of 2017 American Community Survey data (1% IPUMS).

5. Pew Research Center, "U.S. Unauthorized Immigrant Population Estimates by State, 2016," February 5, 2019, http://www.pewhispanic.org/interactives/u-s-unauthorized-immigrants-by-state/.

6. *Source:* Analysis of 2017 American Community Survey data (1% IPUMS).

7. Public Policy Institute of California, "Immigrants and the Labor Market," 2011, https://www.ppic.org/publication/immigrants-and-the-labor-market/https://www.ppic.org/publication/immigrants-and-the-labor-market/.

2 Migration Past, Present, and Future

Frank D. Bean, Susan K. Brown, and Stephanie A. Pullés

California has long symbolized both real and imagined opportunity (Starr 2005; Didion 2003). At least since the Gold Rush in the mid-nineteenth century, California's outsized features have often reflected and reinforced this possibility. Certainly this seems true for the state's geography. Its vast land mass (some 270,000 square miles, a geographic area ranking second only to Texas among the contiguous U.S. states) and its singularly long north-to-south distance (a span of 1,040 miles encompassing considerably more than half of the West Coast shoreline) provide cases in point. More significantly, among all U.S. states, California's population and economy are unsurpassed. In 2019, the state boasted about 40 million people, 10.5 million more than Texas, the second most populous (U.S. Bureau of the Census 2019). Most notable of all, California's 2018 economic output pushed \$3 trillion (U.S. Bureau of Economic Analysis 2019), a figure one-seventh the size of the entire U.S. economy, although the state comprises only one-eighth of the nation's population. Also, California's economic output is more than two-thirds again larger than that of Texas, an achievement that would seem to foreshadow its enduring economic preeminence among U.S. states (see table 2.1).

Indeed, several of the state's economic statistics are consistent with this, even reaching levels that are globally significant. For example, the Golden State has become such an economic powerhouse that were it a country, its economy would tie for the world's fifth largest, trailing only the U.S., China, Japan, and Germany. Texas, whose economy is sometimes seen as gaining on

Table 2.1. Largest national GDPs, California and Texas GDPs, and GDP per capita, 2019

Rank	Country/state	GDP (trillions)	GDP/capita ($)	Rank
1	United States	22.3	67,430	1
2	China	15.3	20,980	8
3	Japan	5.4	46,830	6
4	Germany	4.0	55,310	2
X	**California**	**3.2**	**79,854**	X
5	India	3.2	9,030	10
6	France	2.8	48,640	4
7	United Kingdom	2.7	48,170	5
8	Italy	2.0	41,580	7
X	**Texas**	**1.9**	**50,355**	X
9	Brazil	1.9	17,020	9
10	Canada	1.8	52,140	3

Sources: International Monetary Fund 2019; U.S. Bureau of Economic Analysis 2019; U.S. Bureau of the Census 2019.

Note: GDP is calculated using current prices. GDP per capita reflects purchasing-power parity in international dollars. World data come from the World Economic Outlook, released in October 2019. U.S. data come from third-quarter 2019 estimates, with population estimates from July 1, 2019, to calculate GDP per capita.

California's, stands about ninth when viewed in such terms (International Monetary Fund 2019). Despite its extraordinary success, however, California also suffers enormous economic inequalities, outranking all other U.S. states in the absolute number of persons living in poverty, even after adjusting for cost-of-living differences (Fox 2019). Moreover, the state's economy and public finances in the past have often fluctuated wildly, swinging sharply between boom and bust periods (Pastor 2018), a pattern often befalling places whose economies depend heavily on finance and natural resources and on taxing capital gains. Nonetheless, California's national and global leadership since at least the mid-1990s in innovative job growth (i.e., high-tech, dot-com, digital media, and pharmaceutical industries) underscores the reality that the state remains an exceptionally dynamic place (see Chapter 6 in this volume; also see Atkinson, Muro, and Whiton 2019; Moretti 2019).

Focusing on California as the most populous state in the country and proclaiming that it constitutes the world's fifth-largest economy, however, risks overlooking certain problems that now threaten its further development, such as income inequality, housing unaffordability, labor shortages, and potential rises in ethnoracial tension. Failing to remedy these not only undermines economic strength but also does so at an accelerating pace because each of these problems intensifies the others' negative effects over time. For example, greater housing shortages exacerbate income inequality and ethnoracial tensions, and vice versa. Hence, difficulties that initially may be somewhat manageable grow ever larger over time, thus threatening California's current global leadership in technological innovation and its exceptionally strong economy. Imbalances start to proliferate and exert effects, as happens when high housing costs induce both blue-collar and high-tech workers to leave the state. To find answers to such problems, it is helpful to examine some of the factors that have brought about California's triumphs and vulnerabilities today. This chapter lays out the demographic and economic changes since 1900 that have propelled California to its present crossroads, seeking to shed light on which current problems most need immediate attention if the state is to continue to fulfill the California Dream implied in its nickname, the Golden State.

To accomplish this, we focus on two broad goals. The first is to outline the circumstances and processes through which the state's population and economy have evolved over the past century. This is essential for understanding California's strengths and weaknesses today. The second is to gauge where today's policymakers have yet to address the side effects of prosperity that are now threatening the state's future. We also strive to show how coping with one of the most important challenges—alleviating inequality to forestall the possibility of ethnoracial tension—depends on sustaining factors that have made California's economy exceptionally strong, such as the state's unique high-tech concentrations. This means improving pay levels for middle- and working-class families and improving housing affordability for both lesser- and higher-skilled workers. It also means maintaining and even increasing recent immigration levels to reduce looming shortages of both higher-skilled and lesser-skilled workers, on the one hand, and restoring investments in human and physical infrastructure, on the other (Peri 2019; Bean 2019). One strategy we adopt for gauging the state's past trends and discerning its optimal path forward is to compare it with Texas, another large state with a dynamic economy that is often viewed as an up-and-coming rival to the Golden State (e.g., Wright 2017).

We especially seek to shed light on how international and domestic migrations both influence and are influenced by economic and social change, and on what kind and volume of migration the state needs to ensure a healthy future. Domestic migration refers to movement within the U.S., such as state-to-state moves. Note that domestic migration can occur among foreign-born individuals in the U.S. who previously migrated from a country outside the U.S. On the economic front, we thus ask: When and to what extent has California's economic growth attracted migrants to the state? When has this migration involved substantial domestic or international migration components? Has the latter served mainly to import additional poverty, as is sometimes emphasized (e.g., Martin 2009; Yoo 2008), or has it enhanced the state's workforce with needed manual and service and high-tech workers whose efforts and creative talents constitute integral components of the workforce and have sparked the emergence of both new technologies and employment opportunities (Moretti 2019)?

On the sociodemographic and sociocultural fronts, we ask: What side effects have recent economic booms spawned that threaten to undermine the state's future by fostering an exodus from the state of needed middle- and working-class workers, even as many highly educated newcomers continue to arrive? What do the aging and educational upgrading of the state's baby boomers mean for labor shortages, immigration, and the strength of California's future economy? What are the implications for the state's social welfare of the rise in ethnoracial diversity that often now accompanies domestic and international migration?

Population and Economic Trends

Where did California's success come from, and when did it first emerge? Despite the romantic aura (and force) of the idea of economic opportunity accompanying the 1849 Gold Rush, along with the economic promise emanating from the later construction of intercontinental railroads, California's population did not substantially "take off" until World War II. In the early 1940s, shipbuilding and armament manufacturing on the West Coast expanded rapidly in connection with the large-scale wartime initiatives mounted as part of the country's Pacific Theater military campaigns (Starr 2009a). From around 1940 through 1990, California's population increased notably, with its proportion of the nation's total population rising steadily.

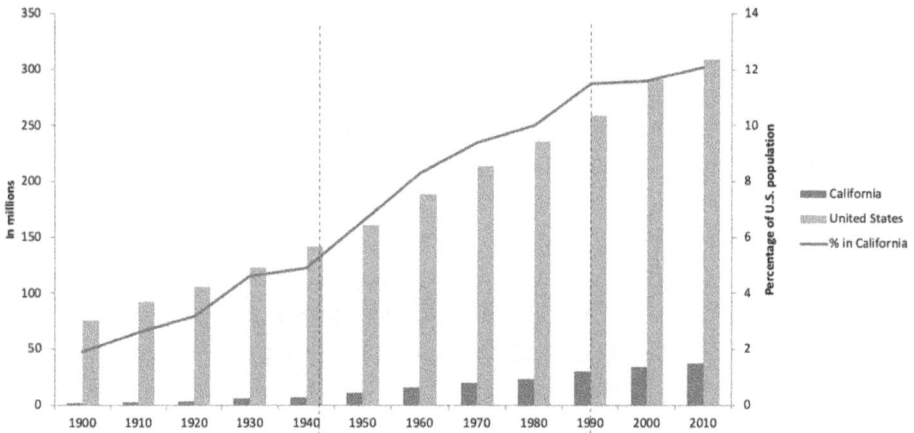

Figure 2.1. Population of California and the United States, total and percentage, since 1900
Source: Authors' compilations from U.S. Bureau of the Census data reported by Ruggles et al. 2019.

This is clear in figure 2.1, where the graph's vertical bars for each decade show the trends in the state's and the nation's total population in millions. The continuous line in the graph displays the *percentage* of the U.S. population that resided in California. From 1940 until 1990, that percentage increased regularly, indicating that California's relative share of the national population was growing faster with each decade. The recession in the early 1990s led to a break in this pattern. Since then, California's share of the national population has leveled off and remained at about 12%. Of course, the state's overall population has continued to increase, albeit just more slowly than during the baby boom years of the 1950s and 1960s.

The extraordinary population expansion during the postwar decades reflected California's continuing economic strength. Beginning and sustaining this growth was not a chance phenomenon. Driving the population growth were remarkable developments in infrastructure, with new large-scale projects involving massive public investments in higher education, transportation, and water retrieval and storage undertaken throughout the state (Starr 2009b). These developments soon spawned sizeable cross-border migrations of both farmworkers and temporary and permanent workers from Mexico, enabling both manufacturing growth in Los Angeles and large-scale agricultural expansion in the San Joaquin Valley. The state's output of fruits, vegetables, and other farm products rose appreciably. As a result, California stands today as the number-one food provider in the country (a recent estimate finding that it accounted for more than 13% of the national agricultural value and as of 2018 grew more than one-third of the nation's vegetables and more than two-thirds of its fruits and nuts. [California Department of Food and Agriculture 2020]).

The state's World War II wartime expansion also set the stage for subsequent industrial development. Providing impetus to population growth were substantial investments in defense and aerospace industries, emphases reflecting the foreign policy and defense commitments associated with the Cold War in general and with the U.S. military engagements in Korea and Vietnam in particular (Hersch 2015). All of this of course contributed to outsized economic growth. By 1990, the California economy had grown to almost the one-seventh share of total U.S. output that it shows today, with manufacturing (including both automobile and defense-related production), agriculture, and natural resources (including oil) predominating (Cohen 2011).

Declines in Federal Spending: Recession and Recovery

With the 1989 collapse of the Soviet Union, however, government spending in 1990 on aerospace and defense began a four-year period of sharp decline, cutbacks that precipitated only a mild *national* recession in 1991, but one that delivered a gut punch to California. For three straight years, the state's overall output shrank, from about one-seventh to one-eighth of total U.S. productivity. At the national level, the recession involved only slightly anemic growth (from 1990 to 1991), before rebounding to about 3% in 1992. In Texas, the economy continued to grow from 1990 to 1993. In California, output fell by 1.4% from 1990 to 1991, and then substantially dropped again in the next two years (figure 2.2). By 1994, the state had suffered about two-fifths of the nation's decline in manufacturing employment during those years, with literally tens of thousands of defense and aerospace blue-collar workers either losing their jobs or taking early retirement (U.S. Bureau of Labor Statistics 2019). Not surprisingly, the outsized population growth in California fell back. Opportunity declined, and tensions ran high. Tellingly, it was in 1992 that the LA riots over the Rodney King beating took place, and it was in 1994 that Governor Pete Wilson campaigned successfully for the passage of Proposition 187, the voter referendum to bar unauthorized immigrants from access to education or receipt of social services, although federal courts quickly ruled the changes unconstitutional (Pastor 2018).

Even as the recession lingered, the effects of the state's earlier investments

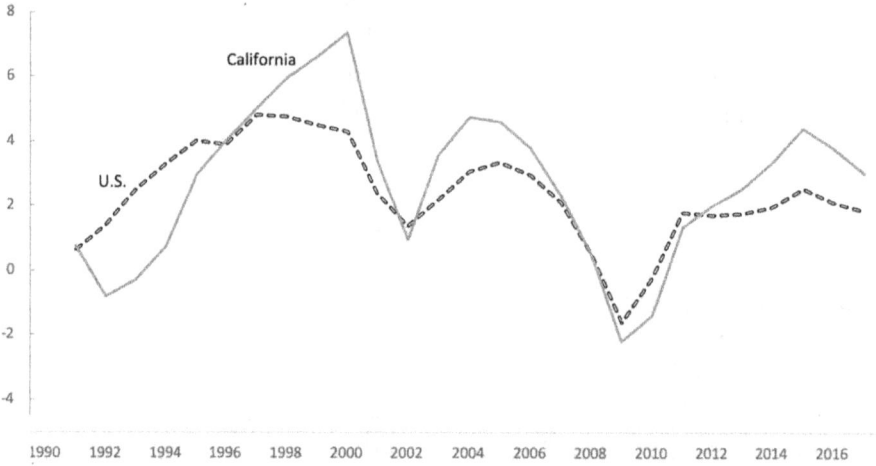

Figure 2.2. Annual percentage change in GDP for the United States and California, 1990–2018, two-year moving average
Source: Authors' compilations of data from the U.S. Bureau of Economic Analysis, 2019.

in infrastructure and higher education were beginning to blossom in the form of nascent high-tech industries in Silicon Valley and elsewhere in the state. At the time, these focused on computer chip manufacturing and assembly, with these concentrations growing to employ almost a third of manufacturing workers (Rhode 2001), even as manufacturing overall was declining. That the substantial fraction of the new high-tech companies then as well as the start-ups that followed in subsequent decades were concentrated in California indicated that the state's outsized investments in higher education compared with other states, including Texas, were paying dividends. More so than the 1940–1990 decades, which were characterized by growth in traditional manufacturing and agriculture, the late 1990s brought forth a high-tech, knowledge-based economy that increasingly required highly skilled knowledge-based workers, although not so many as had been employed in the shuttered manufacturing and defense plants.

After the prolonged bust of the early 1990s, the state's resumption of economic health once again resulted in outsized jumps in GDP. From 1994 until the end of the decade, California's GDP averaged 5.8% growth per year, considerably more than the national average of 4.3%, and more than Texas's average of 5.4% (a level enabled in part by new recovery techniques [fracking] applied to the state's vast but previously difficult-to-tap oil reserves).

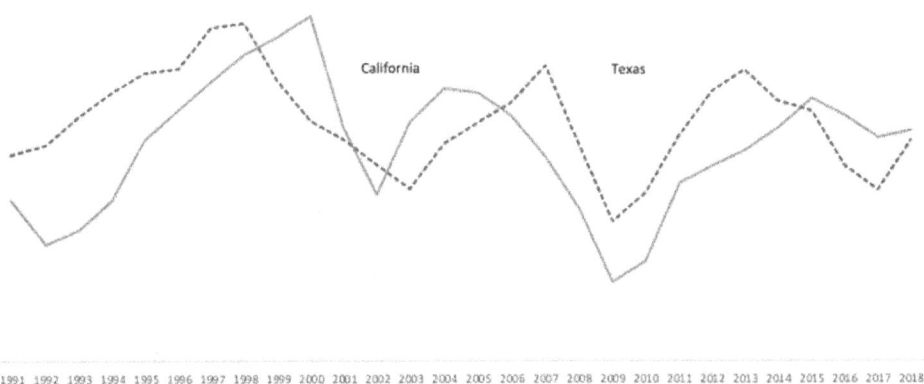

1990 1991 1992 1993 1994 1995 1996 1997 1998 1999 2000 2001 2002 2003 2004 2005 2006 2007 2008 2009 2010 2011 2012 2013 2014 2015 2016 2017 2018

Figure 2.3. Annual percentage change in GDP for California and Texas, 1990–2018, two-year moving average
Source: Authors' compilations of data from the U.S. Bureau of Economic Analysis, 2019.

The higher productivity of high-tech industries boosted economic growth at rates considerably above rates of population increase. Subsequently, after a brief and mild national recession in 2001, induced in part by the uncertainty and trauma resulting from 9/11, California returned to high-tech-fueled economic growth, at that point surpassing even that of the country overall (figure 2.2). Texas, by contrast, recovered faster from the early 1990s recession, owing in part to benefiting from a revolution in oil recovery techniques. This led for a few years to relatively steeper growth in GDP (figure 2.3). However, in 2008, this growth collapsed when a global oil glut drove prices and U.S. crude oil production to their lowest levels in the twentieth century (Wright 2018).

Migration Patterns in the High-Tech Era

Thus, to a great degree, California's economic fortunes spurred both migration patterns and population change up through 1990. Before World War II, California's population and economy grew somewhat faster than the country overall, including components of both domestic and international migration. Although the passage in 1924 of the National Origins Quota Act had limited European immigration to the nation (and California), a nascent stream from Mexico remained unaffected (Bean, Brown, and Castillo 2015). Although the onset of the Dust Bowl in the 1930s had unleashed a substantial domestic migration from Oklahoma, Texas, and New Mexico (Hayes-Bautista and

Rodriguez 1996), it was from 1940 through the 1980s that population growth in California exploded. Exceeding the national average and involving both domestic and foreign sources of migration, the state's population surged. The flows also extended to new kinds of migration, most notably of Mexicans of unauthorized migration status in the 1970s settling in Los Angeles, in part because the 1965 law had reduced their possibilities of legal entry (Bean, Brown, and Castillo 2015). In terms of general patterns, however, the 1940–1990 period was one of disproportionate population growth involving high natural increase (more births than deaths) and large components of domestic migration and immigration (both legal and unauthorized), at least up until the late 1980s. Employment started to diminish in the latter half of the 1980s, however, as deindustrialization (although not yet in defense and aerospace) hit California hard, with more frequent shutdowns in heavy manufacturing, such as for automobiles.

Starting in the late 1980s and continuing during the early 1990s, with the further demise of that part of the state's economy hastened by the defense and aerospace manufacturing crisis, the migration pattern began to shift. Thus the U.S. Bureau of the Census reported that in 1990, only about forty thousand more migrants moved to California than left (figure 2.4), a drop from earlier levels of positive net domestic migration. At the same time, the state's high-tech era was fast developing. Reflecting this, 85% of the state's forty thousand domestic-migrant gain in 1990 involved people with college or advanced degrees. By contrast, Texas suffered a net decrease of domestic migrants in 1990, and this was the case for *both* higher-skilled and lesser-skilled migrants. By 2000, a new pattern had emerged. On a net basis, Texas was gaining both higher- *and* lesser-skilled domestic migrants each decade. By contrast, California, even though gaining more *higher-skilled* domestic migrants, was losing *lesser-skilled* ones. By 2000, the *net* number of working-age domestic migrants had turned negative in California, with over 92,000 more persons leaving than arriving in the state, as manufacturing declines continued. Negative domestic migration has persisted in every period since then, although the level has varied.

The picture of the numbers of persons born abroad and moving into the two states, however, was considerably different. In 1990, over 160,000 lesser-skilled persons born abroad moved to California, versus only 40,000 who went to Texas (figure 2.5). In the case of Texas, this number rose across decades, more than doubling by 2018, although California still was receiving

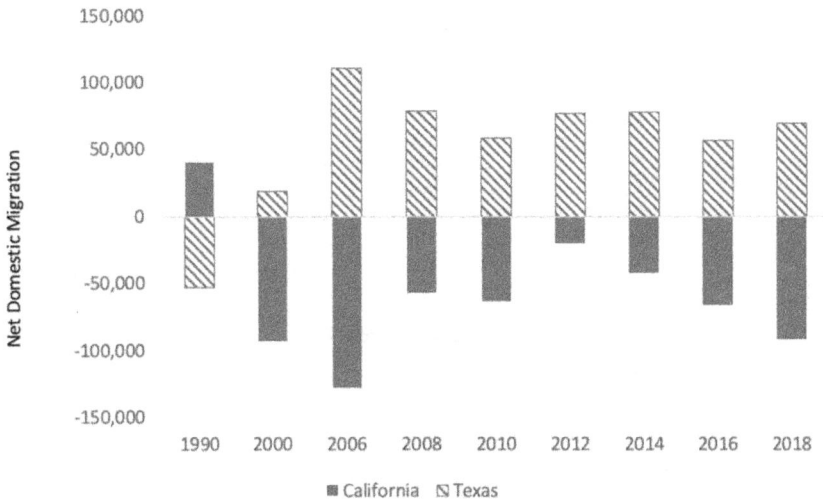

Figure 2.4. Average annual net domestic migration among the working-age population (ages 20–64) to California and Texas, selected years, 1990–2018
Source: Authors' compilations from U.S. Bureau of the Census microdata reported by Ruggles et al. 2019.
Note: Average annual estimates for 1990 and 2000 data are adapted from a different question than that used in later years and may underestimate the actual migration. The timeline for those years is also not drawn to scale.

more lesser-skilled born-abroad persons than Texas in that year. But when it came to the number of higher-skilled born-abroad migrants moving in, California surpassed Texas in 1990 by almost 25,000, a gap that increased to over 40,000 by 2018 (figure 2.5). In short, in 1990, California showed a noticeable vestige of the old industrial-era migration pattern (sizeable positive lesser-skilled migration) *as well as* the high-tech industry's ability to attract high-skilled foreign-born migrants. Texas, by contrast, did not show much of a high-tech pattern until 2010, and then one that functioned at a lower level than in California.

As described in more detail in Chapter 6, higher-skilled persons born abroad (those with college or advanced degrees) also arrived in California in increasing numbers over this period, some as temporary higher-skilled entrants (typically on H-1B visas) drawn by the state's burgeoning high-tech economy. The annual numbers of higher-skilled born-abroad persons in California nearly tripled from 1990 to 2018, reaching almost 120,000, a level

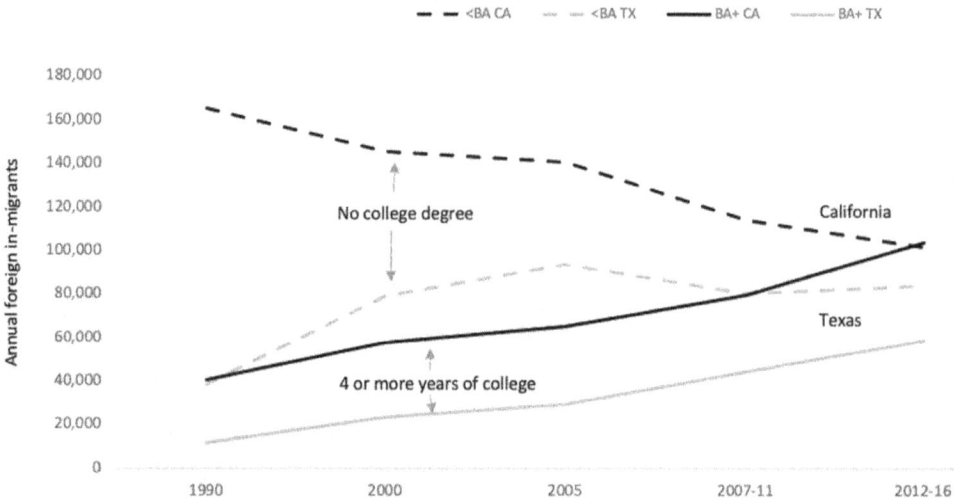

Figure 2.5. Annual migrants from abroad to California and Texas, by degree, ages
20–64, selected years, 1990–2016
Source: Authors' compilations from U.S. Bureau of the Census microdata reported by Ruggles
et al. 2019.
Note: In 1990 and 2000, respondents were asked whether they had moved in the last five years,
whereas in the later years, they were asked whether they had moved in the last year. Responses
for 1990 and 2000 are divided by five. Even so, the counts with later years are not equivalent,
because the five-year question will not pick up multiple moves over that period. The 2005 and
2018 counts consist of American Community Survey data for those years alone. The 2008–2012
and 2013–2017 counts are five-year averages.

appreciably above the number of lesser-skilled entrants. Texas also showed
increases in higher-skilled in-migrants over this period, but with numbers
starting and ending at lower levels than in California (figure 2.5).

These patterns reflect and are consistent with the somewhat different
kinds of economies the two states now have. California is more invested in
knowledge-based, innovation-oriented, high-technology economy activities
than Texas, although in the latter state, the net domestic migration of higher-
skilled workers has grown in recent years, although from a lower base than
in California. Viewed in these terms, California seems at present to be well
positioned to continue future economic growth driven by high-tech, high-
knowledge industries, in some ways more so than Texas, although the latter is
increasing its capacity in this regard (Vara 2015).

Three Distinct Periods of Development

California's economic and demographic growth during the twentieth and twenty-first centuries thus reflects three distinct periods that show different growth and migration patterns. From 1900 until 1940, the state's population grew somewhat faster than did the country's, welcoming during the first third of the twentieth century westward-moving domestic migrants as did many other West Coast states (table 2.2). Domestic and international migration taken together, however, contributed to population gains that were proportional to those of the nation. An apt characterization of this period would be "Early Development." Starting around 1940, however, and lasting until about 1990, a period of considerably more rapid population growth emerged, led as noted earlier by manufacturing, especially defense-and-aerospace and automobile manufacturing, along with agriculture. Substantial migration from other states constituted an important part of this surge, as did international migration, which began to increase during the 1970s, including nonfarm-worker unauthorized Mexican migration to Los Angeles and its burgeoning light manufacturing plants. Much of this consisted of unauthorized migrants taking up permanent residence, unlike earlier-arriving seasonal farmworkers who often came as temporary circular migrants. We term these years the "Industrial Boom" period. It was one that involved substantial growth in both the economy *and* population, with domestic and international migration making up appreciable elements of population growth.

The third period, which runs from 1990 until the present, we term "Postindustrial, High-Tech." Although the period began with the economic slowdown in the late 1980s, followed by the deep California recession of 1990–1994, it has been characterized since by disproportionately high economic growth driven by the emergence of high-tech computer, internet, entertainment, and bio-tech industries. But notably, it has *not* been characterized by disproportionately rapid population growth. Rather, domestic in-migration has decreased, while domestic out-migration increased. Even so, the period's signal feature has been the arrival of high-skilled migrants, both foreign and native born. Although gains in both domestic and temporary international higher-skilled migrants are notable early in the period, domestic in-migration of higher-skilled workers dropped sharply in the last few years. Moreover, net losses of lesser-skilled persons to other states have grown in recent years. The age patterns of the growing out-migration of both lesser-skilled and some

Table 2.2. Change in total California population, percentage of total U.S. population, and growth patterns, 1900–2017

Decade	Population increase (millions)	Percentage point change in California as percentage of total U.S. population	Period pattern
1900s	0.9	0.7	Modestly disproportionate growth
1910s	1.0	0.6	Some domestic and international migration
1920s	2.3	1.4	
1930s	1.2	0.3	
1940s	3.7	1.7	Substantially disproportionate growth
1950s	4.1	1.7	
1960s	4.2	1.1	Large domestic in-migration
1970s	3.7	0.6	
1980s	5.1	1.5	Strong increase in international migration in the 1970s and 1980s
1990s	4.0	0.1	Negligible relative growth
2000s	3.5	0.5	
2010–19	2.3	-0.1	International migration offset by domestic out-migration

Sources: Authors' compilations of U.S. Bureau of the Census data from Ruggles et al. 2019.

high-skilled workers and retirees to other states imply that the driving force behind such moves is diminishing housing affordability.

Housing Affordability and Sustaining the California Dream

Our analysis to this point shows the importance of migration in the growth of California's economy and population since 1900, and substantially from 1940 to 1990. The same has been true over the past couple of decades, although now in a new form. In recent years, it has been the movement into the state of college-educated migrants, both from other U.S. states and abroad, along with increasing numbers of native Californians entering and completing college, that provides much of the lifeblood of the state's high-tech economic vitality. Clearly, California now depends crucially on advanced, innovative, high-tech, knowledge-based industries for its economic growth. Because of increasing productivity in such industries, employment growth, though substantial, has lagged economic growth, although employment increases too have been notable. In short, the state for over two decades has depended more and more heavily on higher-skilled employees, many of whom have been graduates of California's well-respected higher education system. Demand for higher-skilled workers has also been high enough that such employees have also had to come from both elsewhere in the United States and from abroad.

The substantial growth in California's postindustrial economy over the past forty years has been so rapid that the state has come to depend more and more on less-skilled immigrants for manual and service work. Also, its highly paid upper-middle-class workforce has expanded and created further demand for a variety of personal and social services (Clark 1998). Before the COVID-19 epidemic struck in early 2020, the U.S. Department of Labor was projecting that this growth would continue, especially in California, in service and construction, along with food service, health care, and elder care (U.S. Bureau of Labor Statistics 2019). Thus, since 1990, the state has needed and increasingly relied on *both* domestic and international migrants, and there remains little reason to think that a thriving knowledge-based economy would not benefit from these same kinds of migration in the future. But this is not what appears to be happening in the state in terms of migration. California has for three decades experienced net out-migration among lesser-skilled workers (those most likely to be affected by income inequality and housing unaffordability) and recently among higher-skilled migrants as well (for whom unaffordability has also become an issue). What are the likely consequences of California's continuing inequality and recent changes in migration patterns?

The shift in migration patterns resulting from housing affordability suggests that California's economic preeminence may be at risk. Behind the state's extraordinary economic achievements lies another less commendable reality, one that could hamper its future dynamism. Although the state's per capita GDP in 2018 ranked among the top five in the country (exceeded only by Connecticut, Delaware, Massachusetts, and New York), it remained at the very bottom (fiftieth) in the absolute number of people living in poverty households, even after adjusting among states for differences in various cost-of-living measures (table 2.3). Its income inequality is also high and increasing. From 1969 until 2009, California's rank among states in income

Table 2.3. States with the largest numbers of people living in poverty, with and without a Supplemental Poverty Measure (SPM), 2016–2018

State	Number of people (millions)	With SPM*	Percentage in poverty (official)	Rank among states in percentage above poverty (official)	Percentage in poverty with SPM	Rank among states in percentage above poverty (SPM)
United States	39.6	42.3	12.3	—	13.1	—
California	4.9	7.1	12.5	33	18.1	50
Texas	3.8	4.0	13.7	38	14.2	43
Florida	2.8	3.4	13.6	37	16.2	48
New York	2.3	2.7	11.8	27 (tie)	14.0	40 (tie)

Source: Fox 2019.
*After adjusting for cost-of-living measures.

inequality grew from the middle of the distribution to almost the top (Pastor 2018). Estimates of the state's homeless population have been as high as 112,000, which places its rank at number one in the country (Khouri 2018).

Additional insight into California's changing migration patterns emerges from comparing its components of recent population change with those in Texas from 2015 to 2019. Over these years, Texas showed the greater overall average annual population growth (an average of 1.5% per year compared to 0.5% for California). Over this time, California added an average of about 183,000 people per year, whereas Texas added an annual average of about 400,000 (table 2.4). Looking at the component of population change demographers call natural increase (births minus deaths), the two states are quite similar, with California having experienced an average gain of about 210,000 and Texas 195,000. And when we include international migrants, along with births and deaths, each state's increase in all three taken together is roughly in proportion with the relative size of its overall population. Hence, the differences between the two states in births, deaths, and international migration do not appreciably account for Texas's higher recent overall population growth. It is only when we look at the remaining factor, domestic migration, that we see a dramatic difference. From 2015 to 2019, California on a net average annual basis *lost* about 30,000 domestic migrants a year to other states, whereas Texas *gained* about 205,000. In short, more domestic migrants during these years were going to Texas from other states than were leaving. Just the opposite was true in California, where more left the state than arrived.

Table 2.4. Components of population change for California and Texas, 2015–2019

State	Year	Population (July 1)	Percentage change	Numeric change	Births	Deaths	Natural increase	Net migration	Net foreign immigration	Net domestic migration
California	2015	38,918,045	0.83	321,073	500,380	253,798	246,582	76,932	156,870	-79,938
	2016	39,167,117	0.64	249,072	490,358	260,121	230,237	19,523	141,892	-122,369
	2017	39,358,497	0.49	191,380	481,943	265,241	216,702	-24,732	112,814	-137,546
	2018	39,461,588	0.26	103,091	465,017	277,578	187,439	-83,981	71,300	-155,281
	2019	39,512,223	0.13	50,635	462,617	282,520	180,097	-129,386	74,028	-203,414
Texas	2015	27,470,056	1.88	505,723	402,264	187,837	214,427	289,708	117,660	172,048
	2016	27,914,410	1.62	444,354	400,965	188,794	212,171	231,776	110,866	120,910
	2017	28,295,273	1.36	380,863	391,340	194,141	197,199	182,978	98,188	84,790
	2018	28,628,666	1.18	333,393	379,544	201,799	177,745	155,073	71,278	83,795
	2019	28,995,881	1.28	367,215	378,664	202,786	175,878	190,704	65,044	125,660

Source: U.S. Bureau of the Census 2020, *Population, Population Change, and Estimated Components of Population Change: April 1, 2010 to July 1, 2019* (NST-EST2019-alldata).

Note: Revisions compiled by the California Department of Finance slightly increase the overall population in California but do not change the overall trends.

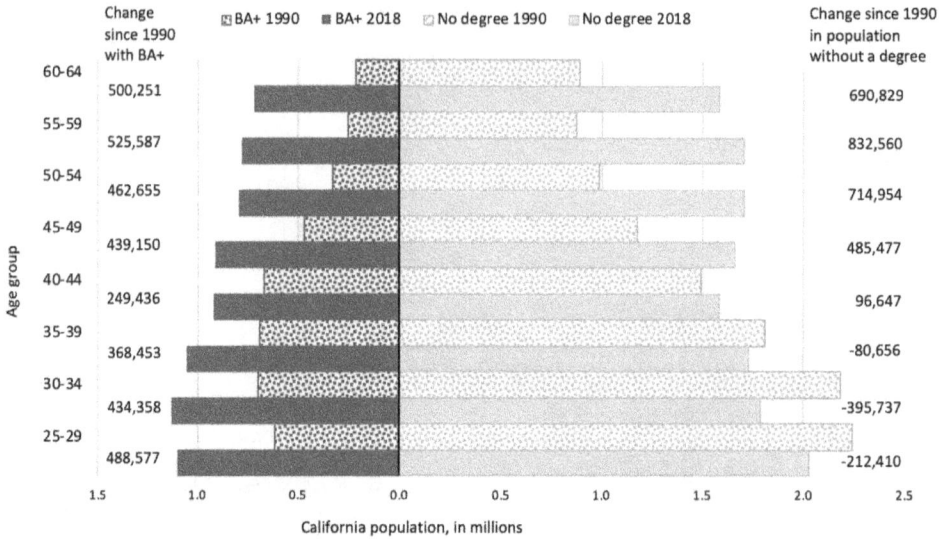

Figure 2.6. California working-age population, by education, 1990 and 2018

Source: Authors' compilations of U.S. Bureau of the Census microdata reported by Ruggles et al. 2019.

Note: Working-age population includes both native born and foreign born.

What explains this pattern? Does it come about because Texas now exhibits a stronger economy than California? This seems unlikely given that the California economy has reached the preeminent levels it attained relative to Texas in the late 1990s. Does the pattern then reflect a saturation effect; that is, does it indicate that California has attracted so many migrants in recent years that it simply no longer needs new ones? This, too, seems unlikely, because California has been subject to the general national trend over the last thirty years of shrinkage in the number of lesser-skilled persons in the workforce because many people are gaining skills through college. For example, when we look at the age and education structure of California, we see a notable reduction in the number of persons without college degrees occurring from 1990 through 2018 (figure 2.6).

This same pattern characterizes the United States as a whole. It stems from the baby boom generation born in the years 1946 through 1965 aging considerably by 1990, then starting to age out of the workforce and starting to retire by 2010. This generation also received considerably more education than did preceding cohorts, meaning that a lower proportion worked in lesser-skilled jobs compared with earlier birth cohorts. Demand for manual and service blue-collar work, however, has not diminished over the period under scrutiny (Bean, Bachmeier, and Brown 2014). The shortfall has been filled by lower-skilled unauthorized Mexican immigrant workers (Bean, Brown, and Bachmeier 2015). Therefore, some other factor must explain California's current pattern of negative net domestic migration, which is taking place even as positive net migration continues among the foreign born.

The factor most plausibly causing this pattern lies in California's disproportionately high housing costs (see Woetzel et al. 2016), which recently seem to be inducing more working-class and middle-class persons to leave the state. This is implied in the results of a recent report documenting net departures from the state of non-college-educated Californians during 2012–2016, but continuing *net* gains of those with a college degree or more (Johnson 2017). If unusually high housing costs have been driving this pattern, we would expect the burden of such costs to fall more heavily on lesser-skilled (non-college-educated) than on higher-skilled (college-educated) domestic migrants. In fact, when we look at net domestic lesser-skilled migration in California in recent years, we see that the state suffered a net loss to other states of 77,000 working-age migrants per year from 2012 to 2016, even as it was incurring a net *gain* of over 27,000 college-educated migrants (table 2.6). By contrast, Texas during this time was continuing to experience net *gains* of lesser-skilled domestic migrants.

This suggests that something that was present in California but not in Texas, such as prohibitive housing costs, might explain the pattern. As indicated by the data in table 2.5, California ranked second highest in the country in various measures affecting monthly housing costs in 2019. In short, the lack of housing affordability appears to be the factor pushing people out of California. That housing costs are notably higher in California than in Texas is consistent with this net loss occurring in the case of the non-college-educated Californians but not such persons in Texas. That greater numbers of older, often retirement-age, lesser-skilled migrants go to Texas than go to California also implies that housing is more affordable in Texas than in California (table 2.6). To afford an average two-bedroom apartment at fair market rate, renters in California must earn over $14 an hour *more* than renters in Texas (National Low Income Housing Coalition 2019).

How critical is California's housing problem? For California to sustain the less-skilled workforce necessary to undergird its presently robust high-tech

Table 2.5. Affordability of renting in ten most costly states and District of Columbia, 2019

State Rank	State/region	Fair market rent (FMR) of 2BR apt. ($)	Hourly wage needed to afford 2BR at FMR ($)	Estimated mean hourly wage for renters ($)	Full-time jobs at mean renter wage needed to afford 2BR FMR
1	Hawaii	1,914	36.82	16.68	2.2
2	**California**	**1,804**	**34.69**	**22.79**	**1.5**
3	Massachu-setts	1,758	33.81	20.72	1.6
–	District of Columbia	1,665	32.01	28.57	1.1
4	New York	1,599	30.76	25.00	1.2
5	New Jersey	1,501	28.86	18.68	1.5
6	Washington	1,445	27.78	20.06	1.4
7	Maryland	1,431	25.40	17.88	1.5
8	Connecticut	1,321	25.33	17.53	1.4
9	Colorado	1,317	25.33	18.69	1.4
10	Alaska	1,292	24.84	18.96	1.3
19	**Texas**	**1,055**	**20.29**	**18.94**	**1.1**

Source: Adapted from National Low Income Housing Coalition 2019.
Note: "Affordability" represents the traditional rule of thumb of spending at most 30% of gross income on rent and utilities. Wages rates assume a 40-hour workweek and 52 weeks of employment.

economy (which the past few years has outranked both Texas and the national economy in growth rate, as noted earlier), it needs soon to formulate and develop policies that can boost affordable housing throughout the urban areas of the state (see Woetzel et al. 2016 and Zuk and Chapple 2016). Evidence that the affordability crisis is growing worse comes from out-migration showing up recently for the first time among older higher-skilled workers. Beginning in 2014, more working-age people over thirty-five with college or advanced degrees left California than arrived, and the net outflow increased from 3,142 in 2014 to 26,613 in 2018 (figure 2.7). Among younger highly educated migrants during these years, net migration remained positive, but the margin peaked in 2016. In that year, 26,221 more arrived than left, but by 2018, only 5,865 more arrived than left. Significantly, these trends took place in a context of an economy continuing to show high rates of expansion. Increasing housing costs thus appear likely to constitute the main factor driving up not only

Table 2.6. Annual domestic interstate migration for California and Texas by age and schooling, average of 2012–2016 and 2018

		California migration			Texas migration		
		In	Out	Net	In	Out	Net
2012–16							
Ages 20–39	No college degree	118,373	165,498	-47,125	141,103	121,982	19,121
	Four years college	92,122	74,356	17,766	66,649	46,739	19,910
	5+ years college	46,663	34,822	11,841	34,250	23,592	10,658
Ages 40–64	No college degree	56,519	86,405	-29,886	74,960	57,502	17,458
	Four years college	24,042	27,578	-3,536	23,177	19,575	3,602
	5+ years college	21,177	19,641	1,536	17,569	13,573	3,996
Total		358,896	408,300	-49,404	357,708	282,963	74,745
2018							
Ages 20–39	No college degree	112,817	166,719	-53,902	130,592	113,429	17,163
	Four years college	98,605	98,024	581	77,269	62,222	15,047
	5+ years college	61,346	48,078	13,268	44,303	27,526	16,777
Ages 40–64	No college degree	47,372	82,379	-35,007	71,492	59,059	12,433
	Four years college	22,610	35,743	-13,133	28,568	23,799	4,769
	5+ years college	22,320	26,038	-3,718	20,932	17,064	3,868
Total		365,070	456,981	-91,911	373,156	303,099	70,057

Source: U.S. Bureau of the Census microdata from Ruggles et al. 2019.

the net numbers of lesser-skilled people departing the state but also the net numbers of higher-skilled persons starting to leave as well. Clearly, something in this situation in California will have to give before too much longer. Either the state must find ways to develop more affordable housing or its economy will likely to start to suffer from lack of workers.

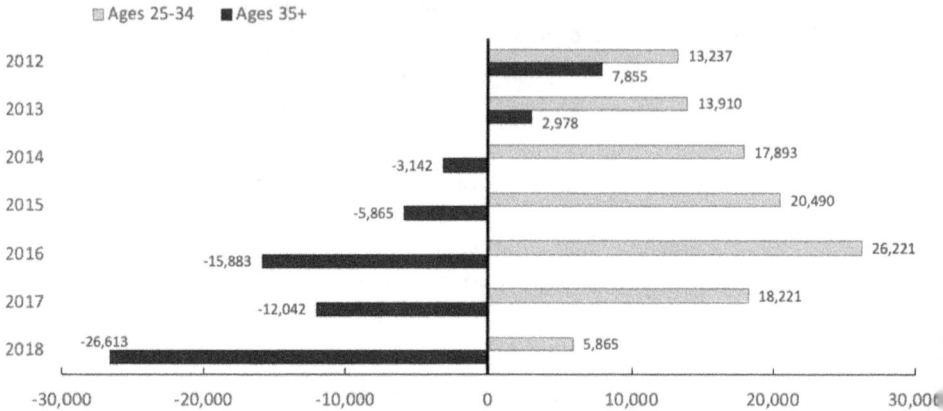

☐ Ages 25-34   ■ Ages 35+

Year		
2012	13,237	7,855
2013	13,910	2,978
2014	17,893	-3,142
2015	20,490	-5,865
2016	26,221	-15,883
2017	18,221	-12,042
2018	5,865	-26,613

Figure 2.7. Net interstate migration to California among those with a bachelor's or advanced degree, by age, 2012–2016

Source: Authors' compilations from the U.S. Bureau of the Census microdata reported by Ruggles et al. 2019.

Immigration, Diversity, and Sustaining the California Dream

We have outlined to this point the trends and forces taking California through three distinct eras of development since World War II, each involving different kinds of economic growth and migration patterns. An Industrial Period lasting from the beginning of World War II until the late 1980s provided many decent-paying manufacturing jobs and attracted sizeable numbers of domestic migrants to the state. The most recent period has witnessed high-tech economic growth that has outstripped employment growth. As substantial numbers of manufacturing jobs disappeared, greater numbers of higher-skilled, better-paying jobs emerged that attracted college-educated workers to the state. In their wake came lower-paying, lesser-skilled service jobs that involved myriad service activities, often directly or indirectly linked to the increases in higher-skilled jobs (Moretti 2012). Many of these jobs have been filled by immigrants who are of nonwhite ethnoracial status.

It is critical to appreciate the roles that entrepreneurship, innovation, and immigration have played in the growth of California's both higher-skilled and lesser-skilled employment. The expansion has not resulted just from more people moving to the state. In other words, the state has *not* been getting richer merely through natural increase and domestic migration, although such growth certainly accounts for a portion of recent economic upswings. Rather, California has recently been prospering fundamentally because the state leads the country and the world in innovation and entrepreneurship (Moretti 2019). Indeed, economic growth as a result of increases in value-added from the innovation-based higher productivity in California's high-tech industries has constituted the hallmark of the state's new economy (see Chapter 6). While such innovation and its ensuing financial success have made California richer, they have also contributed to economic inequality, just as they have throughout much of the United States (Stiglitz 2018).

This inequality, together with such other factors as zoning restrictions, have contributed to the development of substantial housing shortages, raising to even higher levels housing costs that were already exceeding those of other states (Dillon 2018). This has recently begun to induce people to migrate out of the state. The demand for workers at multiple skill levels, however, remains high, for both demographic and economic reasons (Bean, Bachmeier, and Brown 2014), meaning that the need for immigrants is likely to continue to be high in the foreseeable future. Immigration has been accompanied by ethnoracial diversity in the past (Bean, Bachmeier, and Brown 2014), and this is nearly certain to continue. Ensuring that the state will receive needed immigrant workers thus requires taking action to raise living standards for all, not just for highly paid, high-tech workers (Bean 2019). Without such initiatives, and without dealing first with current housing unaffordability, the benefits of immigration and ethnoracial diversity are likely to be undercut by negative forces emanating from an increasingly zero-sum orientation that fosters populist backlash, immigrant scapegoating, and rises in ethnoracial tension and conflict.

It is thus relevant to ask, first, what are the changing demographic reasons why California's higher- and lesser-skilled workforce will continue to need to rely on foreign-born workers? Second, what is the nature and extent of growth in the state's nonwhite population, and to what extent has that population been able to achieve upward educational mobility? Third, what do the results of social science research suggest about the extent to which diversity leads to improvements in general social welfare, especially under circumstances where opportunities for such upward mobility are favorable? An important reason for California's outsized economic expansion over the past few decades compared to elsewhere has been the state's openness to and welcoming of talented and entrepreneurial newcomers from elsewhere in the country and around the world and its capability to provide adequate education for these newcomers and their children.

California's high-tech success and the viability of the state's social infrastructure, however, may now be at risk because increasing inequality is raising housing costs to a considerable extent. Both middle-class and working-class Californians face housing prices they simply cannot afford to pay (Woetzel et al. 2016). This seems to account for more lesser-skilled workers moving to other states compared to those coming to California. More higher-skilled workers also now seem to be leaving because, even though they may be able to pay the escalating prices, they can achieve a higher standard of living by moving to places where housing requires a smaller share of their income, even though the income they receive at these new destinations is not as high as it would have been in California. In short, expensive housing is increasingly undermining the workforce and social infrastructure California needs to sustain itself and its high-tech innovation economy. Without enough teachers, police officers, firefighters, plumbers, electricians, chefs, nurses, and many others, life in California becomes increasingly difficult and unpleasant, so much so that even well-paid high-tech workers are finding reasons to leave for other states.

Changing Demographic Trends Nationally Are Creating Worker Shortfalls

Although California's strong economic growth and out-migration because of high living costs may create labor shortages in their wake, another factor also contributes substantially to recent labor shortages. This has to do with broader patterns of demographic change. For several years, steady shrinkages in the working-age population in the state, and indeed in the entire country, have strongly emerged. Because of low fertility in the late 1960s and 1970s, the aging of baby boomers, and subsequent cohorts attending and graduating from college at higher rates than baby boomer cohorts, fewer native-born, non-college graduates have been available to fill lesser-skilled jobs, such as construction work. As baby boomers have aged and retired over the past twenty-five years, much of the workforce void has been filled by immigrants, many from Mexico (Bean, Bachmeier, and Brown 2014). Because that workforce itself is now less replenished with new migrants, it is becoming harder and harder to fill such labor shortages. This also makes it more difficult to deal with the especially acute problem of housing affordability. In short, California, like the nation in general, will continue to need immigrants if it is just to maintain its lesser-skilled workforce at its present relative size, let alone increase it (Peri 2019). Moreover, the state will continue to need higher-skilled immigrants as well, as it has the past thirty years, in order to sustain its high-tech economy. But as we noted earlier, older (over-age-thirty-five) college-educated migrants are now starting to move out of California much more than they previously did, thus potentially exacerbating shortages of high-skilled workers. In general, if California is to sustain its robust economy, then the state must address *both* its inequality and housing crises, continue to welcome both lesser-skilled and higher-skilled immigrants, and continue to nurture the policies and circumstances that help make ethnoracial diversity a strength rather than a problem.

Ethnoracial Diversity Is Increasing in California

Maintaining existing levels of immigration thus means continuing to strive to harness the benefits of ethnoracial diversity. In the past, immigration has rendered California the most ethnoracially diverse state in the nation, except for Hawaii (Clark 1998; Lee and Bean 2010). Some might think of this as a problem because they assume a zero-sum labor market, with competition for resources occurring among the members of different groups, inevitably sparking debilitating conflict (Esses et al. 2001). Others think this need not be the case, but rather that people often seek to build modes of cooperation and to fulfill common purposes, embracing tolerance and inclusion of others in the process, especially during periods of healthy economic growth (Haubert and Fussell 2006). As noted earlier, California needs newcomers through immigration to meet its workforce needs. Given that most immigration is likely to consist of people of different ethnoracial backgrounds, the challenge of diversity is one that California will have to continue to meet. The extent of California's diversity today can be seen in its present ethnoracial composition (see figure 2.8). Among adults, Latinos are now a plurality, whites are a minority, and Asians are growing as a share of the population. What are the prospects for the state maintaining and improving in the future the reasonably harmonious relations that have emerged in the state after their low point in the 1990s (Pastor 2018)?

To maintain diversity as a positive force, it is important that the socioeconomic attainment of ethnoracial groups continue to improve. In California, the educational attainments of blacks and Latinos in 2018 were considerably higher than they were in 1990 (table 2.7). The percentages of these groups obtaining some college, graduating from college, and securing advanced

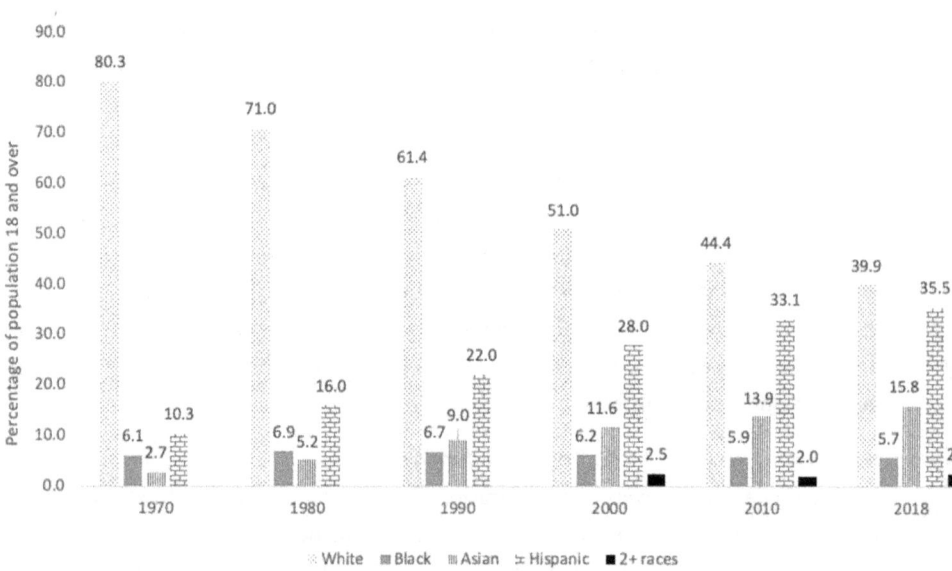

Figure 2.8. Ethnoracial change in California's adult population, 1970–2016 (percentages)

Source: Authors' compilations of U.S. Bureau of the Census microdata reported by Ruggles et al. 2019.

Note: The white, black, Asian, and multiracial populations are non-Hispanic. Non-Hispanics identifying as American Indian, Alaska natives, or other races constitute less than 1 percent of the population across all periods and are omitted. Adults are ages 18 and over.

degrees are notably higher than they were in 1990. For blacks and Mexican Americans, the rates of improvement from 1990 to 2018 (a twenty-eight-year period, or about the length of a full generation) in graduating from college have been nearly as large as they were for whites, with gains of a bit below 50%, which was the increase among whites. In terms of obtaining advanced degrees, blacks and Mexican Americans surpassed the gains of whites, with such proportions more than doubling since 1990. Although such changes have not yet reached parity with whites, they nonetheless indicate that California has closed much of the ethnoracial education gap in just the last generation. The socioeconomic situations of African Americans, Mexican Americans, and the growing multiracial population are appreciably rising, indicating that a much more non-zero-sum situation has emerged in which ethnoracial diversity can continue as a positive rather than negative force in the state (Lee and Bean 2004). And, as native baby boomers continue to age and retire,

Table 2.7. Education by race/ethnicity, U.S.-born Californians, ages 30–39, 1990 and 2018

	White (%)		Black (%)		Mexican American (%)		Asian/Pacific Islander (%)	
	1990	2018	1990	2018	1990	2018	1990	2018
Less than high school	4.5	2.4	7.7	5.3	17.4	9.5	2.7	2.2
High school diploma	23.8	22.7	31.4	31.1	37.7	41.5	13.3	13.9
Some college	40.3	25.1	44.6	35.2	34.9	29.1	34.6	19.6
Bachelor's degree	21.4	31.6	12.0	18.6	7.3	14.4	33.2	40.0
Postgraduate training	10.0	18.1	4.2	9.6	2.7	5.6	16.1	24.3

Source: U.S. Bureau of the Census data reported by Ruggles et al. 2019.
Note: Whites, blacks, and Asian/PI groups consist of only those who identify as non-Hispanic.

workforce voids are providing still further prospects for upward mobility among both Latinos and African Americans (Bean, Lee, and Bachmeier 2013; Alba 2009; Myers 2007).

The General Social Benefits of Diversity
Beyond such educational improvements, what do we know about the effects of ethnoracial diversity in general on social cohesion and solidarity? Both social science theory and research suggest that these are often positive. Theoretically, immigrants bring with them new resources, ideas, and ways of doing things that contribute greatly to improving social and economic life. Rather than emphasizing that newcomers are essentially people of color whose mobility is limited by discriminatory treatment—an orientation that risks self-fulfilling prophecies and fosters anxiety narratives about immigration causing weakened social cohesion and hardened social boundaries among groups—alternative narratives emphasize immigration's social richness and heterogeneity and the positive consequences that diversity often generates. In fact, research shows that ethnoracial diversity boosts people's awareness of alternative cultures and lifestyles, stimulates creativity, leads to the greater development of interpersonal and problem-solving skills, and fosters increases in innovation (Benkler 2006; Chua 2007; Grewal 2008; Herring 2009; Page 2007). These in turn reinforce narratives about the salutary and socially enriching effects that stem from immigration and make for a more resilient and vibrant society (Bean and Stevens 2003; Lee and Bean 2010; Kasinitz et al. 2008).

Sometimes research has overlooked these dynamics. Robert Putnam

(2007) conjectured a decade ago that ethnic heterogeneity might lead natives to be suspicious of immigrants and could thus in general operate to diminish social trust and solidarity. Since then, researchers have conducted dozens of inquiries on the topic in the United States and Europe, concluding overwhelmingly that immigration-induced ethnoracial diversity does *not* on balance negatively influence interethnic social cohesion, except sometimes in U.S. cities containing both immigrants and African Americans (van der Meer and Tolsma 2014; Portes and Vickstrom 2011). In other words, the U.S. case turns out to be affected by prejudicial attitudes toward blacks. Because white Americans perceive a greater threat from and exhibit more prejudice toward blacks than toward other ethnoracial groups, whites living in areas with both large immigrant *and* black populations often report less social solidarity, thereby accounting for the lower solidarity that in some places accompanies the diversity stemming from immigration (Bean, Lee, and Bachmeier 2013; Bean 2016).

A great deal of social science research shows that diversity also reduces the strength of ethnoracial barriers in the United States, including the black–white color line. Numerous studies of ethnoracial intermarriage and multiracial identification have found support for these ideas. For example, in 2015, 9.5% of all U.S. marriages were ethnoracially mixed, and 16.2% of all *new* marriages (those occurring in 2011–2015) were mixed. This represents almost one in every six unions (Frey 2018). Moreover, this latter figure was up from about one in eleven in 2000, a rise of more than half in one decade. Higher levels of intermarriage also occur in tandem with growing multiracial populations. Thus 5.3% of all children ages zero to seventeen were identified as multiracial in 2010, compared to only 1.1% of persons age fifty-five or more (Bean, Lee, and Bachmeier 2013). For white children (i.e., those having some white identification), the percentage multiracial was 6.4; for blacks (those having some black identification), the percentage multiracial was 14.6; and for Asians (those having some Asian identification), it was 27.9%. (Comparable figures for Latinos are impossible to derive because census data do not unambiguously identify mixed Latino/non-Latino origins.)

Most significant of all, research also shows that intermarriage and multiraciality are highest in those parts of the country that are the most diverse, such as California. Moreover, this results from diversity per se, rather than simply from the presence of relatively larger minority populations that provide more opportunities for intermarriage (as well as relatively smaller majority populations that provide fewer) (Bean, Lee, and Bachmeier 2013). The huge post-1965 immigration to the country brought large numbers of immigrants from many countries to California. Their ethnoracial status was mostly neither black nor white, thus elevating ethnoracial diversity. Significantly, most research shows that this diversity appears to be creating multiple color lines, detracting from stark emphases on black-white, white-nonwhite, and black-nonblack divides. Recent rises in intermarriage and multiracial identification—which are more pronounced among Asians and Latinos than among blacks (Frey 2018)—suggest a broad loosening of the boundaries among groups, thus setting the stage for still further increases in intergroup tolerance and social cohesion.

Conclusion

Today California exemplifies a remarkable success story. Its economy, arguably stronger and more innovative than that of Texas (Vara 2015), provides a model that other states and countries often aspire to emulate. Socioculturally, it continues to blaze a trail into the future, embodying new values, practices, and customs (Pastor 2018). Sustaining these tendencies involves several elements: welcoming and offering protection to immigrants (including refugees and unauthorized migrants); celebrating ethnoracial diversity and promoting widespread tolerance for peoples of all kinds; adopting innovative political alignments and election procedures designed to minimize partisan extremism; supporting a strong system of higher education; maintaining a robust health care system and safety net; and reducing economic inequality. Given the state's relative successes in regard to many of these elements in the recent past, it seems incongruous to think that California's economy and future now face serious threats stemming from the state's housing costs being so high. Yet in fact this is the case. Indeed, it is virtually impossible to exaggerate the degree to which this is true. Why do we say this? A major reason is that solutions for the other serious problems California faces—income inequality, poverty, homelessness, insufficient support for early childhood and higher education—take a long time to yield results. Even if authorities adopted programs to deal with trouble spots today, those programs would require several years before substantial improvements in the quantity of housing and reductions in housing prices became evident. In the meantime, given the migration pattern documented earlier of greater numbers of middle-class people starting to leave the state than has been true in the past, the state's economy is likely to suffer. If the presently robust high-tech economy in California were to begin to transfer significant parts of its operations to other states and countries and thus to shrink, the entire California economy would be harmed, and economic growth curtailed.

This could result in many persons in the state adopting the kind of zero-sum outlooks that exacerbate ethnoracial tensions, which in turn would make it harder to sustain the levels of immigration that have contributed substantially to California's current economic strength. The institutional and cultural practices that today still condone the disproportionate incarceration of black males and the practice of black-targeted police violence (Alexander 2012), along with the recent killings by police of blacks in several U.S. cities, spotlight the continuation of racial prejudice toward blacks. This is a major national problem. Our determination now *not* to repeat our past mistake of underestimating racism against blacks (Faust 2015) should not induce us, however, to exaggerate disadvantages among today's other nonwhite immigrant groups. We should not overlook the fact that the second- and third-generation descendants of these immigrants show considerable integration into the country's larger socioeconomic fabric (Waters and Pineau 2015; Frey 2018), as we have noted earlier in the case of California. But these positive long-term trends have taken place in an economy the wage structure of which has more recently stagnated for all but the top 10% of earners.

This kind of inequality underscores the importance of efforts to develop broader and greater opportunities for *all* Californians. And these must be accompanied by housing policies and programs that provide considerably larger numbers of less expensive places to live. Also, diversity today, because of immigration, derives from the presence of many new national-origin groups. Although the reality of this brings real and positive consequences for many Californians (e.g., weaker boundaries among groups, greater social cohesion and solidarity, and more economic opportunity in the state's large metropolitan areas), many Californians, especially those outside large metropolitan areas and often in places without many immigrants, increasingly feel left behind and resentful. Seeking to stifle immigration and punish unauthorized immigrants through deportation, as current federal-level policies tend to do, does little for these overlooked Californians. It only undercuts the social and economic benefits that the new diversity has brought to the state. The challenge now is to develop statewide policies designed to reduce income inequality and substantially improve housing affordability for all Californians, but especially for those in the bottom three-fourths of the income distribution.

Note

This chapter is a revision of one originally prepared for the Ninth Annual University of California International Migration Conference, titled Immigrant California: Policies and Politics, held at the University of California, San Diego, March 2, 2018. The research papers presented at that meeting were commissioned by the California Immigration Research Initiative (CIRI), a five-year multicampus research project supported by a grant from the University of California Office of the President to centers or programs at five UC campuses: the Center for Comparative Immigration Studies (UCSD), the Center for Research on International Migration (UCI), the Center for Latino Policy Research (UCB), the Program in International Migration (UCLA), and the School of Public Policy (UCR).

3   Immigration Policy

Allan Colbern

California began to transform in the late 1990s to the country's model pro-immigration state, after more than a century as a model for passing anti-immigrant legislation. This chapter draws from diverse scholarship on the history of immigrant exclusion and integration to provide an overview of California's long history in passing immigrant policies that date back to the state's founding in 1850. In reviewing California's policy leadership, this chapter weaves together the recurring roles played by demographic diversity and size, economic recession, partisanship, and activism for California's expanding anti- and pro-immigrant policies.

The chapter shows that having a white majority was a critical condition for immigration restrictions to emerge, but white supremacy had to be championed by state officials. Economic recessions provided the important condition for state officials to champion anti-immigrant policies. More than a century later, when California's white majority ended and a more diverse population emerged, the face of its partisan leadership and activism also transformed in favor of pro-immigrant policies. These factors have come together at specific times to make California a historical leader on both anti- and pro-immigrant policies, but this does not preclude other states or localities from achieving similar expansions or transformations.

Indeed, California's model holds special resonance for other jurisdictions. Its anti-immigrant policies have been adopted throughout much of American history for new restrictions in federal immigration law, beginning with the

Chinese Exclusion Act in 1882. Beginning in the late 1990s, this federal–state relationship was redefined by new California policies that prevented state and local officials from actively enforcing federal immigration law and that dramatically expanded the rights of its undocumented residents. The timing of a demographic change and forging of new alliances between immigrant rights organizations and state leaders made California's transformation possible, which now provides a model of pro-immigrant policies for jurisdictions that are becoming more diverse and welcoming to immigrants.

Early Immigration Law in the United States

In early America, the dominant actors in immigration regulation were states, not the federal government. Article 1, Section 9 of the U.S. Constitution created a sunset clause to end the importation of slaves into the country by 1808, and the federal government used its constitutional power to officially ban the international slave trade in 1807, which became effective in 1808.[1] Beyond the international trafficking of slaves, travel into the country was minimally regulated by the federal government under the Steerage Act of 1819 and other passenger acts, which restricted the total number of passengers, set conditions for safe travel, and required ships to report passenger lists and demographic information at ports of entry. States and localities, however, controlled all ports of entry and were the primary enforcers of federal law.[2]

The cause of this federalist arrangement in regard to immigration regulation, as Anna Law and others explain, was the regional conflict over slavery. When drafting the U.S. Constitution and national legislation in the antebellum period, Northern and Southern officials were unwilling to specify who had authority over immigration, in order to preserve free and slave states' control over black migration, demographic diversity, and minority rights (Law 2014, 2015). With the nation growing at a rapid pace, the federal government's primary role was limited to acquiring new federal territories, not regulating migration or setting uniform rights for the country's residents. States controlled who could freely move across national, state, and local borders; set diverse regulations with regard to the internal movement and rights of people; and led in the removal, indenture, or enslavement of persons considered to be unlawfully residing within their jurisdiction (Frymer 2014, 2017; Neuman 1993, 2010).

In early America, state governments (not the federal government) created the patchwork of laws that regulated the movement and rights of free and enslaved blacks, immigrants, paupers, and other classes of people. Seaboard states in the North created and controlled the nation's ports of entry and set up robust social welfare systems, including outdoor relief, public aid, and indoor relief to support its growing, mostly white immigrant population (Katz 1996, 2002, 2013). Despite federal fugitive slave law granting slave owners the right to capture and reclaim their "property," and making it a crime for anyone to harbor runaway slaves, some Northern states enacted personal liberty laws to protect their fugitive and free black residents from being returned to slavery or kidnapped and sold into slavery (Colbern 2017). Southern states, by contrast, passed a range of restrictive slavery and criminal laws to control every facet of black life (Colbern and Ramakrishnan 2020; Hadden 2001).

Scholarship on U.S. immigration law has focused on national development after 1875, particularly on the entry and exit of immigrants, their deportation and removal, and the terms of their residence in the country. Once the federal government entered the field of immigration restriction more fully, passing the Page Act in 1875 and the Chinese Exclusion Act in 1882, scholars often tell the story of immigration regulation from a purely national perspective.[3] As I show in this chapter, however, the lines separating immigration and immigrant policy have always remained somewhat blurred, as states continued to find ways to regulate the movement and rights of their immigrant residents (Gulasekaram and Ramakrishnan 2015, 1–56). California has not only passed its own state laws to regulate the lives of immigrants but also shaped the national direction of federal immigration law, beginning with Chinese exclusion in 1882. Thus, in addition to looking domestically, this chapter demonstrates how California's expansions in immigrant policies have played a significant role nationally and as a model for other states.

Explaining California's Policy Expansions

California's late entrance to statehood in 1850 was significant for ushering in a new era of immigrant restrictions. Bean, Brown, and Pullés (see Chapter 2) demonstrate how California's large and diverse population raises both opportunities and challenges. Indeed, this has allowed the state to become the fifth-largest economy in the world today, with booming industries in agriculture, manufacturing, and technology. This chapter highlights California's diverse population as an important factor in its historical development, but with a different point of emphasis than that of Chapter 2. For most of its history, California's racial and ethnic diversity has fueled its leadership role in passing harsh anti-immigrant state policies. The discovery of gold in 1849 propelled the migration of whites from the Northeast, South, and Midwest, who quickly replaced the Mexican population in California as a new majority. With political power, white Californians immediately enacted a state constitution, followed by a set of laws that restricted the movement and rights of black, Latino, Native American, and Chinese populations (Colbern and Ramakrishnan 2018, 5). Within just a few years, the international and domestic migration patterns that fueled California's formation laid unique demographic foundations for it to become a national leader in setting both anti- and pro-immigration policy throughout U.S. history.

Current explanations of state immigration policies focus on the post-9/11 era, when the number of state policies began to increase across the country: from 27 in 2005 to 437 in 2013 (Johnston and Morse 2013). Gulasekaram and Ramakrishnan argue that the preconditions for this proliferation in the early 2000s occurred through changes in federal law and court decisions ever since 1965, but especially in 1996, which allowed states and localities to regulate immigration despite federal plenary powers. With these conditions set, issue entrepreneurs took up immigration as a major issue in need of national, state, and local reform as a response to the 9/11 terrorist attacks (Gulasekaram and Ramakrishnan 2015). The variation we have seen on the part of states and localities since 2000 is caused by different sets of issue entrepreneurs partnering with Republican jurisdictions to pass mostly restrictive policies and with Democratic jurisdictions to pass mostly integrationist policies (Gulasekaram and Ramakrishnan 2015; Motomura 2014; Hessick and Chin 2014; Chen 2014; Elias 2013; Rodriguez 2008; Varsanyi 2010; Bloemraad and de Graauw 2011; de Graauw 2016; Wong 2012).

With a few exceptions, scholars have not yet examined states' contemporary policymaking in a historical framework. In their historical look at immigration federalism, Daniel Tichenor and Alexandra Filindra (2012, 1245) argue that states have always led in "open combat" with the federal government. In the 1860s, states enacted anti-Chinese immigration laws; in the 1970s, they enacted employer sanction laws prohibiting the hiring of undocumented immigrants; and in the 1990s, California passed Proposition 187, a comprehensive anti-immigrant law that required state and local officials to enforce federal immigration law and banned undocumented residents from all state public benefits including K–12 education. Tichenor and Filindra argue that these instances of state policies are an effort by state officials to "force the immigration issue on the federal agenda" (2012, 1237).

Through examining California's history of immigration policies, this chapter spotlights the continued role of demographic diversity and size, economic recession, partisanship, and activism. California's long history of having a white majority was a critical condition for immigration restrictions to emerge, but white supremacy had to be championed by California's officials for restrictionist immigration policies to become politically viable. Periods of economic recession provided a unique condition for state officials, anti-immigrant activists and native white workers, and employers' interests to align around exclusionary policy expansions. More than a century later, California's white majority ended, and a more diverse population emerged at a critical moment in history that allowed for partisan leadership and activism to redirect the state towards becoming pro-immigrant.

Statehood and Anti-Chinese Laws, 1850–1900

California's 1850 state constitution and early restrictive immigration laws created a racial hierarchy and vulnerable labor force to build its new economy (Colbern and Ramakrishnan 2018, 357–360). Chinese immigrants were actively recruited for mining, railroad construction, manufacturing, and farming, and were replaced in the early 1900s by Mexican immigrants for similar purposes. The need for an exploitative, cheap source of labor led to two distinctive logics of exclusion: one where native white workers sought to keep out immigrant groups altogether and to constrain their activities once they arrived, and another where native employers sought only to constrain their rights and activities. State policies were often framed around the threat of economic competition between Chinese workers and native white workers (Takaki 1998, 92, 95–99, 110–12; Marks 1998, 300–301; Salyer 1995; Mann 1982, 188–93; Saxton 1971, 72–75). Scholars explain, however, that employers' desire for low-wage labor remained an important countervailing factor against state exclusions of Chinese laborers (Brown and Philips 1986; Chiu 1963, 129–32). This meant that during periods of economic growth, employers pressured state officials to preserve access to cheap labor, while allowing for harsh crackdowns and restrictive policy expansions in periods of economic recession. Most of California's restrictive laws benefited employers' access to and control over cheap immigrant laborers, in periods of both growth and recession.

During the 1860s, labor leaders in San Francisco organized large anti-Chinese clubs in every ward of the city, which spread to other cities and towns throughout the state (Kanazawa 2005; Miller 1969). State officials, in collaboration with the anti-Chinese movement, pushed for restrictive state policies while also pressuring for restrictive federal immigration laws (Tichenor and Filindra 2012, 1217). Republican governor Leland Stanford led this effort, successfully pressuring the state legislature to discourage immigration by the "degraded" Chinese immigrants and to pass the state's Anti-Coolie Act of 1862, which was a tax placed on Chinese workers to "protect Free White Labor," despite the fact that Stanford employed them as cheap labor on his farms and in his railroad enterprise (Tichenor and Filindra 2012, 1226). Over the next few years, California led the country by enacting many anti-Chinese laws designed to restrict new immigration to the state and to deprive Chinese immigrant residents of civil, economic, and social rights (Colbern and Ramakrishnan 2020; Tichenor 2002, 89–92; Daniels 1990).

In 1877, the transcontinental railroad increased white migration to California at a time when there was a slowdown in gold mining and an economic recession, which increased support for organized violent riots and expulsion campaigns against Chinese residents throughout the state. Leadership by Denis Kearney, who organized the Workingmen's Party under the slogan "The Chinese Must Go," was critical, as nearly one-third of the delegates selected to the 1878 state constitutional convention belonged to the party (McClain 1994, 316n6). This presence of an anti-Chinese political party had a tremendous impact on the 1879 state constitution, which empowered state officials for the first time to remove immigrants considered detrimental to the well-being of the state and to impose conditions on their residency. The constitution went much further, by barring Chinese from being employed by any corporation or government entity, allowing cities and towns to expel or segregate their Chinese immigrant residents, and banning all Chinese persons from holding property rights and voting rights (Colbern and Ramakrishnan 2020).

Transition to Anti-Mexican Laws, 1900–1930

The year before gold was discovered, the United States signed the 1848 Treaty of Guadalupe Hidalgo that granted U.S. citizenship rights to eighty thousand Mexican nationals and classified them as "white." Meanwhile, in California, Mexican Americans' large population translated into their winning state, county, and local elections and providing eight of the forty-eight delegates to California's state constitutional convention (State of California Office of Historic Preservation 1988, 209). This political power was short lived. Continued white migration to the state led to the formation of a white majority in the early 1850s, just after the state's constitution passed. White leaders such as Senator Thomas Jefferson Green began the process of subjecting Mexicans Americans and immigrants to constitutional restrictions on voting rights and other restrictive state laws, including a foreign miner's tax.[4] Green framed the tax law as an issue over free labor, specifically seeking to restrict foreign capitalists' employment of Mexican "peons" in California's mines (Smith 2013, 87).

Without effective federal protection of U.S. citizenship, California's laws were able to disenfranchise, target and expel Mexican Americans based on their *mestizo* (Indian or Spanish) descent (Gulasekaram and Ramakrishnan 2015, 19; Molina 2014, 26; Menchaca 2010; Castillo 1992). California and its localities, particularly Los Angeles, used racial identity rather than U.S. citizenship status to control the lives of its Mexican residents. Scholars highlight that even after naturalizing, Mexican Americans lost voting rights, trial-by-jury rights, and property rights under California laws (Molina 2014, 23). California's 1855 anti-vagrancy law specifically targeted "persons who are commonly known as 'Greasers' or the issue of Spanish and Indian blood," subjecting Mexican Americans and others considered to be vagrants to either jail or hard labor (Bender 2003).[5] Mexican Americans and immigrants existed between two worlds, classified under federal law as white but treated culturally as nonwhite (Molina 2014). State commissions and courts removed land from Mexican Americans, then legally banned them from owning property (Menchaca 2010; Gómez 2007; Chavez-Garcia 2004). As one scholar put it, "Despite de jure [U.S.] citizenship status, Mexicans could not exercise the franchise [in California] with anything close to the same ease of lighter-skinned Angelenos" (Deverell 2004, 16).

Soon after the federal Chinese Exclusion Act of 1882, Mexican immigrants replaced Chinese immigrants as California's primary source of recruited laborers. First, they were recruited to construct southern railway lines for the Santa Fe and Southern Pacific Railway companies in the 1890s. Over the next thirty years, Mexicans became the backbone of the state's growing seasonal farm workforce (McWilliams and Meier 1990; Reisler 1976). California and other southwestern states experienced an economic boom, and high demand for cheap labor pressured the federal government to preserve an open southern border during national debates on immigration (Zolberg 2006; Ngai 2004; Massey, Durand, and Malone 2003; Tichenor 2002). In 1921 and 1924, federal laws for the first time put quotas on immigration from southern and eastern Europe, but left Mexican immigration uncapped to ensure the Southwest's access to seasonal immigrant laborers (Molina 2014, 2).

From 1929 to 1936, when the country faced the Great Depression, it became clear that despite the emergence of federal exclusivity over setting immigration law (beginning in 1882), states remained central actors in immigrant regulation. California was permitted to expand its anti-Mexican policies, with state officials leading a repatriation movement targeting and forcibly removing nearly four hundred thousand Mexicans, including many U.S. citizens (Hoffman 1974). It simultaneously restricted the labor rights and access to social welfare of Mexican immigrants, all while pushing for greater federal restrictions. The ebbs and flows of California's economy, and its continued access to Mexican immigrant labor, placed the state's political parties and activists in the role of leading the nation on immigrant policy throughout the twentieth century.

Restricting Social Welfare Rights

From 1900 to the 1930s, California's county-level relief offices used social welfare policy to control Mexican and Japanese farmworkers, making them dependent on employers. Growers worked with county relief offices to manipulate their relief rolls in ways that constructed "a fluid and mobile population of farm workers sustained in the off-seasons but ready to be deployed at harvest time" (Walsh 1999, 398). Support from government agencies facilitated agricultural workers' ability to find temporary work in urban industries during off-seasons, while growers' control over relief rolls ensured that these workers returned to farming (Monroy 1981).

Exclusion from social welfare soon emerged through a concerted campaign by California's Governor Young, who initiated a fact-finding mission from 1924 to 1928 to support his view that Mexicans were disproportionately reliant on local relief and depleted the state of resources. Young directed the California Commission of Immigration and Housing (CCIH), which was originally established in 1912 to identify solutions for employment and housing of immigrants in the state, to paint the image of Mexicans as burdens and paupers. The CCIH issued a report in 1926, stating: "The Mexicans as a general rule become a public charge under slight provocation and have become a great burden to our communities" (Walsh 1999, 406). George Clements, who headed the Los Angeles Chamber of Commerce's Agricultural Department, praised Mexican laborers early on, but in 1928 assured Governor Young that "[f]rom a social service standpoint, the Mexican laborer is an alien possible of deportation should he become indigent or a social menace" (Walsh 1999, 408). Relief agencies responded to Young's campaign with local regulations that for the first time required proof of U.S. citizenship, but applied this rule against all Mexican paupers regardless of their citizenship status.

A few years later, in the 1930s, Franklin D. Roosevelt's New Deal created America's federal welfare system with de facto racial exclusions (Katznelson 2006). Many more restrictions emerged, however, because states were placed in control of administrating federal welfare programs. For example, the Federal Emergency Relief Administration (1933) appropriated $500 million to states (as matching grants) to spend on either direct relief or work relief (Fox 2012, 190). Throughout the South and Southwest, this meant that state and local officials were able to shut down their local relief offices during harvest seasons, with the goal of securing growers' control over both black and immigrant labor (Fox 2012, 195). Meanwhile, in California, Governor James Rolph appointed an avid anti-immigrant conservative, Archbishop Hanna, as the state's head social welfare administrator; Hanna made Mexican exclusion the centerpiece of implementing federal relief in the state (Fox 2012, 197).

California simultaneously led the push for more restrictive federal welfare policies. The Social Security Act of 1935 barred agricultural and domestic workers from Social Security and unemployment insurance, disqualifying large numbers of blacks, Mexicans, and other minorities. However, it made no mention of citizenship or immigration status. In fact, between 1935 and 1971, no federal laws barred noncitizens from access to Social Security, unemployment insurance, Old Age Assistance, Aid to Families with Dependent Children, the Food Stamps program, or Medicaid (Fox 2012, 214–49). California pressured Congress to change federal policy throughout the twentieth century, and under Governor Ronald Reagan's leadership, succeeded in 1972 when federal law began to restrict immigrant access for the first time (Fox 2016). California leaders and the state's restrictive policies continued to influence the direction of federal social welfare policy—specifically the Personal Responsibility and Work Opportunity Reconciliation Act (PRWORA) of 1996, which barred states from using federal funds to provide Medicaid and welfare to legal and undocumented immigrants, among other exclusions (Fox 2016, 1052–53; Jacobson 2008; Fujiwara 2008).

Restricting Labor Rights

The New Deal's federal programs for work relief, such as the Public Works Administration and Civil Works Administration, were highly inclusive of immigrants (Fox 2012, 210). Even the most ambitious and largest federal work relief program, the Works Progress Administration (after 1929, renamed Work Projects Administration), did not restrict access based on citizenship or legal status (Fox 2012, 215). Moreover, from the 1930s and through the American civil rights era, federal labor rights were granted to citizens, legal immigrants, and undocumented immigrants alike, including the Fair Labor Standards Act of 1938 (FLSA), Title VII of the Civil Rights Act of 1964, the Occupational Safety and Health Act of 1970, and the Migrant and Seasonal Workers Protection Act of 1983 (Weil 2012; Fisk and Wishnie 2005).

It was the leadership of a California-led coalition of southern and southwestern congressmen that pressured the federal government to place industry-specific restrictions into FLSA labor rights, which excluded black and immigrant workers in agriculture, domestic service, retail, and restaurants. This coalition also succeeded in changing existing federal policy by adding restrictions on employing "unauthorized" immigrants on WPA projects in 1936 and eventually adding restrictions on all immigrants on WPA projects in 1939 (Fox 2012, 215). Banning immigrant laborers from WPA projects and from being able to receive federal relief worked in favor of California's agricultural employers, who preferred a dependent labor force that lacked basic rights. Thus, while California leaders worked hard to prevent its immigrant residents from having rights, they joined leaders in other southwestern border states to request that the federal government still allow them to recruit Mexican immigrant labor during the 1940s to support their expanding economy (Calavita 1992). President Truman agreed and negotiated a bilateral agreement with Mexico to provide for seasonal migration of *braceros*, a program that continued from 1942 until 1964.

In 1970, when California's economy faced a recession, anti-immigrant political leaders redirected their energy from labor recruitment to passing the first employer sanctions law, AB 528, which banned the hiring of undocumented immigrant labor. California Assemblyman Pete Chacon, a prominent member of the Assembly Committee on Labor Relations, argued, "For too many years the illegal entrant has been the tool of unscrupulous employers who capitalize on his willingness to work long hours for minimum wages. The widespread use of illegal entrant workers . . . deprives unskilled and semi-skilled Mexican-Americans, citizens and aliens alike, black and white workers, of decent employment" (Calavita 1983, 211). State leaders attacked illegal immigration as the primary cause of California's economic problems and the reason for regulating who could be employed in the state (Portes 1977, 36). Sectors of the labor movement also supported restricting the hiring of undocumented workers, including the California Teamsters, California's Federation of Labor (AFL-CIO), UFWOC, and California Rural Legal Assistance, Inc (CRLA) (Calavita 1983, 213).

On November 8, 1971, California's Republican governor Ronald Reagan signed AB 528 into law, which states: "No employer shall knowingly employ an alien who is not entitled to lawful residence in the United States if such employment would have an adverse effect on lawful resident workers" (Calavita 1983, 205).[6] The irony of AB 528 is that it did not prevent employers from hiring undocumented labor. Rather, it further increased employers' control by making immigrant workers vulnerable to having their immigration status reported to officials for possible deportation. A decade later, in 1986, President Reagan led a bipartisan Congress to enact the Immigration Reform and Control Act (IRCA), establishing the first federal employer sanction law, modeled after California's 1971 law.

Labor rights movements did exist in California, but were unable to push the state in a pro-immigrant direction. César Chávez's United Farm Workers (UFW) led a grassroots resistance movement that engaged in walkouts, consumer boycotts, hunger strikes, long-distance marches, vigils, and disruptions; it won collective bargaining rights and contracts for farmworkers in California, and even forged temporary ties to California's political leadership. UFW-backed Democrat Jerry Brown replaced Reagan in 1974, and created the Agricultural Labor Relations Board (ALRB) to oversee farm labor disputes. However, Brown governed as a moderate from 1974 to 1983 and only took on a leadership role in immigrant rights temporarily, when it served his electoral interests. California was undergoing significant demographic change as well, with 40% of the total national increase in the U.S. foreign-born population during the 1970s occurring in the state (Pastor 2018, 72–73). Not only did Republicans mobilize its majority-white voter base through painting immigrants as a demographic threat, but to avoid losing white voters, Democratic leadership avoided taking a strong leadership role on immigrant rights. Meanwhile, the UFW split in the mid-1970s over internal issues between its leaders and members on how to protect migrant worker rights. Governor Brown severed his partnership with UFW as a result (Neuburger 2013). Soon after, small gains in California's immigrant labor rights faded, and its new generations of farmworkers remained legally unprotected, with few political allies in state and local government (Pawel 2010, 2015).

Today, undocumented immigrants do have basic federal labor rights, but they face the risk of deportation any time they exercise these rights (Nissen, Angee, and Weinstein 2008; González-López 2006; Williams 2005; Loh and Richardson 2004; Vellos 1996). The Supreme Court ruled in *Hoffman Plastic Compounds, Inc. v. National Labor Relations Board* (2002) that undocumented workers are not entitled to back pay, making them more vulnerable to employer abuse and severing immigrants from access to rights established under the National Labor Relations Act of 1935. Worker centers and nonprofit organizations have filled the void left by a general lack of federal and state-level protections by providing information to immigrant workers about their rights, helping them navigate the process of submitting a claim, and serving as a firewall to avoid revealing their legal status to employers during this process (de Graauw 2015; Fine 2006, 2015; Gleeson 2012, 2015; Milkman 2006, 2000, 2011).

Policing and Immigration Enforcement within States

After the federal government took control over immigration law in the late 1880s, states no longer controlled entry, exit, and removal, but continued to have roles in immigration enforcement. To expand its reach and capacity to enforce immigration law in the interior of the country, the federal government partners with states and localities. This includes issuing federal detainer requests to state or local law enforcement by providing formal notice that the federal government intends to take custody of detainees believed to be unauthorized. States seeking to enforce immigration law cannot act alone. Criminal and civil violations under current immigration law are enforceable only by the federal government: unauthorized entry is a misdemeanor, and reentry (after being previously deported) is subject to a possible felony, but unlawful presence inside the country is considered only a civil violation (not a crime) subject to removal from the country (Wong 2016, 7). Although federal detainer requests can incentivize and encourage compliance, under the Tenth Amendment's anti-commandeering principle, the federal government cannot force or mandate state or local officials to use their own resources and personnel to keep noncitizens in their custody or to enforce federal immigration law.[7] Thus American federalism allows for state and local governments to partner with the federal government in policing immigrants or to sever their role in immigration enforcement to protect their immigrant residents.

During the 1980s, hundreds of thousands of Salvadorans, Guatemalans, and Nicaraguans fled their countries to escape civil war. President Reagan and GOP allies in Congress considered Central Americans not as refugees to be welcomed under the Refugee Act of 1980 but rather as economic migrants who unlawfully entered the U.S. and were therefore subject to removal by federal immigration officials. This led to a nationwide sanctuary movement by individuals and churches to protect Central American asylum seekers from deportation. On March 24, 1982, Southside Presbyterian in Tucson and five churches in Berkeley, California, led the country by publicly declaring themselves as sanctuaries for Central American "refugees," whom the federal government deemed unlawfully present (García 2006, 99). By 1985, the movement developed into a national network of churches and synagogues that harbored and transported Central Americans to protect them from being deported.

California was home to the largest number of church-declared sanctuaries in the 1980s (over one hundred), forty of which were in the San Francisco Bay Area. San Jose enacted the first city resolution in 1984 to show its support for the church-led sanctuary movement. This grew to eleven cities in California and twenty-seven cities nationally by 1989, when the movement came to an end (Colbern 2017; Colbern, Amoroso-Pohl, and Gutiérrez 2019). Despite the symbolic significance of this resistance movement, few jurisdictions actively protected undocumented immigrants from immigration enforcement. In California, the Los Angeles Police Department issued Special Order 40 in 1979, preventing local police officers from reporting undocumented immigrants to federal immigration authorities, unless they committed serious crimes. Leaders in the 1980s Central American sanctuary movement and pro-immigrant activists in the 2010s often referred to Special Order 40 as a model sanctuary policy, but it was created to establish community policing practices in the city, not as a local form of resistance to federal immigration law.

California also remained the nation's leader in anti-immigrant policies, despite the role of its local jurisdiction in the 1980s sanctuary movement. In 1983, Governor Brown was replaced by George Deukmejian, a conservative Republican governor who served until 1991, with an agenda that largely avoided the issue of immigration. However, his conservative agenda cut the size of government and taxes, weakened the Agricultural Labor Relations Board, and relaxed labor law enforcement. This further weakened the political power of the UFW to advocate for farmworker rights ("Latinos in Twentieth Century California: National Register of Historic Places Context Statement" 2015, 81). In the early 1990s, California resumed its role as a national leader in restricting immigrant rights under Republican governor Pete Wilson—who notoriously partnered with anti-immigrant activists in Orange County to become the face of Proposition 187 in his 1994 reelection campaign.

Restricting Voting Rights

Ever since statehood, California has been unique among other states in its relation to immigrant residents: In its 1850 constitution, it placed U.S. citizenship as a requirement for voting, in contrast to most early American states that expressly permitted immigrant voting and office holding in order to attract immigrant settlers. Meanwhile, California's constitution mirrored those of other states by also restricting voting rights along racial and gender lines, by excluding blacks, Native Americans, and women. It wasn't long before the white population grew into a majority in the early 1850s that state leaders expanded California's restrictions by subjecting Mexicans Americans (despite being U.S. citizens) to the same constitutional restrictions on voting rights applied to immigrants. Racial exclusions were later formalized under state laws requiring literacy tests, poll taxes, early registration, and residency requirements to vote (Fox 2012, 46–47).

Following World War I and heightened national anti-immigrant sentiment, every state in the country followed California's model of requiring U.S. citizenship in order to expressly deny immigrants the right to vote (Hayduk 2012; Keyssar 2009). Scholars note that the 15th, 19th, 24th, and 26th Amendments prevent states from denying U.S. citizens voting rights, but the "one person, one vote" jurisprudence on suffrage leaves open whether or not states can grant immigrants voting rights (Raskin 1993). Political barriers, not constitutional law or federal law, has prevented states and localities from offering voting rights to immigrants (Kini 2005).

The movement to extend voting rights to immigrants reemerged first in New York City, which enacted a law in 1968 allowing noncitizen parents of schoolchildren the right to vote in community school board elections and to hold office on school boards (Hayduk 2012, 76). Local initiatives have spread throughout major cities in California with little success, lacking support from public opinion and effective framing of the value of noncitizen voting rights (Hayduk 2012; Coll 2011). California's most progressive city, San Francisco, began its efforts in 1996, and it took two decades for it to make history as the first jurisdiction in the state to ever extend immigrants the right to vote.

In February 1996, San Francisco's supervisor, Mabel Teng, sponsored a proposal to grant two groups of legal permanent residents (LPRs, or green card holders) the right to vote, including giving parents the right to vote in school board elections, and community college students the right to vote for City College trustees (Kini 2005). Teng explained that her motivation was "to extend the right to legal residents who live here, work here, have kids that go to school here, or who go to school themselves" and "encourage people to participate in the political process" (Walsh 1996). San Francisco's 1996 attempt, and another two ballot measures in 2004 and 2010, failed to pass due to public opinion and failures in strategic campaigning. Finally, Proposition N passed in 2016, allowing all immigrant parents the right to vote in the city's school board elections.

California's Transformation: Expanding Immigrant Rights

California transformed after a last hurrah in expanding restrictions on immigrants. In the early 1990s, the state faced growing expenses for developing its public infrastructure to support a rapidly growing immigrant population and was hit by another economic recession. This led to military base closures and cuts in defense spending, public infrastructure projects, and local public services. Unwilling to increase local taxes because of local political constraints, and dependent on national and state funds that were no longer available, Orange County filed for bankruptcy in 1994 and made national headlines. Cities throughout California were similarly hurting and susceptible to another racialized campaign for immigration exclusion.

Anti-immigrant activists forged a partnership with political leaders and capitalized on the recession and fiscal problems California faced, with the intention of targeting immigrants (Gulasekaram and Ramakrishnan 2015, 51). Republican governor Pete Wilson and state officials politicized immigration by asking Congress to repay California for providing immigrants social services, and then passed a new set of state laws in 1993, barring unauthorized immigrants from obtaining driver's licenses, mandating cooperation between state prisons and federal immigration authorities, and mandating employment agencies to verify immigration status (Pastor 2018, 74).

The following year, Governor Wilson pushed for the passage of Proposition 187 as part of his reelection campaign, which was enacted by voters in November 1994 by a wide margin of 59% to 41% (Gulasekaram and Ramakrishnan 2015, 54). Prop. 187 sought to limit access to public services for undocumented persons, required state officials at all levels to report suspected unlawful presence, and barred primary and secondary education for undocumented children. A federal district court held most of it unconstitutional.[8] This included preempting Prop. 187's ban on K–12 education, which the U.S. Supreme Court in *Plyler v. Doe* (1982) protected under the Fourteenth Amendment's equal protection clause, regardless of a child's immigration status. It also included preemptions on California's verification, notification, and cooperation/reporting requirements in Prop. 187, which were considered exclusive powers of the federal government under U.S. immigration law.

Beyond gaining a court victory, Latino voters responded by greatly increasing their participation in state elections, leading to a new era of Democratic Party dominance and a new generation of Latino leaders, who were able to secure staff positions and legislative offices (Gulasekaram and Ramakrishnan 2015; Ramírez 2013). Grassroots organizing around immigrant rights also began to build a strong advocacy network of activists, allies, and policymakers in state and local government (Colbern and Ramakrishnan 2020; Gulasekaram and Ramakrishnan 2015, 119–50; Cha 2014). These top-down and bottom-up developments set the conditions for California to become a pro-immigrant state.

The counterresponse to Proposition 187 was long-term investment in organizing from the mid-1990s through the 2000s that made reversing course in California possible (Colbern and Ramakrishnan 2016, 3). As California was transforming, federal reforms to immigration law in 1996, made through the Illegal Immigration Reform and Immigrant Responsibility Act (IIRIRA) and the Personal Work Opportunity and Reform Act (PWORA), created new openings for states to begin regulating areas such as education, health care, and professional licenses. California extended many benefits and protections for undocumented immigrants, including granting in-state tuition in 2001, banning restrictive local landlord ordinances in 2007, and granting access to postsecondary financial aid in 2011, driver's licenses in 2013, and professional licenses in 2014.

California banned local governments from being able to mandate employer use of E-Verify in 2011 and enacted laws in 2015 to limit all employers in the state from using E-Verify on existing employees or those who have not yet received a conditional job offer. These policies were a response to federal developments in enforcing IRCA restrictions (passed in 1986) on employment through a new federal E-Verify system—first piloted in 1996 and then required in 2007 for all federal contractors and vendors—which uses Department of Homeland Security and Social Security Administration databases to verify the identity and work authorization of employees. California similarly passed a noncooperation law in 2013, called the Transparency and Responsibility Using State Tools (TRUST) Act, which stipulates that officers can only enforce immigration detainers issued by ICE for persons convicted of serious crimes (Colbern and Ramakrishnan 2016, 5–6).

In regard to health care, as Shimkhada and Ponce show (see Chapter 4), California made national headlines by providing all immigrant children access to full-scope Medicaid in 2015 and began mobilizing political support for expanding coverage to all immigrants. To fill gaps in federal labor rights and protections, California passed three laws in 2013 that expanded the definition of extortion to include a threat to report immigration status; empowered the California Labor Commission and courts to suspend business licenses for employers who retaliate against workers by using their immigration status; and made it a "cause for suspension, disbarment, or other discipline" for lawyers to report suspected immigration status. It also passed two laws in 2015 to empower the California labor commissioner to pursue cases against employers who steal employees' wages and to ensure that all injured workers have access to compensation benefits, regardless of their legal status (Colbern and Ramakrishnan 2016, 8–9).

In 2016, California passed the Truth Act, which provides additional due-process protections to detained immigrants. It requires local jails to provide advance written notice of ICE hold requests to immigrants and their legal representatives before transferring immigrants to federal custody. The law adds new accountability and review processes for local detainer compliance practices. In 2017, California passed SB 54, the California Values Act, severing state and local resources and officials from "performing the functions of a federal immigration officer" and requiring that ICE obtain a court warrant before a transfer of violent offenders can be made by any state or local official to federal custody for deportation. It also created "safe zones" that prohibit immigration enforcement on public school, hospital, and courthouse premises, and requires state agencies to review and update confidentiality policies to protect immigrants.

Conclusion

The contrast between California's past and present is stark. It altered its historical trajectory on immigrant policy and has become a leader for other progressive states when it comes to immigrant integration. By 2017, and following California's lead, seventeen states passed laws to offer in-state tuition, and thirteen states passed laws to offer driver's licenses to undocumented immigrants. Other states have led as well, including Illinois, which passed the first E-Verify bans in 2007 and 2009, preceding California by four years; and Connecticut, which passed the first TRUST Act just months before California in 2013. States are turning to California as a model for developing their own versions of a statewide advocacy coalition and policy agendas. Most recently, in 2017, the New York Immigrant Coalition (2017) issued a blueprint outlining short-term (by 2020), mid-term (by 2023), and long-term (by 2028) sets of policy goals that draw on California's achievements as a model. Democratic leadership and powerful immigrant rights organizations in diverse states have led to major changes in Connecticut, Illinois, and New York, often in parallel to the policy developments in California.

At the same time, California's radical transformation is unique. As Bean, Brown, and Pullés highlight in Chapter 2, its large and diverse population contrasts many other states, with important implications for its economic leadership. This diversity has also placed California at the forefront of the nation on immigration policy, especially in times of demographic change. Most illustrative of California's demographic and political story is Prop. 187 in 1994. Whites had lost their majority status in the 1990s with large increases in the state's Latino and Asian populations, leading California to become a minority-majority state (Schevitz 2000). Unlike in the past, when California had a predominately white leadership that could be leveraged during economic recessions to enact anti-immigrant

policies with little consequence, Prop. 187 fueled a major increase in naturalization, activism, and political participation by Latinos in the state. This reaction to
state politics in 1994 solidified the political conditions for radically transforming
California into a pro-immigrant state today.

California is now solidly Democratic, with over two decades of coalition
building connecting a highly organized statewide advocacy movement to state
officials. The Latino population increased to 14.99 million in 2014, replacing
whites as the state's largest group (Panzar 2015). This new majority is likely to
support immigrant-friendly policies, as a reaction to the racialized quality of the
state's past and in response to escalating attacks on immigrant rights by President
Trump's administration (Jacobson 2008, 60). California's radical transformation
has ushered in a new era of what scholars call progressive state citizenship (Colbern and Ramakrishnan 2020).

Notes

1. US Const. art. I, sect. 9, cl. 1; Act of March 22, 1794, ch. 11, 1 Stat. 347 (1794); Act
of May 10, 1800, ch. 51, 2 Stat. 70 (1800); Act of Feb. 28, 1803, ch. 10, 2 Stat. 205 (1803);
"An Act to Prohibit the Importation of Slaves," ch. 22, 2 Stat. 426 (1807).

2. "An Act Regulating Passenger Ships and Vessels," ch. 46, 3 Stat. 488 (1819).

3. Page Act of 1875, ch. 141, 18 Stat. 477 (repealed 1974) (prohibiting the immigration of prostitutes, contract laborers, and convicts from "China, Japan, or any Oriental
country"); Immigration Act of 1882, ch. 376, 22 Stat. 214 (codified as amended at 8
U.S.C. §§ 1551–1574 (2012)) (transferring authority over the landing of immigrants
from individual states to the U.S. Treasury Department); Chinese Exclusion Act of
1882, ch. 126, 22 Stat. 58 (repealed 1943) (prohibiting the entry of Chinese laborers
into the United States for a period of ten years); Contract Labor Act of 1885, ch. 164,
23 Stat. 332 (repealed 1952) (prohibiting the immigration of any foreigner who had
entered into an employment contract with an American employer prior to departing
his country of origin).

4. State of California, *Journal of the Assembly*, 1st sess. (1849/50), 1147, 1165; state
of California, *Journal of the Senate*, 1st sess. (1849/50), 257–58; Act of April 13, 1850,
ch. 97, *SC*, at 221–23.

5. 1855 Cal. Stat. ch 175 § 1.

6. Eleven states and one city followed California's lead in adopting employer sanctions: Connecticut, Delaware, Florida, Kansas, Maine, Massachusetts, Montana, New
Hampshire, New Jersey, Vermont, Virginia, and the city of Las Vegas, Nevada (Calavita 1983, 226n3).

7. *Galarza v. Lehigh County*, No. 12–3991 (3rd Cir. Mar. 4, 2014).

8. *LULAC v. Wilson*, 908 F. Supp. 755 (C.D. Cal. 1995).

4 Federal Policies and Health

Riti Shimkhada and Ninez A. Ponce

The provision of health care insurance coverage in the United States has produced fierce debates (Obama 2016). Through the use of premium subsidies for private coverage purchased in a health insurance exchange, an individual health insurance mandate, and Medicaid expansion, the Affordable Care Act (ACA) in 2010 was a major policy shift for the country and has expanded both public and private health insurance coverage of individuals in the United States. Under the ACA, noncitizen immigrants, both lawfully and not lawfully present, constitute the largest group facing various forms of exclusions—enrollment, language access, and eligibility for subsidies—from federally financed health coverage programs.

The ACA retains many of the same exclusions for eligibility in public programs that were introduced decades earlier. The Personal Responsibility and Work Opportunity and Reconciliation Act (PRWORA) of 1996 and related immigration reforms in the same year excluded most noncitizens from federally funded Medicaid eligibility as well as other federally funded public benefit programs. (Only "qualified aliens" are eligible for public benefits according to PRWORA. This includes lawful permanent residents, refugees, Cuban and Haitian entrants, asylees, aliens paroled into the United States for a period of at least one year, aliens granted withholding of deportation, aliens granted conditional entry into the United States, and certain battered spouses and children.) PRWORA also introduced a five-year waiting period for eligibility for benefits after immigrants obtain qualified status.

This chapter provides the backdrop to the conversations on public charge—defined as being primarily dependent on the government for subsistence (U.S. Department of Homeland Security 2019a)—and health care use by immigrants, beginning with federal health care policies and the inclusion of immigrants in these federal laws, and California's response to these policies. California has introduced expansive policies to extend and promote health care access to its population (Weil 2018; Melnick, Fonkych, and Zwanziger 2018; Ko et al. 2018), where 27% are foreign-born immigrants (Migration Policy Institute 2018). In the particular case of linguistic access in health care settings, California helped form the basis for federal language access laws, including new requirements for language assistance services under the Patient Protection and Affordable Care Act (ACA).

We use the California Health Interview Survey (CHIS) to describe the populations affected by potential new federal policies that present threats to immigrant health. We look specifically at the expansion of the public charge rule published by the U.S. Department of Homeland Security on August 14, 2019, and implemented on February 24, 2020, which expanded the benefits that could be considered in a determination of whether an immigrant seeking permanent residency would become dependent on the government for subsistence, also referred to as a public charge. CHIS data provide an opportunity to examine the immigrant communities that remain vulnerable to potential changes in public benefit exclusions and are highly sensitive to an anti-immigrant policy climate.

Federal Law—The ACA

The Patient Protection and Affordable Care Act (ACA) was signed into law by President Obama in 2010 and upheld by the U.S. Supreme Court in 2012 (132 S. Ct. 2566). With premium subsidies for individuals to directly purchase private coverage in the federal or state established health insurance exchanges, a requirement by law for individuals to obtain health insurance (known as the individual mandate), and Medicaid expansion, the ACA's explicit goal was to increase insurance coverage. The ACA also included provisions to require the coverage of "essential health benefits" (e.g., mental health), to reform payment systems, and to improve the quality of care.

Under the ACA, most individuals who are U.S. citizens, U.S. nationals, or "lawfully present immigrants" are required to have health coverage.

Lawfully present individuals in the United States include U.S. citizens and U.S. nationals; lawful permanent residents (LPRs), or "green card holders"; lawful temporary residents; persons fleeing persecution, including refugees and asylees; other humanitarian immigrants, including people granted temporary protected status; and nonimmigrant status holders (including people with worker visas and student visas). Individuals who are lawfully present in the United States are subject to the health insurance mandate and are eligible, if otherwise qualified, to participate in the health insurance exchanges and to receive the premium tax credit and cost-sharing subsidies. As of 2019, although the individual mandate under the ACA is still intact by law, the tax penalty is zero for individuals who do not have health coverage and who do not qualify for an exemption. Individuals who are not lawfully present are exempt from the requirement to have health insurance. Under the federal law, unauthorized immigrants are not allowed to purchase health insurance through the state exchange.

California's Response to the ACA Transformed Immigrant Health in California

Immigrants in California, particularly unauthorized immigrants and the uninsured among them, have fewer or similar numbers of doctor, emergency room, and preventive service visits compared to U.S. citizens and other immigrant groups (Pourat et al. 2014). Immigrants tend to arrive in the United States when they are young and healthy. However, as they continue to work and grow older, there is an increasing need for care, treatment, preventive screening services, and emergency health care, especially given the risk stemming from poor living and work conditions (Ponce et al. 2008).

California has been at the forefront of instituting immigrant health protection policies, especially as a countervailing force in the face of more exclusionary federal policies that have direct, indirect, and sometimes unintended consequences for immigrant health. California has gone further than most states in providing access to health insurance coverage by expanding eligibility for the state's Medicaid program (Medi-Cal) to all low-income adults earning up to 138% of the Federal Poverty Line (FPL) guidelines (up to $34,638 for a family of four in 2018). In May 2015, in his release of the California state budget, Governor Jerry Brown formalized the extension of full-scope Medi-Cal coverage (as well as In-Home Supportive Services and Cash Assistance Program for

Immigrants) to unauthorized Californians protected from deportation under the Deferred Action for Childhood Arrivals (DACA) program.

California's policies under the ACA expanded coverage for lawfully present immigrants in the state who have been LPRs for at least five years. Those with incomes at or below 138 percent of the FPL became eligible for Medi-Cal. For recent LPRs in their first five years of residence, those without children and who have household incomes below 139 percent of the FPL are able to obtain Medi-Cal. Recent LPRs with household incomes between 139 and 400 percent of the FPL were allowed to purchase subsidized insurance through the state's health insurance exchange, Covered California. California became the fifth state to expand health insurance coverage to unauthorized children in 2015 when Governor Brown signed into law SB 4, the Health for All Kids Act. California joined the small group of states that had already expanded coverage to all children regardless of the immigration status of the child—Washington, New York, Massachusetts, Illinois, and the District of Columbia. With the Health for All Kids Act law in place in California, it has been estimated that about 170,000 unauthorized children became eligible for Medi-Cal coverage in 2016 (California Department of Health Care Services 2015). With SB 75 (Full Scope Medi-Cal for All Children) in place, starting May 2016, children under nineteen years of age are eligible for full-scope Medi-Cal benefits regardless of immigration status, as long as they meet all other income eligibility requirements (Welfare and Institutions Code section 14007.8). In 2019, under California's new governor Gavin Newsom and Democratic-controlled state legislature, Medi-Cal was expanded to unauthorized adults under twenty-six years of age starting in 2020 via the Young Adult Expansion, modeled after SB 75, which also amends the California Welfare and Institutions Code 14007.8. In Governor Newsom's budget proposal released in January 2020, he plans to expand Medi-Cal to all people age sixty-five and older regardless of immigration status starting in 2021 (Newsom 2020).

Medi-Cal and Covered California eligibility based on citizenship and immigration status is summarized in table 4.1. In 2016, California overturned the federal exclusion of unauthorized immigrants from purchasing health insurance through the exchange, suggesting that Covered California would soon offer a health insurance solution for unauthorized immigrants in the state. But, in early 2017, Covered California withdrew its request to sell unsubsidized health plans to unauthorized immigrants when it became more apparent that the chances of federal approval were slim under the Trump administration. The sponsor of the

Table 4.1. Medi-Cal and Covered California eligibility based on citizenship and immigration status

Full-Scope Medi-Cal Eligibility	Covered California Eligibility
Per California Code of Regulations section 50301 (Citizenship or Immigration Status for Full Medi-Cal Benefits), to be eligible for full Medi-Cal benefits, an applicant or beneficiary must be a California resident who is one of the following: • A citizen of the United States. • A national of the United States from American Samoa or Swain's Island. • An alien lawfully admitted to the United States for permanent residence. This includes conditional permanent residents who have been granted a two-year period of lawful admission for of permanent residence in accordance with section 216 of the Immigration and Nationality Act (8 USC 1186a). • `An alien permanently residing in the United States under color of law (PRU-COL). • `An amnesty alien (lawful temporary resident or lawful permanent resident) whose status has been adjusted in accordance with section 210, 210A, or 245A of the Immigration and Nationality Act (8 USC sections 1160, 1161 or 1255a) if the alien meets one of the following conditions: o The alien is aged, blind, disabled, or under 18 years of age, or o More than five years have elapsed since the date the alien was granted lawful temporary resident status. The date of granting is the date the alien filed his or her application for lawful temporary resident status. All children and young adults under the age of 26 years are eligible for full-scope Medi-Cal regardless of immigration status, starting in 2019 (California Welfare and Institutions Code 14007.8).	To be eligible for health insurance through Covered California, an applicant or beneficiary must be a California resident who is one of the following: • U.S. citizen or U.S. national • Lawful permanent resident (green card holder) • Lawful temporary resident • Person fleeing persecution, including refugees and asylees • Other humanitarian immigrant, including those granted temporary protected status • Non-immigrant status holder (including worker visa and student visa) Federal Tax Credits and the State Subsidy for Covered California To qualify for federal tax credits and the state subsidy, you must • Be a U.S. citizen, a U.S. national, or be lawfully present in the United States. • Not have access to affordable, minimum-value health insurance through an employer. • Not be eligible for other public health coverage, including full-scope Medi-Cal, premium-free Medicare Part A or military coverage. • File taxes for the year that you will receive premium assistance. • File taxes jointly if you are married. • For federal tax credits, have an annual household income between 100 and 400 percent of the federal poverty level. • For the state subsidy, have an annual household income between 0 and 138 percent or over 200 and up to 600 percent of the federal poverty level.

Note: The information in this table is directly quoted from the original sources (California Code of Regulations and Covered California).

Sources: California Code of Regulations 50301. Citizenship or Immigration Status for Full Medi-Cal Benefits: https://www.cdss.ca.gov/shd/res/pdf/50301.pdf and Covered California Immigration Status and Health Coverage: https://www.coveredca.com/individuals-and-families/getting-covered/immigrants

bill, State Senator Ricardo Lara, also expressed concern that the federal administration might use information gleaned from Covered California for the purpose of identifying and deporting unauthorized individuals. Covered California had estimated that about seventeen thousand Californians would have gained coverage if the legislation had passed (Covered California 2016).

ACA Impact

Since the ACA coverage expansion went into effect in 2014, the uninsured rate in California declined from 15% in 2013 to about 8% in 2018. Figure 4.1 shows health access indicators for the period from 2006 to 2018, using data from the California Health Interview Survey (CHIS). The downward trend in the number of individuals of all ages who are uninsured began after the implementation of the ACA in 2014. The number of individuals covered by Medi-Cal increased at the same turning point.

Unauthorized Immigrants

Unauthorized immigrants were excluded from coverage under the ACA, including the health benefit exchanges. Among workers in the labor market that employs unauthorized immigrant wage earners, employers are less likely to offer benefits in the absence of legal labor protections, and even for legal immigrants, limited English proficiency can impede access to government programs and jobs that offer insurance (Ponce et al. 2008). Legal status is associated with health risks, such as stress, poor working conditions, and limited access to health services and resources (Torres and Young 2016). Legal status also shapes economic and educational integration, social mobility, and isolation (Dreby 2015; Gulbas et al. 2016; McCabe et al. 2017; Zhou et al. 2008).

Using data from the 2001 and 2009 CHIS, Pourat et al. (2014) found that unauthorized immigrants in California, and the uninsured among them, had fewer or similar numbers of doctor, emergency department, and preventive service visits compared to U.S. citizens and authorized immigrants. California is home to more than two million unauthorized immigrants, representing 6% of the state's population. About 12% of school-age (K–12) children in California have an unauthorized parent; most children with an unauthorized parent—about 80%—are U.S. citizens (Hayes and Hill 2017).

In 2017, the California legislature considered various state policies to address fear and anxiety related to immigration enforcement actions that particularly impact unauthorized populations. For example, SB 244 (Lara), which passed and was approved by Governor Brown, tightens the restrictions on what state and local government agencies can do with data, including prohibitions on sharing citizenship or immigration status information with federal immigration authorities. Another bill, SB 613 (De León), which also passed and was approved by Governor Brown, repealed the mandate for the State Department of State Hospitals to cooperate with the U.S. Bureau of Immigration and Customs Enforcement in arranging for the deportation of immigrants who are confined, admitted, or committed to any state hospital.

Federal actions continue to be a concern in California. Lawmakers in California have thus become adept in responding to the federal policy climate by proposing legislation that seeks to provide health care and related services to all, regardless of immigration status. The actions taken by California to date move the state closer to providing full-scope health care coverage to all individuals regardless of immigration status.

Another Major Step Forward with Language Access

According to the 2016 CHIS, nearly seven million Californians (19%) report speaking English "less than very well," which is referred to as limited English proficiency or as being limited English proficient (LEP). Limited English language proficiency and low income are associated with limited access to care among immigrants (Ziol-Guest and Kalil 2012; Muñoz-Blanco et al. 2017; Lu et al. 2017; Hall and Cuellar 2016; García-Pérez 2016). Existing laws require federally funded health care organizations and insurers to provide the individuals who are LEP with access to language services, including utilizing qualified interpreters. In 2003, California SB 853, the Health Care Language Assistance Act, began requiring health plans to collect data on race, ethnicity, and language to identify health disparities and to implement interventions, including providing enrollees with interpreter services and translated materials (Ko et al. 2018). In an effort to increase access to language services in health care for individuals with limited English proficiency, Governor Brown approved California SB 223, Chapter 771 (health care language assistance services) in 2017. SB 223 requires that similar services be provided by any organization that accepts Medi-Cal. The law also required the provision of a written notice of the availability of free language-access services in the top fifteen languages spoken by LEP individuals living in the state, as well as a written notice of the availability of interpretation services.

Medi-Cal

U.S.-born citizen — Naturalized citizen — Noncitizen

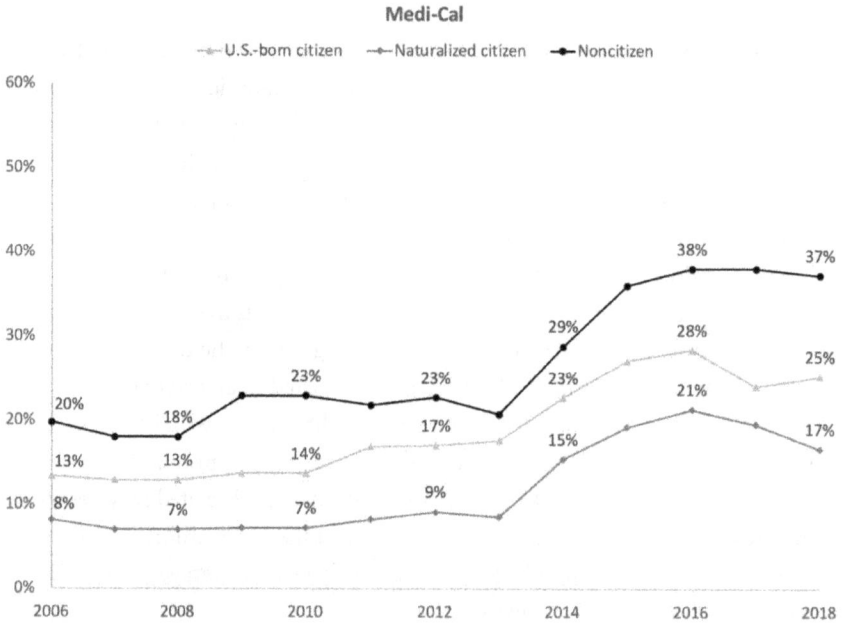

Privately Purchased Insurance

U.S.-born citizen — Naturalized citizen — Noncitizen

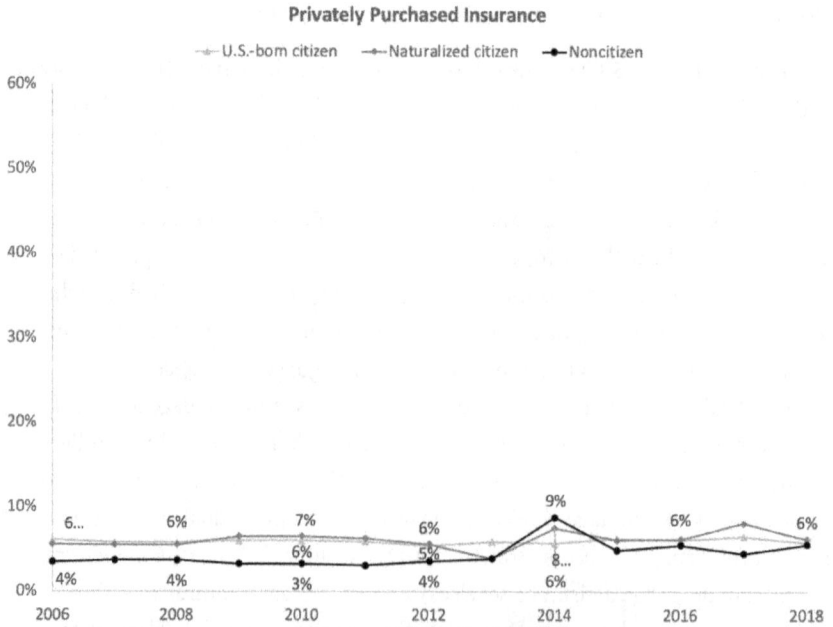

Figure 4.1. Health insurance coverage in California, all ages
Source: California Health Interview Survey 2006–2018.

Employer Sponsored Insurance (ESI)

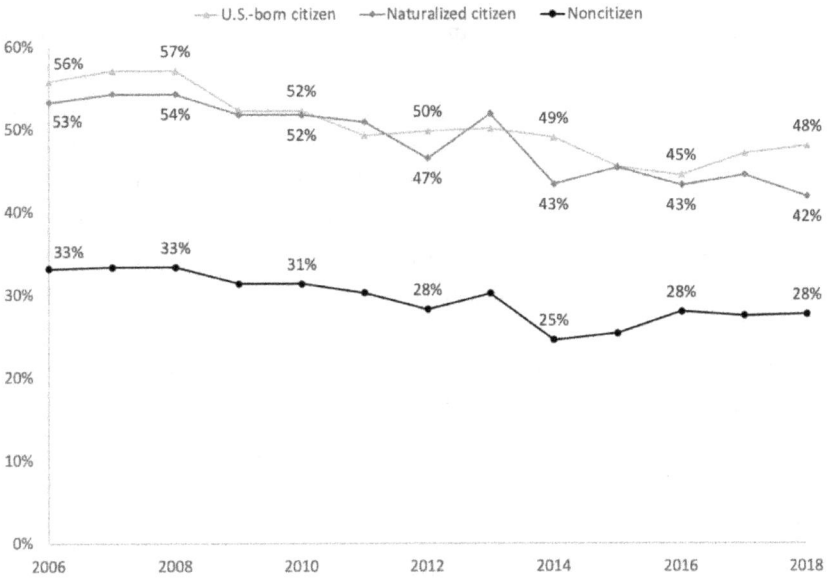

Legend: U.S.-born citizen · Naturalized citizen · Noncitizen

U.S.-born citizen: 56%, 57%, 52%, 50%, 49%, 45%, 48%
Naturalized citizen: 53%, 54%, 52%, 47%, 43%, 43%, 42%
Noncitizen: 33%, 33%, 31%, 28%, 25%, 28%, 28%

Uninsured

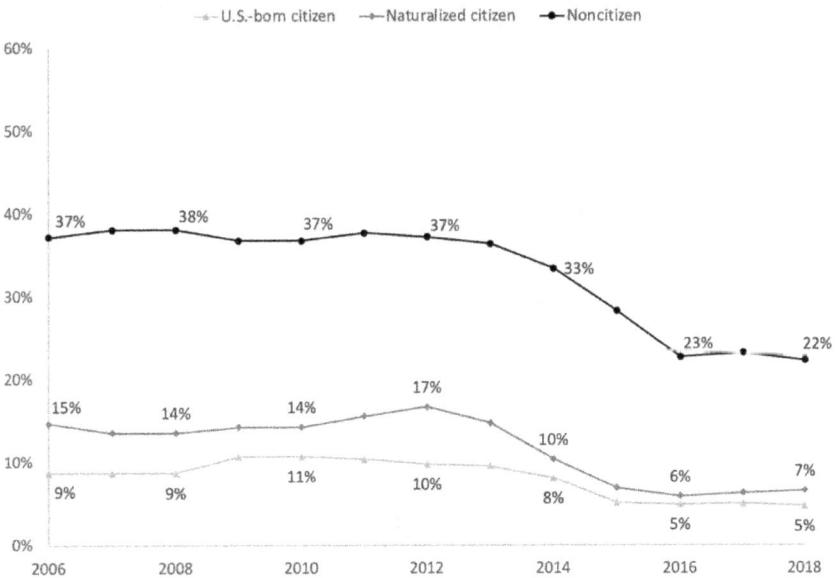

Legend: U.S.-born citizen · Naturalized citizen · Noncitizen

Noncitizen: 37%, 38%, 37%, 37%, 33%, 23%, 22%
Naturalized citizen: 15%, 14%, 14%, 17%, 10%, 6%, 7%
U.S.-born citizen: 9%, 9%, 11%, 10%, 8%, 5%, 5%

The California law states that individuals must be notified of the availability of language access at least once each year in notices and other regular communication, as well as on easily accessible platforms, such as insurer websites. The law also specifies standards that define "quality interpreting." It requires that interpreters working with California health care organizations must demonstrate proficiency in English and the target language, have knowledge of terminology and concepts relevant to health care and health care delivery systems in both languages, and adhere to ethical principles and client confidentiality. SB 223 has made it clear that LEP individuals are not required to provide their own interpreter or rely on other people for interpreting services unless it is an emergency and a qualified interpreter is not immediately available, or unless the LEP individual specifically requests that an accompanying adult facilitate communication. Table 4.2 offers a visual summary and timeline of the major federal and state laws impacting immigrant health in California as discussed here.

California's Safety Net

Even with the reduction in the numbers of uninsured in California due to the ACA, there were still approximately three million uninsured in 2017, with about 59% (1.8 million) uninsured due to ineligibility because of their immigration status (Dietz et al. 2016). Unauthorized adults in California are generally eligible for only emergency and pregnancy-related services through Medi-Cal. Thus many of California's counties provide primary and preventive health care services to low-income unauthorized residents through safety-net programs. Healthy San Francisco in San Francisco and My Health LA in Los Angeles are the largest county-based programs in the state offering a range of services, including systems-of-care coordination, to uninsured individuals regardless of legal status. County health programs in California are an important safety net for unauthorized immigrants.

Since 1933, California's Welfare and Institutions Code Section 17000 has required counties to make available a safety net to individuals who have no other recourse for their health care needs. The understanding of this obligation varies among counties regarding whether or not unauthorized individuals are included in this responsibility. As of 2016, forty-seven of the fifty-eight counties in California had programs that provide health care services to unauthorized immigrants (Jacobs and Lucia 2018). Health services are delivered through a variety of safety-net providers including Federally Qualified Health Centers (FQHCs), public hospitals, community health centers, and other facilities. The range of services

Table 4.2. Timeline of major federal and California state policies affecting immigrant health, 1996–2020

1996	2003	2010	2014	2015	2016/2017	2019/2020
U.S. Personal Responsibility and Work Opportunity and Reconciliation Act ("Federal Welfare Reform")	CA Senate Bill 853 Health Care Language Assistance Act (requiring health plans to collect race/ethnic data to identify health disparities	U.S. Patient Protection and Affordable Care Act (ACA)	CA ACA Medicaid expansion/Covered California launch	CA Senate Bill 4 Health for All Kids (health insurance coverage for unauthorized children under 18 years)	CA Assembly Bill 635 (2016) Medical Interpretation Services for Medi-Cal CA Senate Bill 223 Health Care Language Assistance Services (2017), expanded language assistance	CA State Budget agreement in 2019 to expand Medi-Cal to unauthorized adults under 26 years starting in 2020

covered under country programs can vary quite significantly across counties in the state. An unauthorized individual in San Francisco or Los Angeles, for example, can obtain access to primary, preventive, specialty, behavioral, and hospital care through Healthy San Francisco or My Health LA, but the same person in another, often rural county may *only* be eligible for emergency care.

Other Major Public Health and Nutrition Safety-Net Programs That Serve Children

The nutrition assistance programs offered to children in California overlap in goals and eligibility criteria: CalFresh (California's SNAP), National School Lunch Program (NSLP), and Special Supplemental Nutrition Program for Women, Infants, and Children (WIC). These programs are part of the safety net for children. In order to qualify for CalFresh, children must be documented as legal residents or citizens. By contrast, WIC and school lunch programs do not require such documentation. It is estimated that the majority of children of unauthorized immigrants are citizens and thus likely eligible for safety-net programs if income-qualified (Passel and Taylor, 2010).

Immigrant Barriers to Public Benefits

For low-income and uninsured patients—many of whom are unauthorized immigrants—safety-net hospitals and community health centers remain the main source of care (Chokshi, Chang, and Wilson 2016). Under current federal law, the only federal payments that can be used for the health care of unauthorized immigrants include hospital reimbursement for uncompensated care, community health center grants, and Medicaid funds just for emergency services. Any financial shortfalls incurred by safety-net hospitals have been addressed through the use of state Medicaid waivers (Kelley and Tipirneni 2018). Researchers have called for greater attention to finding innovative models to address health care for unauthorized immigrants, as it is possible there will be an increase in the number of people who will lose temporary protected status (TPS). Without this status, they lose access to lawful employment and employer-sponsored health insurance. Although the administration expects that all who lose TPS will leave the United States, it is possible that many families will not move despite becoming unauthorized, as the cost of moving back to their home countries may include the risk of violence and economic distress. The participants in the DACA program are another group at risk of becoming unauthorized if their protected status is revoked. On June 18, 2020, the U.S. Supreme Court denied the Trump administration's attempt to end the DACA program; however, the program may face future legal challenges, and DACA recipients have not yet been given a path to citizenship.

A looming threat to the use of public benefits by lawfully present immigrants is the change to the public charge ground of inadmissibility (*Lancet* 2019; Zallman et al. 2019b; Ku 2019). On August 14, 2019, the U.S. Department of Homeland Security (DHS) published the Inadmissibility on Public Charge Grounds final rule that codified regulations of Section 212(a)(4)(A) of the Immigration and Nationality Act (INA) that allows for the denial of entry to, or permanent residence in, the U.S. of any applicant who is considered likely to become a public charge at any time (U.S. Department of Homeland Security 2019b). In August 2019, California's attorney general (AG) Xavier Becerra, leading a multistate coalition with AGs of Maine, Oregon, Pennsylvania, and the District of Columbia, filed a lawsuit and a motion for a preliminary injunction to block the final rule (U.S. District Court for the Northern District of California 2019). Other state AGs also filed lawsuits challenging the final rule (one led by AGs of Washington and Virginia along with eleven other states, and another by AGs from Connecticut, New York, and Vermont). By October 2019, several U.S. district judges (from the Southern District of New York, Eastern District of Washington, Northern District of California, Northern District of Illinois, and District of Maryland) issued injunctions blocking the final rule from moving forward. On February 21, 2020, the U.S.

Supreme Court allowed DHS to implement the new public charge rule nationwide starting on February 24, 2020. The public charge rule changes the 1999 Interim Field Guidance by significantly expanding the types of public benefits that if taken, or deemed to be likely to taken in the future, by a lawfully present immigrant not holding a green card (i.e., a non-LPR). Individuals subject to the public charge rule include individuals applying for either immigrant or nonimmigrant visas abroad, individuals seeking admission to the U.S. on immigrant or nonimmigrant visas, and individuals seeking to adjust their status from within the U.S. Under the new rule, public benefits that are considered in the public charge determination process include Supplemental Security Income, Temporary Assistance for Needy Families, Supplemental Nutrition Assistance, Section 8 Housing Assistance, public housing, and federally funded Medicaid (with some exceptions for Medicaid benefits for emergencies and for certain disability services related to education).

Further, the public charge rule requires immigration officials to look at all factors that relate to noncitizens' ability to support themselves and thus not become a public charge in the future, including an individual's age, health, income, assets, education, family members he or she supports, and family who will support this individual. Immigration officials may also consider whether a sponsor has signed an affidavit of support promising to support the noncitizen applying for legal permanent residence. Because the determination includes the individual's overall circumstances prospectively, no one factor is definitive. DHS calls this prospective determination a consideration of the "totality of the circumstances." In making this determination, DHS would consider current and past receipt of included public benefits as a negative factor in the totality of the circumstances. The final rule also contains a "heavily weighted negative factor" for current receipt of public benefits or past receipt (above DHS-designated thresholds outlined in the final rule) within the past thirty-six months preceding the time of submission of an application or petition.

Changes to the public charge determination affect two types of immigrants: (1) individuals who are lawfully present in the United States and seeking permanent residency, and (2) individuals wanting to enter the United States, including those seeking reunion with family members in the U.S. Certain immigrants—refugees, asylees, survivors of domestic violence and trafficking, and other protected groups—are not subject to public charge determinations and would not be affected by the rule if they sought

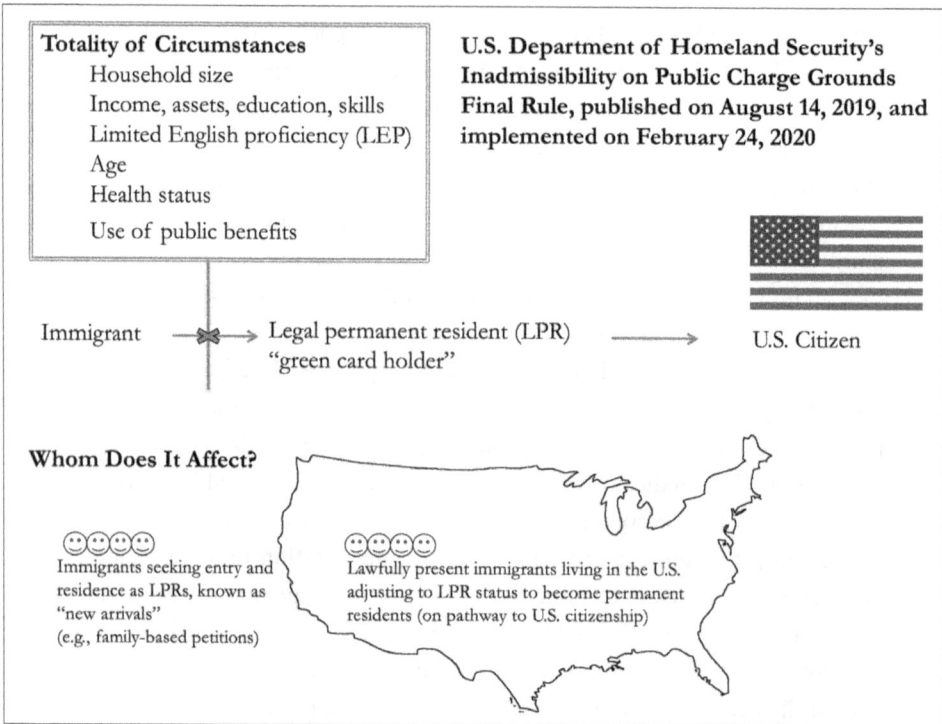

Totality of Circumstances
  Household size
  Income, assets, education, skills
  Limited English proficiency (LEP)
  Age
  Health status
  Use of public benefits

U.S. Department of Homeland Security's Inadmissibility on Public Charge Grounds Final Rule, published on August 14, 2019, and implemented on February 24, 2020

Immigrant ⟶ Legal permanent resident (LPR) "green card holder" ⟶ U.S. Citizen

Whom Does It Affect?

Immigrants seeking entry and residence as LPRs, known as "new arrivals" (e.g., family-based petitions)

Lawfully present immigrants living in the U.S. adjusting to LPR status to become permanent residents (on pathway to U.S. citizenship)

Figure 4.2. Summary of the public charge determination proposed in the U.S. Department of Homeland Security's Inadmissibility on Public Charge Grounds final rule, published on August 14, 2019, and implemented on February 24, 2020
Note: The totality-of-circumstances test is a barrier to permanent residence and eventual citizenship for those seeking LPR status. In 2016, 1,183,505 individuals obtained LPR status in the U.S. (223,141 in California): 618,078 new arrivals; 565,427 immigrants living in the U.S. who adjusted to LPR status. The number obtaining LPR status each year is based on a quota and makes up a small proportion of all who have applied for LPR status and are waiting.

status or a green card through those pathways. Figure 4.2 offers a summary of the August 14, 2019, final rule.

Use of Public Benefits in California: 2016

California has the most to gain or lose from the DHS rule changes to public charge determination. California, which holds the title of fifth-largest economy in the world, is made up of thirty-eight million people, 27 percent of whom are immigrants (that is, not U.S. born; nationally, 13 percent of the population is not

U.S. born). According to the DHS, California is the leading state of residence for LPRs, with an estimated 3.3 million in 2014—a number that has held steady over the past decade. We question whether immigrants, specifically LPRs, in California have in fact relied heavily on public benefits as insinuated by the public charge draft rule. In an analysis conducted prior to the proposed public charge rule that was leaked to the media in 2017, we examined public benefits use among immigrants in California using 2015–16 CHIS data weighted to the 2016 population (Ponce et al. 2018). CHIS, an instrument of the UCLA Center for Health Policy Research, is a population-based survey of California's population. CHIS data provide an opportunity to examine the immigrant communities that remain vulnerable to potential changes in public benefit exclusions and are highly sensitive to the immigrant policy climate. We focus on enrollment in four public programs assisting low-income Californians: Medicaid/Medi-Cal (health care coverage), Supplemental Nutrition Assistance Program/CalFresh (food and nutrition benefits), Temporary Assistance for Needy Families/Cal-WORKS (cash assistance for families with children), and SSI (cash assistance for the aged, blind, and disabled).

Immigrant Enrollment in Public Programs in California

According to the CHIS, the majority of enrollees for public programs are U.S.-born citizens: 69 percent of Medi-Cal, 73 percent of Cal-Fresh, 78 percent of CalWORKS, and 67 percent of SSI recipients are U.S.-born citizens. By contrast, LPRs make up 9 percent of Medi-Cal, 7 percent of CalFresh, 6 percent of CalWORKS, and 5 percent of SSI. The CHIS estimates that 1.15 million LPR adults and an additional 760,000 U.S.-born children with at least one LPR parent participated in at least one of the programs examined here (Medi-Cal, CalFresh, CalWORKS, or SSI). This is less than two million of California's population of thirty-eight million.

Figure 4.3 presents participation in public benefit programs among adults in California with incomes below 200% of the federal poverty level (FPL) (which is equivalent to $24,120 annual income for an individual or $49,200 annual income for a family of four in 2016) by immigration status in 2016. Noncitizens with income below 200% of the FPL make up about 7% of the Asian and 19% of the Latino population in California. Among this low-income group of Californians, U.S.-born individuals have the highest participation rate in Medi-Cal, CalFresh, CalWORKS, and SSI compared to naturalized citizens and LPRs. Compared to that of U.S.-born Californians, participation of LPRs in these programs is lower for Medi-Cal, CalFresh, and CalWORKS, but not for SSI.

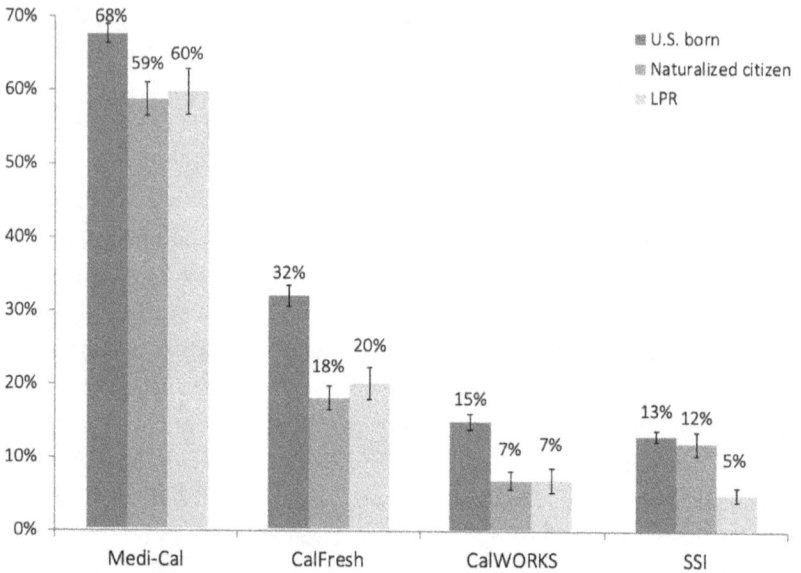

Figure 4.3. Participation in public benefit programs by Californians with incomes below 200% of federal poverty level (FPL), by immigration status in 2016
Source: California Health Interview Survey 2015–16.
Note: Error bars in figure are the standard errors associated with each estimate of the mean; adults eighteen years and older (SSI) and all ages (Medi-Cal, CalFresh, CalWORKS).

Potential Impacts on Health of Limiting Public Benefits to Immigrants

Public charge is not a consideration when lawful permanent residents (green card holders) apply to become U.S. citizens. Families with mixed legal status, such as families with U.S.-citizen children and noncitizen parents, might find these new rules particularly confusing. Confusion, along with fear stemming from an ancillary anti-immigrant social climate, may contribute to wider reach of the rule (Migration Policy Institute 2018). This confusion and fear manifesting in disenrollment in programs by individuals fully qualified to receive benefits is often referred to as the *chilling effect*.

The Chilling Effect
As mentioned earlier in this chapter, PRWORA made fundamental changes to the federal system of public assistance in the United States and specifically

limited the eligibility of immigrant households to receive many types of public aid. The welfare law made many legal noncitizens ineligible for certain public benefit programs, including Medicaid, SNAP, TANF, and SSI. One of the rationales for the welfare reform laws cited by its supporters was that immigrant families use welfare at higher levels compared to people born in the United States. Researchers show that program participation and poverty go hand in hand and that with greater proportions of immigrants in poverty, there will naturally be greater participation in public programs (Borjas 2011). Many studies have shown that noncitizens' participation in these programs significantly declined after the law's enactment (Joo and Kim 2013; Gubernskaya, Bean, and Van Hook 2013; Viladrich 2012; Gerst and Burr 2011; Nam and Jung 2008; Fix and Passel 1999, 2002; Kandula et al. 2004). Studies note that the largest declines were seen in California, and may be attributable to the anti-immigrant climate of the early 1990s in the state, which eventually led to the public voting favorably for Proposition 187 (Kandula et al. 2004; Borjas 2002).

Although eventually struck down by a U.S. District Court judge for being unconstitutional, California's Prop. 187—a 1994 ballot initiative that would have prohibited nonemergency health care, public education, and the use of other public services by "illegal aliens" (a term used widely at the time to refer to immigrants who were not lawfully present)—likely contributed to the fear that the use of public services may risk categorization as a public charge and lead to deportation. Clinical reports find that even though citizen children of unauthorized-immigrant parents are eligible for Medicaid coverage, they are less likely than children of citizens to have health insurance. Unauthorized immigrant parents may believe that their exclusion from public programs extends to their children, or they fear that applying for benefits for citizen children could jeopardize their residence in the U.S. Fear of deportation and lack of literacy with regard to the availability of health and social programs in the U.S. may stimulate a chilling effect on the use of health care resources (Page and Polk 2017).

Even though most children of immigrants are U.S. citizens or LPRs, misunderstanding of eligibility rules and parental fears about accessing benefits can lead to underuse of benefits (Perreira et al. 2012). Immigrants who are qualified for public benefits may also fail to enroll in benefits for which they legally qualify due to the chilling effects arising from an unfriendly immigrant policy climate (Page and Polk 2017; Cohen and Schpero 2018; Viladrich 2012; Gerst and Burr 2011; Fix and Passel 1999, 2002).

Quantifying Potential Impacts of the
2019 DHS Public Charge Rule

California attorney general Xavier Becerra's motion for a preliminary injunction to block the DHS's Inadmissibility on Public Charge Grounds final rule (U.S. District Court for the Northern District of California 2019) and comment letter (Becerra 2018) detail how the rule targets working immigrants and their families by creating new barriers to lawful admission and residence in the U.S. and discourages eligible immigrants and their families from accessing health, nutrition, and housing programs. AG Becerra's comment letter cites research conducted by Ponce (chapter author) and colleagues from the UCLA Center for Health Policy Research with the UC Berkeley Labor Center and California Food Policy Advocates (Ponce, Lucia, and Shimada 2018). Our analysis of the DHS public charge rule found that as many as 301,000 Californians could drop out of the CalFresh nutrition assistance program and up to 741,000 Californians could disenroll from Medi-Cal with the rule in place. Nearly 70% of California residents projected to disenroll from Medi-Cal and CalFresh would be children under eighteen years of age. Our estimates are based on CHIS 2015–2016 data on eligibility and enrollment for CalFresh and for Medi-Cal among noncitizens and citizen children with a noncitizen parent. For this analysis, the "chilling effect" population was defined as noncitizens who are (1) eligible and enrolled for CalFresh and/or full-scope Medi-Cal with federal funding and (2) may or may not be legally affected by the final rule, but who may be indirectly affected because of confusion or worry over the regulation (including citizen children with at least one noncitizen parent). We estimate that this population facing the chilling effect includes up to 2.2 million Californians in immigrant families. Estimates of potential disenrollment of the chilling-effect population were based on evidence of disenrollment after the enactment of PRWORA (as discussed earlier in this chapter) (Fix and Passel 1999), forming the basis for using three disenrollment scenarios: 15%, 25%, and 35% disenrollment from Medi-Cal and/or CalFresh. These disenrollment scenario estimates have also been used in other notable analyses of the public charge rule published by the Kaiser Family Foundation (Artiga, Garfield, and Damico 2019), the Migration Policy Institute (Batalova, Fix, and Greenberg 2018; Ziol-Guest and Kalil 2012), the California Health Care Foundation (Zallman et al. 2019b), and the Fiscal Policy Institute (2018).

Because state funding by the federal government is tied to enrollment in public programs, disenrollment in Medi-Cal and CalFresh translates into

losses in federal funding for California. We multiplied the number of dis-
enrollees from Medi-Cal and Cal-Fresh estimated from the CHIS with the
average per-member per-month federal support for CalFresh and Medi-Cal to
obtain losses to the state. Using these estimates, we modeled the subsequent
reduction in employment, output, and state and local tax revenue. We found
that if 35% of the chilling-effect population disenroll from Medi-Cal and Cal-
Fresh, California could lose about $1.67 billion in federal benefits. The loss of
federal funds due to this disenrollment in Medi-Cal and CalFresh is estimated
to trigger a reduction in economic output in California by as much as $2.8 bil-
lion, leading to a loss of 17,700 jobs. An estimated 57% of the job losses would
come from California's health care sector (8,400 jobs) and food-related industries (1,800 jobs). This research highlights how changes to the public charge
rule can have large ripple effects that would be felt statewide. The potential
loss in health care coverage and food benefits has significant consequences for
both the short-term and long-term health of children in particular.

Impacts of Medicaid and Food Benefits on Child Health

A number of studies have documented health improvements attributable to the
expansions of Medicaid and the Children's Health Insurance Program (CHIP) by
states. A 2015 study examined state variation in Medicaid expansion and linked
administrative data on individuals' adult earnings and tax information to residence and family income in childhood. A single additional year of Medicaid/
CHIP eligibility reduced Earned Income Tax Credit (EITC) receipts in the future,
because those who had access to Medicaid as children ended up with higher
incomes and required fewer tax credits than those who were not eligible for Medicaid (Brown, Kowalski, and Lurie 2015). The study found that Medicaid-eligible
children were more likely to attend college and have lower mortality compared
to their counterparts. A study examining the 2008 Medicaid expansion in Oregon found that children's Medicaid and CHIP coverage increased when parental
access to Medicaid coverage was expanded. Apart from improving access to care,
the Oregon Medicaid expansion suggested that Medicaid also improved overall
health status (Finkelstein et al. 2012; Sommers, Baicker, and Epstein 2012; Baicker
et al. 2013), improved mental health (McMorrow et al. 2016), and reduced mortality (Sommers, Baicker, and Epstein 2012). Wherry, Kenney, and Sommers 2016
found that expansions in Medicaid for low-income children and adults were associated with reduced out-of-pocket spending for medical care, increased financial
stability, and improved well-being. They conclude that Medicaid not only plays a
"significant role in decreasing poverty for many children and families" (S98) but

also helps connect families to other opportunities for social support, such as food assistance programs, which also help lift families out of poverty.

Children in immigrant families who lose or forgo access to nutrition assistance through SNAP benefits are at risk of poor outcomes, given the broad evidence that SNAP benefits have positive impact on health and educational attainment (Beharie, Mercado, and McKay 2017; Berkowitz et al. 2017; Gundersen and Ziliak 2015).The impact of other public benefit programs, such as SNAP, have been studied using historical data when the programs were introduced to varying degrees across states and counties. Their impact has been examined by looking at health impacts of the introduction of food stamps in the 1960s to 1970s. One such study found that children born in counties that were early adopters of food stamps had lower incidence of low birth weight than children in counties that introduced the food stamp program later (Almond, Hoynes, and Schanzenbach 2011). Another found that children who used food stamps during the first five years of life experienced a reduction in adult metabolic syndrome conditions such as obesity, high blood pressure, heart disease, and diabetes (Hoynes, Schanzenbach, and Almond 2012). The study also found that disadvantaged girls with access to food stamps from conception to age five were more likely to be financially self-sufficient in adulthood than those who did not have access.

Similarly, the impact of cash assistance programs has been examined extensively using data from the Earned Income Tax Credit (EITC) program, which has undergone a number of expansions since 1975. The EITC program provides a refundable tax credit to low-income working families. The credit amount is based on the number of dependent children and the family's earnings. EITC has been found to encourage work, reduce poverty, help families meet child-care expenses, improve financial assets and savings, and improve school achievement and employment outcomes (Spencer and Komro 2017; Rehkopf, Strully, and Dow 2014; Muennig et al. 2016; Markowitz et al. 2017; Hamad et al. 2016; Hamad and Rehkopf 2016).

Contributions of Immigrants to Health Care and the Economy

Recent studies suggest that immigrants may contribute more financially than they get out of health care (Flavin et al. 2018; Zallman et al. 2018). In an examination of premiums for private coverage in 2014, Zallman et al. (2018) found that immigrants paid more than their insurers paid out for their health care.

Premiums for immigrants were found to be similar to those for U.S.-born enroll-ees, but working-age immigrants incurred significantly lower expenditures than their native-born counterparts. The authors state that their findings suggest that immigrants subsidize U.S. natives in the private health insurance market, and that federal policies that limit the number of immigrants to the U.S. may result in a declining number of "actuarially desirable" persons (i.e., working-age adults who are relatively young and healthy) in the insurance pool (Zallman et al. 2018). Because immigrant contributions may be critical to the health care market, the authors suggest that a compelling economic argument can be made that health care be provided to all immigrants (Flavin et al. 2018). Immigrants also contrib-ute significantly to the U.S. health care industry, which has been hit with work-force shortages throughout the country, particularly in rural and inner-city areas. In 2017, immigrants accounted for 18% of health care workers overall and 23% of long-term-care workers; further, immigrants are make up about 30% of nursing home housekeeping and maintenance workers (Zallman et al. 2019a).

In 2017, the National Academies of Sciences, Engineering, and Medicine (Blau and Mackie 2017) published a report in which the authors estimate the costs versus benefits of immigration. They estimate that first-generation immi-grants are "costly" (i.e., they incur a net cost to state and local budgets) due to use of public benefits. Subsequent immigrant generations, however, result in a net positive to state and local budgets. For the United States in 2011–2013, the net cost of first-generation adults to state and local budgets, on average, was about $1,600 each. However, second-generation and third-plus generation indi-viduals created a net fiscal gain of about $1,700 and $1,300 each, respectively, to state and local budgets. California has better net positives compared to national estimates. In California, the cost of first-generation immigrants was estimated to be about $2,050. By the second generation, the net positive of immigrants was $1,550, and $3,100 for the third generation, thus resulting in net positive of $1,050 averaged over all three generations. The Partnership for a New Ameri-can Economy, which includes Republican, Democratic, and Independent may-ors and business leaders, estimated that in 2014, immigrant-led households in California earned $323.2 billion—or almost 29 percent of all income earned by Californians that year (New American Economy 2016).

Legal status and economic mobility have an important relationship (Keister, Vallejo, and Borelli 2014; Keister and Aronson 2017; Benton and Keister 2017). Researchers suggest that evidence of upward mobility may be a key measure of class transformation, particularly among Mexican Americans, given that Mexicans are often the most disadvantaged of immigrants in the U.S. (Keister, Vallejo, and Borelli 2014). Legal status may be a critical mechanism that allows parents to move up the economic ladder (Keister, Vallejo, and Borelli 2014). In a study on Mexican Americans, researchers found that parents of children raised in middle-class households were more likely to obtain legal status shortly after or upon arriving in the U.S. (Keister, Vallejo, and Borelli 2014). However, these authors note that the respondents in their study arrived in the U.S. during an era when legalization pathways were more widely available than today; namely, the 1986 amnesty under the Immigration Reform and Control Act (IRCA), which aided in stabilizing families economically and offered access to education. Legalization may facilitate the opportunity for parents to move toward middle-class status and have the finances to invest in education, an important mechanism that leads to greater economic stability among the first generation, which helps accelerate the mobility of the second generation (Benton and Keister 2017; Keister, Vallejo, and Borelli 2014).

Conclusion

Although the Affordable Care Act (2010) improved access to health care for non-citizen immigrants, those not lawfully present in the United States faced various forms of exclusions—enrollment, language access, and eligibility for subsidies— from federally financed health coverage programs. However, California has been at the forefront of implementing immigrant health protection policies, especially as a countervailing force against more exclusionary federal policies that have direct, indirect, and sometimes unintended consequences on immigrant health (Wallace and Young 2018). Given California's legacy of generally anti-immigrant policy proposals in the 1990s—Prop. 187 being the poster child for this period of time—it is especially notable that about two decades later, California became the fifth state to offer public health insurance to children and young adults regardless of immigration status and is poised to offer it to its seniors in the future.

California, along with the rest of the country, is facing a new era in immigration where the pathway toward obtaining legal status appears to be much more tenuous than it has in the past. The implications of impeding the pathway to citizenship—with policy changes to the public charge determination, for example—include threats to the health and economic well-being and opportunities for growth for first-generation immigrants and even their U.S.-born children. As California moves forward with health policies that are generally friendlier toward immigrants than those at the federal level, the state will have to find ways to continue on this path as more restrictive federal policies may be introduced.

5 Naturalization

Roger Waldinger

Immigrants cross the territorial boundary, only to face a series of other, internal, often invisible, but vitally important boundaries, each one of which demarcates a zone corresponding to a distinctive set of rights. The first stages of a migrant's life—and more often than not, the entirety of the migrant's experience in the new country—take place in that conceptual space between the external territorial boundary and the internal boundary demarcating citizens from aliens. Consequently, immigration yields additional migrations, this time not spatial but rather political, as the migrant moves from one status to another. Unlike the move that brought migrants to the United States, impelled by their own initiative and their willingness to sacrifice for a better life, the migrants have limited control over their ability to cross status boundaries. Moreover, the resources that helped them get from there to here—whether their willingness to assume risk or their ability to receive help from relatives and friends already present in the United States—prove much less useful when politicians and state officials are the people determining who can cross status boundaries and under what conditions.

Citizenship is a multidimensional phenomenon, involving formal membership, or status citizenship; participation, or the orientation usually described as "good citizenship"; and identification, a subjective recognition by both the self and by others that one belongs to the national people among whom one lives. Understandably, the members and leaders of democratic societies value citizenship, seeing its acquisition as an integral part of the process of immigrant integration or incorporation. Indeed, that view has considerable merit, as residence requirements are universally a prerequisite for the acquisition of citizenship, and settlement almost always helps generate resources that facilitate naturalization.

In the United States, nonetheless, almost one-third of the population eligible to naturalize remains foreigners, retaining the citizenship of their country of origin. Although citizenship rates among the eligible have risen in recent years, advancing from 62% in 2005 to 67% in 2015, the pace of change varies greatly from one group to another, as does the overall rate. Thus, among Mexican immigrants—the overwhelmingly largest component of America's foreign-born population—only 42% of potentially eligible persons had become citizens as of 2015, representing only a 3% increase since 2005 (Gonzalez-Barrera and Krogstad 2018). Of course, naturalization rates are depressed because many foreign-born U.S. residents are not legally present and are thus ineligible to apply for citizenship, despite years of residence in the United States. Even so, among Mexican and other Latin American immigrants, many lawfully present residents decide not to opt for U.S. citizenship, citing poor English language proficiency, the high costs entailed in a citizenship application, limited English, and continuing home-country loyalty as among the constraining factors.

Citizenship acquisition is a matter of particular importance to California. Home to 25% of all foreign-born U.S. residents and the nation's largest concentration of Mexicans and Central Americans, the state contains just under a quarter of the country's eligible-to-naturalize population. In this context, increasing naturalization rates would yield disproportionate effects on the state, deepening the state's democracy by expanding the number of potential voters and enhancing the earning capacity of those same potential new voters. Consequently, this chapter seeks to understand the factors facilitating and constraining immigrants' passage over that internal, formal boundary separating aliens from formal, status citizens. By focusing on foreign-born residents of Los Angeles County and using a high-quality dataset uniquely well suited to the topic at hand, I will show that prevailing approaches, which understand citizenship acquisition as driven by the same mechanisms that propel assimilation, are incomplete. Additional, important influences derive from the underlying system of migration control, as even among persons legally resident in the United States, those who were earlier assigned more favorable migration statuses at different points in their U.S.

sojourn prove more likely to gain citizenship. Moreover, national and ethnic background strongly affects citizenship trajectories, with Latinos far less likely to become U.S. citizens, even after controlling for features of their U.S. experience and socioeconomic characteristics that generally prove conducive to naturalization.

Acquiring Citizenship: Perspectives

Research typically conceptualizes the acquisition of citizenship as an individual decision, one that responds to the perceived costs and benefits of gaining a new (and possibly losing an old) citizenship. From this perspective, naturalization is at once the result and an indicator of assimilation, as extended residence generates the motivation, skills, and resources needed to acquire a new citizenship and the cognitive effort and material means required to cross the threshold of citizenship, signaling the desire to gain membership in a new people. Consequently, individual characteristics, whether related to socioeconomic resources, on the one hand, or changes in affect that produce greater identification with the host country, on the other hand, are seen as the best predictors of naturalization.

Conceptualizing naturalization as a matter of individual choice reflects the prevailing tendency in migration scholarship, which positions immigrants as strangers, whose strangeness diminishes with time and social learning, which in turn facilitates movement across the internal boundary of citizenship (Alba and Nee 2003). By contrast, this chapter develops an institutional approach, motivated by the understanding that immigrants are not just newcomers who need to learn an unknown environment. Rather, they are persons who enter the country of immigration as foreigners, noncitizens who get slotted into different formal statuses that differ in entitlements and rights. Because citizenship is a resource that states deliberately render scarce, and because eligibility for naturalization rests on acquisition of just one of the many statuses by which immigrants enter a territory, legal permanent residence, whether acquired at the time of initial entry or after some later period of residence, exercises the greatest influence on citizenship acquisition. The remainder of this section will outline these two perspectives and then turn to the empirical analysis.

Naturalization as Assimilation: Cost-Benefit Approach

Conventional approaches to naturalization emphasize the importance of costs and benefits. Although the point is rarely made, citizenship's costs derive from the politically generated obstacles to its acquisition. On the most practical level, applying for citizenship in the United States requires navigating a long bureaucratic process that—as famously summarized in the title of David North's "The Long Grey Welcome"—may repel as much as, if not more than, it appeals (North 1987). As Irene Bloemraad (2006) argued in her comparative study of citizenship acquisition in the United States and Canada, as an agency, the Immigration and Naturalization Service prioritized its enforcement function over its integrative one, with an organizational culture stamped by the preoccupation with control. Although border and interior enforcement have since been spun off to a new entity, the ethos prevailing in the INS's successor agency is unlikely to have changed greatly. Among migrants, the INS/USCIS suffers from the image of an organization to be avoided whenever possible, with stories about negative treatment abounding (Alvarez 1987).[1]

Applicants seeking U.S. citizenship need to ready themselves to take a test of English ability and basic facts about the United States. Although the vast majority of applicants passes—about 91% in 2016 (Waters and Pineau 2015, 167)—the ordeal may discourage some potential citizens, especially those with little or no prior test-taking history. Because the process also entails a thorough review of an applicant's immigration history and record, which in turn could uncover a problem, heretofore invisible, that could threaten permanent residence status—concerns over the negative consequences of close scrutiny clearly lead some potential citizens to stay clear of the entire process (Gilbertson and Singer 2003). Costs entail a further deterrent, one of ever greater weight since the late 1980s, when the INS and then the USCIS were transformed into agencies funded not by the U.S. Treasury but by user fees; between 1988 and 2015, fees rose fivefold in constant terms, with barely 3% of applicants granted waivers (Stringer 2016).

Immigrants' capacity to absorb these costs is closely linked to the competencies and resources that they acquire in the pursuit of socioeconomic mobility. Proficiency in English ranks especially high among those competencies, not simply because the citizenship exam tests for familiarity with English, but because that skill makes the U.S. political and institutional environment accessible.

Whereas significant material and informational barriers confront potential citizens, the benefits conferred by citizenship have remained mainly symbolic. The rewards of citizenship include the economic, which are modest at best: Estimates of wage gains range from 1% to 8% (Bloemraad 2017; Pastor and Scoggins 2012). Yet, even at the maximum, these gains are not produced immediately by the one-time act of naturalization, but rather occur over an extended period, an outcome that, from the perspective of the prospective citizen, is freighted with uncertainty.

Naturalization does provide the ticket of entry to the polity, an outcome that could yield significant effect if large numbers of naturalized citizens voted and even more so if naturalization numbers were to grow. Yet if some new citizens clearly prize voting—as suggested by Aptekar's (2015) interviews with applicants waiting for their naturalization interviews—others prove indifferent, as indicated by the relatively low level of electoral participation among Asian immigrants, who naturalize at high levels but then only occasionally go to the polls (Ramakrishnan and Baldassare 2004; Wong et al. 2011).

Beyond the vote, new citizens gain some employment opportunities in addition to those they already possessed as lawful permanent residents, though mainly in selected branches of government (Plascencia, Freeman, and Setzler 2003). By contrast, a U.S. passport may offer both greater security when traveling and greater freedom of international movement, a question of importance to immigrants from countries whose passport holders need visas to enter the developed world. And whereas permanent residents need to return to the United States every six months, U.S. citizens can remain abroad indefinitely without risking loss of citizenship. A more powerful motivation may be the impact of U.S. citizenship on facilitating the immigration of close relatives still abroad—a goal substantially facilitated once citizenship is in hand, as there is no numerical limitation on the number of spouses, minor children, and parents sponsored by U.S. citizens.

Yet the most compelling of citizenship's concrete benefits may derive from its quality as an insurance policy, guaranteeing against the risk of deportation. In contrast to citizenship, legal permanent residency is a conditional status, revocable by the state without much legal recourse, with the 1996 Illegal Immigration Reform and Immigrant Responsibility Act (IIRIRA) in conjunction with the Antiterrorism and Effective Death Penalty Act (AEDPA) greatly increasing the number of violations that could trigger deportation. Indeed, the absolute number of permanent residents experiencing deportation has soared in the years following these acts, climbing from 15,539 in 1994 to 24,702 in 2004.[2] For the individual legal permanent resident, however, the risk of deportation remains very low. Given an estimated legal permanent resident population of 11.5 million in 2003 (Rytina 2005), this translates into a probability of just 0.2% per year.

Naturalization and Civic Stratification: The Impact of Migration Control Policies

As emphasized by the rational-choice approach advocated by neo-assimilation theory, adaptation is driven by the rewards it yields. But the pursuit of the good life yields its effects through its constant action, invisible effects, and compatibility with a range of migrant plans—which is why settlement and assimilation so often happen whether wanted or not. Not so the acquisition of citizenship, for which a deliberate effort is required. Unlike mastering the dominant tongue—or at least enough of it to get by—citizenship is not a quotidian concern, as it can't be reliably read from the everyday encounter. Indeed, it is often *mis*read, to the dismay of the naturalized citizen whose accent gives away his or her foreign origin. Yet precisely because, in the near to medium term, citizenship provides neither much help nor hindrance, its acquisition is likely to be postponed.

Hence, immigrants may spend years—perhaps the entirety of their lives in the United States—in that conceptual liminal zone between the territory of the state and the internal boundary of citizenship. Indeed, in 2010, roughly 8 million of an estimated 12 million legal permanent residents living in the U.S. were eligible to naturalize (Rytina 2011), yet just shy of 620,000, or 5%, opted to acquire citizenship (Lee 2011).

The stickiness of noncitizen status is not an anomaly; rather it stems from the very nature of citizenship as an institution. Citizenship is simultaneously a mechanism of inclusion and exclusion, both an instrument and an object of citizens' social closure, to borrow the concepts formulated by Rogers Brubaker (1992). Citizenship no longer serves as the potent instrument of internal closure against resident noncitizens that the U.S. state utilized during the mid-twentieth-century era of low immigration. As Colbern (Chapter 3) and Shimkhada and Ponce (Chapter 4) show in this volume, California has been particularly active since the 2000s in creating access to health care for legally resident noncitizens, and driver's licenses and access to public colleges for residents regardless of legal status.

Nonetheless, citizenship is more than a status and an activity; it is also an identity, the symbol linking the individual to the nation or people to whom he or she belongs. Although home-country citizenship may not prove of much use, its emotional valence often makes it hard to discard. Hence, the reluctance to give up the citizenship of one's native people may deter one from taking on the citizenship of a previously foreign people, although the passage of dual-nationality laws diminishes the conflict by making new and old allegiances compatible. However, membership has symbolic value for the people of the receiving state as well; numerous surveys, for example, have shown that Americans rate citizenship as an important dimension of American identity (Schildkraut 2010). Not surprisingly, citizenship is a status to which immigrants often aspire, as its acquisition provides reinforcement for one's social standing. Yet when naturalization rates begin to climb, the very same public that makes citizenship a condition of full acceptance starts to worry that citizenship's value is being diluted, an anxiety to which policymakers respond by raising the hurdles over which prospective citizens must jump (Schneider 2001).

Hence, status citizenship remains a powerful object of closure, as even the U.S.—a state with a comparatively liberal citizenship regime—compels would-be citizens to vault over an increasingly high wall. However, eligibility is not available for each and every immigrant who might want to gain U.S. citizenship, though the terms of eligibility have changed over time. Right from the beginning of its history as an independent country, the United States has offered immigrants easy access to citizenship while promising their U.S.-born children citizenship upon birth. Although not often noticed, these practices constituted a *de facto* immigration incentive program, reflecting the new republic's need to attract a population that could fill up its land mass and help wrest territory from the indigenous population. Although conflict over naturalization requirements emerged almost instantly—with the minimum wait period set at two years by the first naturalization law passed in 1790, increased to fourteen in 1798, and then lowered back to five in 1802—residence requirements have remained at that level ever since. From its outset and through the early twentieth century, the procedures for naturalizing took ad hoc form, varying from one locality to another, with approval heavily influenced by the degree to which local political regimes perceived immigrants as likely friends or foes. Those practices were then transformed at the turn of the twentieth century, when the growing wave of anti-immigrant animosity eventuated in the Naturalization Act of 1906, shifting responsibility to the national level, imposing requirements for rudimentary knowledge of English and American civics, and mandating payment of a $6 filing fee—the equivalent of $120 in 2016 currency. The contours of naturalization practices have since then remained roughly stable, though standardizing the naturalization test took protracted form and fees have fluctuated—most recently increasing from $60 in 1989 to $725 as of this writing, or 1.17% of median family income (Parker 2015; Schneider 2001).

For much of U.S. history, prospective citizens also had to fulfill racial criteria. Legislation passed in 1790 restricted applicants to "free white" persons. Due to the Treaty of Guadalupe Hidalgo, persons born in the territories taken from Mexico were absorbed by the United States as full-fledged citizens and, despite subsequent efforts at imposing a racial barrier that would impede naturalization, courts interpreted the treaty as granting Mexican-born immigrants the same rights to naturalize as immigrants from Europe. Following the Civil War, an important piece of Reconstruction legislation, the Naturalization Act of 1870, made foreign-born blacks eligible for naturalization, but was deliberately written to bar Asian immigrants from citizenship. A few decades later, the Supreme Court ruled that all persons born on U.S. soil possessed citizenship from birth, regardless of race, ethnicity, and parents' place of birth, making a contemporaneous decision that all persons born in East and South Asia—even if classified by the "racial science" of the time as "Aryan"—lacked eligibility for citizenship. Racial barriers to naturalization were not stricken until 1952, by which time World War II and the succeeding Cold War environment had made discrimination on the basis of origins politically intolerable.

Scholars have paid much attention to the rise and fall of racial restrictions on naturalization; by contrast, the rise of civic stratification as spurred by the development and thickening of systems of migration control has tended to be neglected. As long as immigrants needed inducements to take on the costs and risks of migration to America, citizenship policy was implemented so as to diminish the scope of immigrants' sojourn in that liminal space between the outer boundary of the territory and the inner boundary of citizenship. Thus for most of the nineteenth century, as Hiroshi Motomura (2006) has argued, immigrants were "Americans in waiting," a condition that often included voting in state and local elections even before citizenship was attained. Yet alien voting disappeared by the mid-1920s, a casualty of the same circumstances that ended mass migration across the Atlantic (Ueda 1980).

As Aristide Zolberg (2006) pointed out, immigration control creates the undocumented immigrant, a person residing on the territory of the state of immigration, but living outside its law. The very first to be excluded from legal entry into the United States, the Chinese were also the first to engage in undocumented migration, a practice that in turn influenced migration-control strategies. By requiring all immigrants from the Eastern Hemisphere to enter the United States with visas, the legislation of the early 1920s extended the illegal immigrant phenomenon from the Chinese to the European born, as the historian Mae Ngai (2014) has noted. But whereas the Asian immigrants upon whom efforts at restriction were first focused were not eligible to become citizens, national origins never served as an obstacle to Europeans. Hence, by creating that new category of person—the undocumented immigrant—restriction changed the relationship between residence and eligibility for naturalization, as the clock only started ticking when and if the unauthorized immigrant gained legal permanent residence.

An incipient development prompted by the Chinese Exclusion Act of 1882 and subsequent efforts to exclude Japanese, Korean, and Indian immigrants, the imposition of the quota laws in 1924 marked the full emergence of the U.S. as a "gatekeeping state," to borrow a concept from the historian Erika Lee (2003). Ever since, those gates have functioned so as to separate the relatively few who are wanted or tolerated from the far more numerous who are seen as undesirable or unacceptable. However, the demand for migrant workers—whether of the high- or low-skilled sort—almost always supersedes the levels of permanent migration that American voters are prepared to accept. Consequently, the United States, like other developed states, has elaborated a complex, often contradictory set of policies that seek to reconcile the conflicting pressures of business demand for labor with consistently negative popular views of immigration.

In the United States, reconciling those conflicting pressures has taken the form of a divergence between policy on the books and policy in practice that has made undocumented migration a protracted feature of the environment. Serving the material interests of domestic groups eager for cheap labor, but also the ideal interests of humanitarians and ethnic advocacy groups that seek to protect undocumented immigrants and stabilize their situation, that disparity has waxed and waned in ways that shape access to citizenship. In 1986, passage of the Immigration Reform and Control Act (IRCA) allowed roughly three million to acquire lawful permanent residence and thereby become eligible for naturalization. Up until the early 2000s, undocumented persons could also avail themselves of a "do-it-yourself" legalization process, as marriage to U.S. citizens or lawful permanent residents triggered transition to legal status, in turn setting the preconditions for possible later transition to citizenship. Since the turn of the millennium, however, the undocumented population is increasingly caged: With few and contested opportunities for escape to a status that would allow legal presence, this population increasingly comprises a set of persons who experience de facto Americanization as a result of extended residence, but lack the opportunity to become Americans de jure.

Other arrivals are not quite so constrained, but nonetheless experience a disjuncture between their entry into the United States and the moment their residence on U.S. soil begins to count for the purposes of naturalization. Although responding to domestic forces, U.S. migration policies are also embedded within a broader control structure, seeking to accommodate the far larger and ever-growing people flows produced by globalization. These movements involve the legal crossing of borders by tourists, intracompany transferees, students, or temporary workers, who arrive for legally sanctioned sojourns that are usually of very limited duration, but that can sometimes prove highly protracted. As these flows are generated by the ever-tighter economic links among countries, they can't be stopped, only managed and regulated (Sassen 1996). Moreover, once activated, these migrant flows connect to economic sectors that find temporary but legal migrants to be highly desirable, whether as students in universities looking for foreigners to pay full tuition, engineers for high-technology companies seeking greater labor force flexibility, or employees of private clubs and golf resorts—such as those owned by current president Donald Trump—for whom the availability of legally present guestworkers reduces pressure on wages.

And thus the advent of a system of migration control that sifts arrivals into a growing number of temporary but legal statuses has broken the close relationship between residence and eligibility for citizenship experienced by the European migrants of the nineteenth and early twentieth centuries and that has been taken for granted by most analysts. Although time spent in the host society, regardless of legal status, yields exposure and thereby directly facilitates language acquisition or socioeconomic mobility, its impact on an immigrant's acquisition of citizenship is far more conditional, as the clock only starts ticking with the acquisition of lawful permanent residence. As most new legal permanent residents are not new immigrants but rather persons who previously came to the U.S. in some other status—whether as legal "non-immigrant" tourists, students, temporary workers, or intercompany transferees, or as unauthorized entrants—disparities in status upon arrival are the key factors that yield differences in the rate at which immigrants take up citizenship.

Data, Methods, Variables

This chapter draws on the Los Angeles Family and Neighborhood Survey (LAFANS), a panel study of a representative sample of all neighborhoods and all households in Los Angeles County, constructed so as to oversample poor neighborhoods and families with children. Although the survey involves two waves, one collected in 2000–2001 and a second wave in 2006–2008, this chapter relies uniquely on wave 2, which contains a far richer set of migration-related questions than were asked in wave 1. The second wave consists of two different subgroups: persons interviewed in wave 1, whether they moved out of the original neighborhood or not, and new entrants who moved into the neighborhood in the years (six years on average) since the first wave was selected and interviewed.

Wave 2 of LAFANS surveyed 839 foreign-born persons, of whom 61% had been born in Mexico, 20% born in Central America, 3% born elsewhere in Latin America and the Caribbean, 9% born in South and East Asia, with the remaining 7% coming from all other regions of the world. As of wave 2, 38% of the foreign-born respondents had become naturalized citizens, 33% then held a green card, and 35% were unauthorized. One-third of the naturalized citizens and one-tenth of the green-card holders originated from countries outside the Americas; by contrast, all of the unauthorized respondents were from Mexico and elsewhere in the Americas.

For the multivariate analysis of naturalization, the sample was limited to those persons who might have ever been eligible to naturalize: persons who had at one point received the green card and had lived in the United States for at least five years following its receipt. The information collected by LAFANS is utilized to construct naturalization histories and then analyzed using a complementary log-log discrete-time event history analysis (Allison 1995). The analysis models the probability of a respondent naturalizing in each year following the receipt of the green card until the respondent either naturalizes or is no longer followed in the sample. This model analyzes the "risk" of naturalization in each person-year after the individual receives his or her green card. That is, immigrants enter our dataset the year they receive their green card and then they are removed from the dataset once they naturalize. The analysis considers those who receive their green card and have not naturalized by the time the second wave of LAFANS is measured as left-censored and assesses the probability that an immigrant naturalizes in each year that he or she is eligible by controlling for individual, parental, and demographic characteristics. Each covariate reports whether it increases or decreases the hazard or risk that an individual naturalizes in a given year.

As predictors in the event history analysis can only include events that were certain to have occurred before the acquisition of citizenship, the number of variables available for analysis is limited, despite the wealth of information collected by LAFANS. As emphasized earlier, standard approaches to the study of naturalization emphasize the importance of socioeconomic and cognitive resources that might help defray and reduce the material and informational costs of naturalization. Conventional analyses of naturalization using cross-sectional data employ a respondent's occupation and education as predictors of naturalization, yet do so mistakenly, as cross-sectional data typically provide no information on the time order of the relevant events, allowing for the possibility that education as measured at the time of the survey is a consequence, not a cause, of naturalization. As LAFANS did not collect information regarding the time when schooling was completed, the same problem afflicts this dataset.

Consequently, the predictors used in the event history analysis all involve events occurring *prior* to the acquisition of U.S. citizenship. These independent variables include the following:

Place of birth. This is a dummy variable distinguishing respondents with origins in Mexico, Central and South America, and the Caribbean from respondents originating in all other parts of the world.

English language competence. LAFANS included a question asking respondents whether they spoke any English at the time when they first came to the United States to live or work. Although respondents were then asked to rate their English on a four-point scale ranging from "very good" to "not so good," only 17% reported speaking English at the time of arrival. Therefore, English language competence is coded as a dummy variable, with a score of 1 for those who reported speaking any English at the time of arrival, and a score of 0 for those who answered no.

Parents' level of education. LAFANS contains an extensive battery of questions related to both the respondents' level of education and the place in which it was received—U.S. or abroad. However, as the survey did not inquire into the timing of respondents' schooling, these data cannot be used, as the information needed to know whether the relevant schooling was obtained before or after the acquisition of citizenship is lacking. However, the survey did collect information on parents' level of schooling; as parents' schooling was almost surely completed before respondents arrived in the U.S., and as parents' schooling is generally a powerful predictor of their children's education, we include this variable in the regression. To reduce missing data, parents' education is defined as the number of years of schooling achieved by the parent—mother or father—with the highest level of schooling, substituting mother or father when information on both parents is not available.

Age at arrival. If citizenship is to be understood as an investment, it is best amortized by immigrants who arrive at a young age. The analysis uses answers to questions regarding date of birth and year of last arrival to live and work to construct a variable measuring the respondent's age at the time of last arrival.

Child migrant. As child migrants are likely to adapt at a quicker pace than adults and are also less likely to retain home-country patriotic or emotional attachments, an indicator variable to distinguish respondents whose last arrival occurred before the age of thirteen from all other respondents is used.

Settlement. The cognitive and material resources needed to acquire citizenship are likely to rise with years of residence in the United States. However, as access to better opportunities and greater exposure to natives are likely to vary depending on legal status, the analysis breaks up settlement into two variables, one measuring the years between receipt of the green card and the year of the interview (either 2006, 2007, or 2008), and the second measuring the years between the last migration and the receipt of the green card. The analysis also includes squared terms for both variables.

Repeat migration. Although residence is likely to generate relevant resources, residence is often discontinuous, interrupted by return travel that, if it reinforces attachments to the home country and/or diminishes competencies previously generated by residence, could adversely affect the acquisition of citizenship. The analysis includes an indicator variable for repeat migration, coded 1 if a respondent reported that a trip to the United States for living or working preceded the last such trip and 0 if the answer to this question was no.

Visa status at the time of last arrival. To detect unauthorized entries, an indicator variable is generated, measured 1 if yes, 0 if no, indexing responses to the question, "Did you have a visa or other entry document when you entered the US this last time?"

Legal status at the time of receipt of the green card. A person's status can change from the time of entry, whether because the migrant decides to maintain residence beyond the period allowed by the visa and thus becomes unauthorized or because the migrant succeeds in transitioning to an authorized status. The analysis measures legal status at the time of receipt of the green card with an indicator variable, measured 1 if yes, 0 if no, indexing responses to the question, "At the time you got your Green Card, did you have a visa, work permit, or another document which permitted you to stay in the United States?"

Unauthorized entrance. Undocumented or unauthorized persons fall into two categories: those who cross a border without authorization and those who enter with authorization to remain for a limited period of time, but then remain in the United States rather than returning home. Transitioning to permanent residence is significantly more difficult for persons who enter without authorization as opposed to those who overstay the terms of their visa. Therefore, the analysis uses responses to the question, "Have you ever entered the United States illegally or without documents?" to generate an indicator variable that indexes illegal entry by coding persons who answered yes as 1 and those who answered no as 0.

Migration and Documentation

A residence requirement lay at the heart of the citizenship regime put in place at the founding of the American republic. Today, as in 1802, prospective citizens must achieve five years of near continuous residence in the United States before applying for citizenship. As residence yields both the cognitive and material resources that facilitate the acquisition of citizenship, the citizenship regime and the underlying process of immigrant settlement would seem to neatly align.

However, the assumption that settlement is a linear, steadily ongoing process stands in contrast to the uncertain and often discontinuous nature of the migration experience. Globalization produces a huge cross-border flow of persons intending short-term stays abroad; in 2016, for example, sixty-one million persons entered the United States as tourists (Teke and Navarro 2018)—some small portion of whom make several trips before eventually settling for good. In developing societies, as a large quantity of literature shows, emigration is often undertaken without the goal of immigration. Rather, emigrants relocate to a developed society in order to gain the access to the resources that can only be found there, channeling those resources back home in order to stabilize, secure, and improve the options of the kin network remaining in place, and possibly returning to make good on the assets and skills acquired abroad. A somewhat similar pattern often characterizes more highly resourced persons—such as foreign students in American colleges or graduate students—who, in applying for legal admission to the United States, tell U.S. authorities that their sojourn is meant to be followed by a return home.

That pattern of repeat migration and extended return to the home country appears among the immigrants surveyed by LAFANS: 12% made a first trip to the United States before returning a second time to live or work. Roughly one out of every four undocumented respondents reported that a first trip had preceded the trip after which they settled to work or live; a little more than one out of every ten green card holders and a little under one of every ten citizens, respectively, reported a similar gap. In addition, a still larger percentage—25% of the entire sample—reported that after this last trip to the United States to live and work, they returned again to the country of origin for a stay lasting at least two months.

Although repeat migrants were more likely to enter the United States without authorization, most interviewees reported lacking a visa or entry document at the time of their last trip to the United States. As to be expected, unauthorized entry was most common among persons in an unauthorized status at the time of the survey (86%), less so among the green card holders

(47%), and least so among the citizens (30%). Yet those answers also show that almost 40% of the respondents who were lawfully present as of the survey (either as green card holders or naturalized citizens) had previously transitioned from an initially unauthorized status. As immigrants from Mexico and elsewhere in Latin America accounted for almost all (98%) of all the unauthorized entries in the sample, those transitions from an unauthorized to an authorized status were overwhelmingly concentrated among the Latin American respondents.

Not surprisingly, among respondents who eventually obtained legal presence, arrival in the United States to live or work typically preceded acquisition of legal permanent residence: only one out of every six respondents reported receiving the green card at the time of their last move to the United States to live or work; the average respondent who was lawfully present as of the survey had lived in the United States for a little over seven years before receiving the green card. Although that gap was most common among the Latin Americans, it also emerged among 60% of lawfully present respondents with origins elsewhere in the world who, on average, obtained the green card within less than three years of arrival in the United States. Statuses also changed in between that interval separating arrival and acquisition of the green card, shifting from authorized to unauthorized as well as in the other direction. Indeed, only a minority of the lawfully present respondents had both entered the United States with authorization *and* possessed a visa allowing for legal temporary residence at the time of receiving the green card. Roughly 14% of the lawfully present respondents had entered without authorization, but subsequently transitioned to a temporary visa; a larger fraction had actually fallen from authorized into unauthorized status. A fifth of the lawfully present respondents had neither entered with authorization nor possessed a visa allowing for temporary residence at the time of receiving the green card; almost all (88%) of these respondents answered yes to a question asking, "Have you ever entered the United States illegally or without documents?"

Given the long history of Mexican and Central American undocumented migration to Los Angeles—Mexicans principally arriving as labor migrants, Central Americans first moving to escape violence and then shifting to a labor migration—patterns of entry and documentation among LAFANS respondents vary by place of origin. Among respondents who received a green card, roughly two-thirds of the Latinos had entered the United States at least once without authorization, half lacked the visa when they last entered the United

State to live or work, and just over half (54%) had a permit allowing for temporary residence at the time when the green card was received. Among the respondents from other parts of the world, by contrast, only two persons (less than 2%) had ever entered without authorization, and the great majority (95%) possessed a visa at the time of their last entry into the United States. Nonetheless, a slightly smaller fraction (87%) had a permit allowing for temporary residence at the time when the green card was received, again highlighting the potential for slippage from one status to another.

Multivariate Analysis

As of wave 2, 60% of all respondents who had received a green card and had fulfilled residency requirements had become citizens. Nonetheless, national origins were strongly associated with citizenship take-up rates: Only 53% of eligible Latinos were citizens, as opposed to 86% of eligible respondents from elsewhere in the world. Given the striking disparity in citizenship take-up rates—with 2% of Latinos likely to become citizens in any year versus 10% of respondents from elsewhere in the world—the analysis focuses on the comparison between Latinos and others, reporting results from two separate regressions of these two subgroups among the LAFANS respondents.

As noted earlier, LAFANS provides two variables that capture relevant resources possessed by respondents at the time of arrival: parents' level of education and respondents' assessment of their English language competence at the time of their last trip to the United States. Latino respondents arrived with far fewer of the resources enjoyed by their counterparts from elsewhere in the world: Among the former, the median parent had acquired five years of schooling, in contrast to fifteen years among the latter; among the former, 20% of the parents had received no schooling at all, whereas among the latter, none of the parents entirely lacked education. Similarly, 27% of the Latinos reported that they spoke at least some English at the time of their last trip to the United States, as compared to 93% of respondents from elsewhere in the world. Nonetheless, and as shown in figure 5.1, which displays a plot coefficient for the theoretically most relevant variables, these measures of resources strongly influenced citizenship take-up rates among Latinos but *not* among respondents from elsewhere in the world. Thus, among Latinos, 6% of those with some English language capacity were likely to naturalize in any given year, as opposed to 2% without English language competence; by contrast,

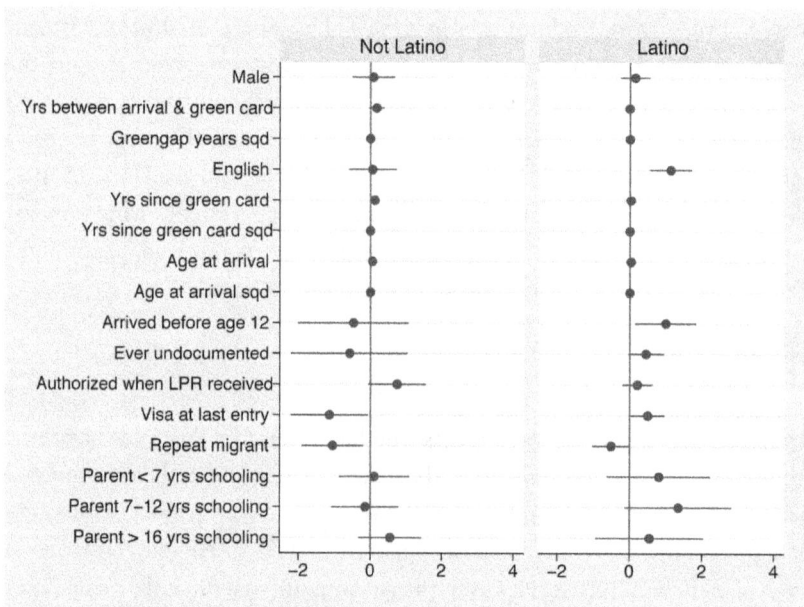

Figure 5.1. Effect of selected variables on acquisition of citizenship
Source: Los Angeles Family and Neighborhood Survey, 2006–2008.

and net of other variables, 6% of respondents from other parts of the world were likely to naturalize in any given year, regardless of whether or not they possessed any English language at the time of last arrival. Likewise, although higher levels of parental education were associated with a higher probability of naturalization among Latinos, the effect was slight.

Settlement is a powerful driver of many aspects of immigrant progress, because as years of residence cumulate, immigrants gain competencies and dispositions that make them increasingly like natives, thus diminishing the upon-arrival disadvantages incurred when confronting a strange world as a stranger. Yet, as displayed in figure 5.1, the event history analysis demonstrates that additional years of residence yield almost no impact on citizenship take-up rates among Latinos, with *none* of the variables measuring years of residence—whether between arrival and receipt of the green card or years after the green card—yielding statistically significant effects on naturalization rates among Latinos. Consequently, as displayed in figure 5.2, predicted probabilities show that take-up rates remain low and virtually unchanged over three decades of residence among eligible Latino residents: even ten years after receipt of the green card, naturalization was only likely to occur among 2% of the Latino respondents; enlarging the interval to thirty years after receipt of the green card only increases the probability of naturalization to 3%. As with the rate for Latinos, at an early period of eligibility, naturalization rates among respondents from elsewhere in the world were also low—with just over 2% likely to acquire citizenship after ten years of residence. With further years of settlement, however, take-up rates rose such that after thirty years of residence, 16% would be likely to gain citizenship in any given year. The impact of settlement is further blunted by the disruptive impact connected to home-country ties: among both Latino and non-Latino migrants, repeat migration slows the acquisition of citizenship, although continuous U.S. residence has stronger effects among the latter than among the former.

Prospective citizens need to acquire both the competencies necessary to obtain citizenship as well as the specific information required to successfully navigate the procedure. Although these demands might weigh heavily on persons who arrive as adults, they are less likely to impinge with the same force among those who immigrate as children, because youth facilitates language learning, and child migrants acquire at least some U.S. schooling, which should facilitate navigation of the institutional barriers to naturalization. Moreover, the costs of naturalization are likely to be lower for child than for adult immigrants, and those who arrive as children also enjoy the prospect of amortizing those costs across the entirety of their working careers.

Not surprisingly, the analysis of citizenship take-up rates among Latinos demonstrates the advantages associated with child migration, as child migrants were about twice as likely as adults to naturalize in any year. By contrast, among respondents from elsewhere in the world, child migrants were less likely to naturalize than adult migrants.

Prospects for naturalization open with acquisition of the green card, but as noted earlier, a large proportion of respondents legally present as of the survey had only received the green card *after* their last move to the United States. The eligibility clock ticks at the same rate for all green card holders, regardless of prior status or mode of entry. Nonetheless, in contemplating an application for citizenship, persons who were previously in an unauthorized status—especially if they had entered the United States without authorization—might prove hesitant, given the heightened scrutiny attendant upon an application for citizenship. The analysis does indeed point to legal status effects, though the results vary from one subgroup to another and in ways

Status and home country visit

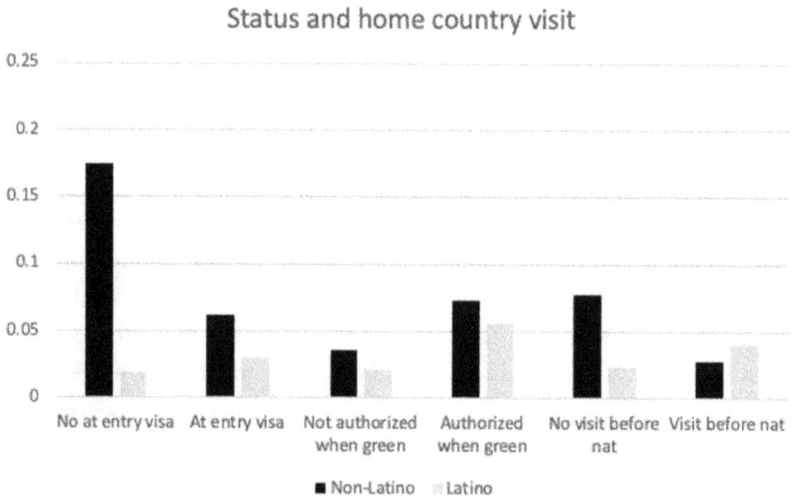

Years after receipt of green card

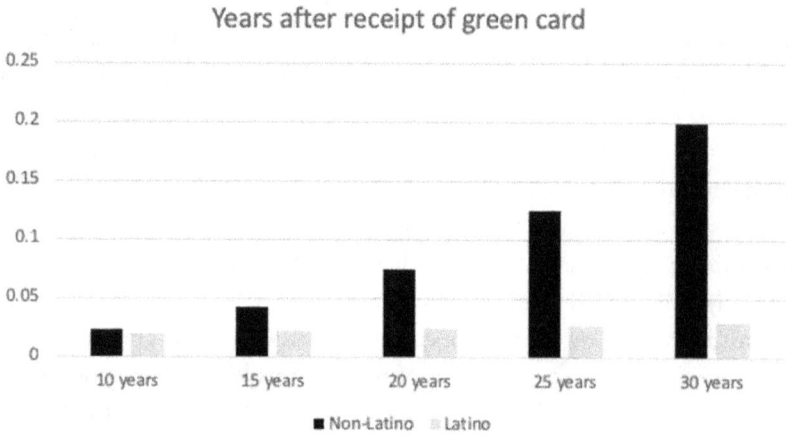

Figure 5.2. Predicted probabilities of naturalization in a given year: Effect of selected variables

Source: Los Angeles Family and Neighborhood Survey, 2006–2008.

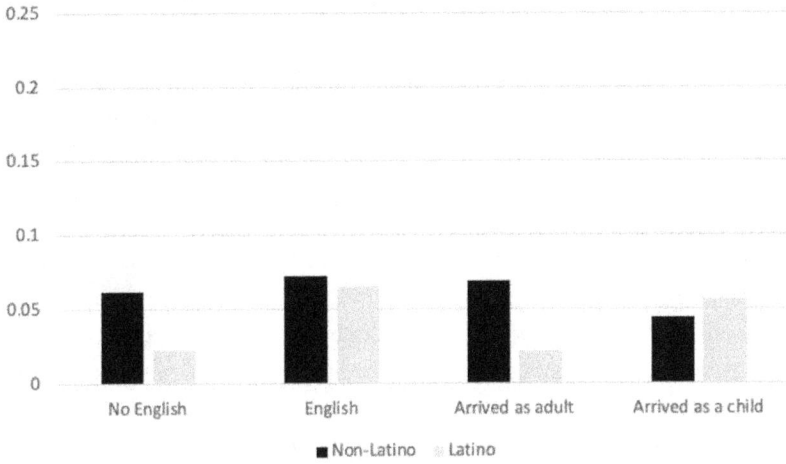

Language and age of arrival

Non-Latino   Latino

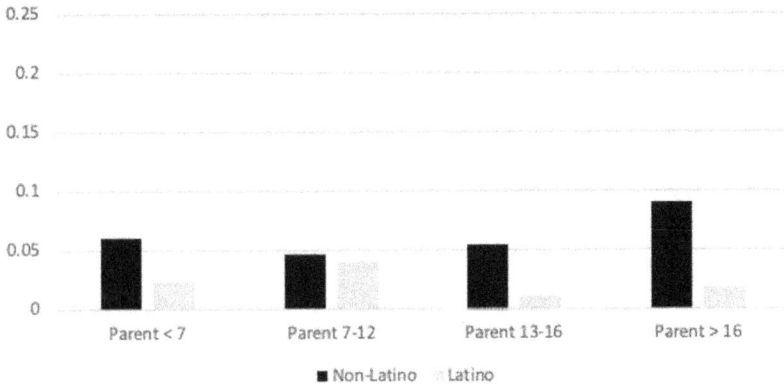

Parent's education

Non-Latino   Latino

that are somewhat counterintuitive. Just over half of all legally present Latino respondents had last entered the United States with a visa or entry document; citizenship rates were higher, at statistically significant levels, among these respondents than among their counterparts who had arrived without an entry document, but the impact was slight (.018 v .03). The survey shows considerable slippage in status between that moment of last entry and receipt of the green card, with Latino respondents more likely to slip *out* of status than *into* status. Most legally present Latino respondents were out of status at the time of receiving the green card, a condition reflected in the weak, positive effect for having once entered the United States "illegally" or without documents. Among respondents from elsewhere in the world, persons in status at the time of receiving the green card were twice as likely as their formerly out-of-status counterparts to become citizens (.073 v .035). Surprisingly, among non-Latino of respondents, lack of a visa or other entry document at the time of last entry was associated with significantly higher rates of naturalization; as this mode of entry was very rare (pertaining to only 6% of the non-Latino respondents), this result may reflect the idiosyncrasies of a very small number of people and the limited power of a small sample.

Conclusion

When we look at citizenship from a global perspective, the United States stands at the liberal end of the spectrum: It requires a relatively short period of near continuous residence; it obliges applicants to take a test, but one that is fairly simple, emphasizes knowledge, and does not screen for values lying close to some putative mainstream; it allows for dual citizenship; and it celebrates the acquisition of citizenship as both an achievement and a contribution to the society that the immigrant formally joins through naturalization.

Yet a large proportion of immigrants fail to acquire U.S. citizenship, even when circumstances allow. Nationwide, 66% of those immigrants who meet the residence requirement have naturalized, though as the denominator includes lawfully present persons as well as unauthorized immigrants, citizenship take-up among persons eligible to naturalize goes well above 66%. Even so, many prospective, eligible immigrants opt to remain outside the circle of citizenship, a pattern particularly prominent among persons from Mexico and Central America.

This chapter, analyzing data from Los Angeles County, home to almost one-third of the state's eligible-to-naturalize adults, highlights the impediments that keep naturalization rates depressed. Unlike most other studies, which derive from sources that lack data on immigrants' legal and citizenship status, LAFANS contains the information needed to delineate the population truly eligible to naturalize, not simply on the basis of residence, but by virtue of lawful presence. Although this group of lawfully present respondents are longtime U.S. residents—with twenty-one years of U.S. settlement on average—only 60% were U.S. citizens as of the time of the survey in 2006–2008.

The analysis confirms what previous research has shown—namely, that naturalization rates among Latinos lag far behind the rates for other immigrant groups. Not only is the disparity in take-up rates large—with rates averaging 2.2% per year for Latinos and 9.9% per year for others—exposure yields far less impact on Latinos than on immigrants from elsewhere in the world. Thus, settlement, which barely alters take-up rates among Latino respondents to LAFANS, speeds naturalization among their counterparts from elsewhere in the world, with the probability of becoming a citizen in any given year following receipt of the green card rising from 2.7% after 10 years to 6.7% after 20 years to 15.7% after 30 years.

The analysis provides several hints as to the factors delaying naturalization. To begin with, among Latino respondents, acquisition of the green card did not precede or coincide with their immigration, but rather occurred well after they had crossed U.S. borders. Moreover, unauthorized presence is a pervasive background factor among Latinos but not among others. Thus, of all the respondents legally present as of the interview, only 30% of the Latinos but 93% of immigrants from elsewhere had never previously entered the U.S. without authorization *and* also possessed a visa at the time when they received the green card. Moreover, before securing lawful presence, Latinos commonly slipped from an authorized to an unauthorized status, doing so with much greater frequency than their counterparts from elsewhere in the world. The strong effects associated with childhood migration and with knowledge of English at the time of arrival further suggest that the complexities of the naturalization process weigh particularly heavily on this disadvantaged population, with exposure adding little in the way of needed cognitive resources among those who came to the U.S. as adults.

Although high in quality, rich in migration-relevant information, and abundant in the number of foreign-born respondents, LAFANS contains relatively little national-origin diversity, which is why our analysis has concentrated on the simple contrast between the two populations of immigrants from Mexico and Latin America, on the one hand, and immigrants from all other regions of the world, on the other. Hence, for additional insights I turn to a new study of naturalization patterns among a highly diverse group of 1.5-generation persons surveyed in Southern California in 2004, appearing in *Origins and Destinations: The Making of the Second Generation* (Luthra, Soehl, and Waldinger 2018). As does this chapter, *Origins and Destinations* found significant intergroup differences in naturalization rates. But leveraging the sample's internal national-origin diversity to assess how differences in the context of immigration affected naturalization, *Origins and Destinations* also showed that naturalization trajectories proceed more slowly among those groups, such as Mexicans or Central Americans, characterized by a prevalence of disadvantaged immigrant statuses. For example, among groups with the most positive status prevalence score, 50% of the 1.5-generation respondents naturalized after roughly fifteen years, whereas it took more than twenty years for those with the least favorable group-level context to reach that same level.

As argued in *Origins and Destinations*, differences in status prevalence at the early stages of a migration's life cycle are likely to exercise long-terms effects for a variety of reasons. From the outset, the incidence of more protected (refugee) or more vulnerable (unauthorized residence) statuses affects both societal perception and the overall level of resources on which members of the same ethnic group can draw if and when they turn to one another for support. Members of groups most likely to enter with rights of permanent settlement get put on the quickest path to citizenship; groups among whom unauthorized migration is common or even prevails count many fewer members who might even be eligible for citizenship; hence, average intergroup differences in legal status and citizenship prevalence widen over time. These differences in status prevalence are likely to exercise the greatest effects on the unauthorized members of groups among whom unauthorized status is particular prevalent. But as we have seen in this chapter, possession of authorized status does not in and of itself necessarily accelerate the path toward citizenship acquisition.

Can changes in policy make a difference? History provides grounds for guarded skepticism. At the individual level, gaining the legal status that makes one eligible for naturalization clearly matters. Yet examination of the naturalization records of the immigrants who gained legalization as a result of the 1986 Immigration Reform and Control Act (IRCA) shows that inter-group differences remain large. Twenty-five years after IRCA, fewer than half of the legalized Mexican immigrants still living in the United States had been naturalized, a rate that fell significantly below the levels attained by legalized immigrants from all other countries of the world (Baker 2010).

Citizenship campaigns might alter the situation. In the mid-1990s, the Clinton administration launched Citizenship 2000, a campaign designed to increase naturalization rates, especially among IRCA beneficiaries who were just beginning to gain eligibility to naturalize at that point in time. As the program was never systematically assessed, hard evidence of its effectiveness is lacking. Nonetheless, that campaign, targeted at Southern California, did coincide with a notable defeat of a Republican Orange County congressman, provoking a Republican reaction that led to the campaign's abandonment (Schneider 2001). Given that firestorm of controversy, it does seem reasonable to think that active governmental promotion of naturalization could drive rates higher. Although citizenship requirements and procedures are a matter of federal policy and hence untouchable by measures taken at the state level, the experience of Citizenship 2000 does suggest that efforts funded and promoted by the government aimed at encouraging naturalization, increasing awareness of citizenship procedures, and publicizing the benefits of acquiring U.S. citizenship could push naturalization rates upward. A fund that would partially subsidize the cost of the citizenship application would also put naturalization in reach of a broader cross-section of California's citizenship-eligible population. The state's extensive infrastructure of immigrant rights and advocacy organizations, already invested in naturalization activities, could undoubtedly benefit from additional state help. Ultimately, the large number of noncitizen Californians eligible to naturalize, as well as the broad benefits—for individuals, families, and Californians statewide—that occur upon naturalization make efforts oriented at boosting citizenship acquisition a priority.

Notes

1. The Homeland Security Act of 2002 dismantled the Immigration and Naturalization Service, separating it into three units within the newly created Department of Homeland Security. U.S. Citizenship and Immigration Services took over responsibility for the immigration service functions previously undertaken by the INS.

2. "Removal Orders under Aggravated Felony Provisions," http://trac.syr.edu/immigration/reports/175/include/table_graph1.html.

6 The Innovation Economy

Natalie Novick and John D. Skrentny

At an event in late 2007, the cofounder and CEO of Cupertino's Apple Computer took to the stage to share his company's latest offering. Steve Jobs stepped forward to announce that he was releasing not one product but three—a phone, an internet communicator, and an iPod—a follow-up to the 2001 music player that became one of the company's best-selling products. On stage, Jobs teased the enraptured crowd, "A phone, an internet communicator, an iPod," he repeated, and repeated again, to ever rising applause from the audience. At the perfect moment, Jobs paused to announce, "These are not three separate devices. This is one device." The crowd went wild. Weeks later, lines of people waited outside shops across America to pick up the first-generation iPhone. On the side of the box, just under the barcode, it read, "Designed by Apple in California, Assembled in Taiwan." On the shiny backplate, again it read "Designed by Apple in California," as it had on the iPods that came before it. Competitors would follow, but Apple—and California—would do it first. Apple has continued labeling its devices as "designed in California"—a practice that not only distinguishes the state as its home but also highlights the brand of technological progress for which the state is known.

Today, many companies contribute to California's innovation brand, as proudly displayed by Apple. People across the globe are familiar with places such as Google's Mountain View or Facebook's Menlo Park thanks to the firms creating some of the most popular, valuable, and innovative products used around the world every day. Beyond consumer products, California

Table 6.1. California state gross domestic product (GDP), 2008–2016 (millions of dollars)

Year	Current Dollars	2012 Dollars	Deflator 2012 = 100	Annual Percentage Change		
				Current $	2012 $	Deflator
2008	1,990,678	2,111,138	94.3	1.8	0.4	1.4
2009	1,920,062	2,026,487	94.7	-3.5	-4.0	0.5
2010	1,974,615	2,058,138	95.9	2.8	1.6	1.3
2011	2,050,057	2,091,586	98.0	3.8	1.6	2.2
2012	2,144,497	2,144,497	100.0	4.6	2.5	2.0
2013	2,262,771	2,220,868	101.9	5.5	3.6	1.9
2014	2,395,162	2,312,540	103.6	5.9	4.1	1.7
2015	2,553,772	2,428,598	105.2	6.6	5.0	1.5

Source: Adapted from U.S. Bureau of Economic Analysis, "Gross State Product." http://www. dof.ca.gov/Forecasting/Economics/Indicators/Gross_State_Product/.

technology enables the world's technical devices, pharmaceuticals, information technologies, semiconductors, and entertainment centers. Innovation, typically understood as the creation of new products, services, and business models, is a major pillar of the state's economy and key driver of growth (see table 6.1). It is in this creation that some of the world's best and brightest minds assemble in California to think, build, and design.

Many of those involved in creating and supporting these innovative companies are immigrants. The focus of this volume is on immigrant integration, and we focus here on immigrants' economic integration in the technology sector. However, two notes on terminology are important at the outset. First, in this sector, both immigrants (that is, foreign-born workers who have settled in the U.S. permanently) and temporary (nonimmigrant) foreign workers are relevant and important, for reasons we explain later. In this chapter, we therefore use the more general term *foreign workers* to refer to both categories of non-U.S.-origin workers employed in this sector.

Second, *economic integration* has multiple meanings. A report from the National Academies of Sciences, Engineering, and Medicine (Waters and Pineau 2015) defined *integration* as "the process by which members of immigrant groups and host societies come to resemble one another," which in turn "depends upon the participation of immigrants and their descendants in major social institutions such as schools and the labor market, as well as their social acceptance by other Americans" (19). Here, we focus only on how non-U.S.-native workers are employed in California's technology sector (as opposed to ethnic enclaves in particular cities or regions, or other highly specialized niches within the mainstream economy). Using firm-level data, we can measure foreign workers' wages and their roles in this major growth sector of the economy. Are foreign workers contributing to California's technology and innovation sector, and if so, how can we characterize this contribution? Is there evidence that foreign workers are earning incomes equivalent to native workers?

The employment of highly skilled foreign workers across the telecommunications, computer, software, and biomedical industries in the United States has become commonplace over the last twenty years (Kerr 2019), and California fits this pattern. We argue, first, that California's innovation economy would look very different without the contribution of highly skilled foreign workers, and its future success now appears dependent on it. Technology firms indicate a demand for foreign workers' skills across the state, not just within the innovation hubs of Silicon Valley and San Francisco. Second, although the picture is complex, it appears that demand for the flexibility afforded by skilled foreign workers is correlated with the development of new technologies. Finally, and relating to the question of integration, available evidence indicates that temporary visa holders are largely divided into two main groups: those who fulfill short-term, flexible staffing needs, and those whom employers value as permanent residents and long-term employees—and who are paid on par with native workers.

This chapter begins with a generalized overview of the features of the innovation economy, and then proceeds to develop a picture of California's demand for the labor of foreign workers. The second section highlights California's role in the innovation economy, and the unique architecture that has allowed the state's innovation economy to flourish in specific local labor markets. The third section develops the connection between technological creation and foreign workers, highlighting how foreign workers contribute toward sustaining innovative activity. The fourth section showcases California's demand for high-skilled talent, utilizing a pooled dataset of Labor Condition Applications (LCAs; required of firms that wish to hire foreign workers on H-1B visas) from 2008 to 2015. This dataset brings together all the LCAs filed by California worksites during this time period. These filings correspond to over one million different positions. Here, we show the requests for foreign workers by city and by firm, showcasing how employers in different regions have sought to augment their local labor pool with specialized talent. Next, we see how these requests for skilled foreign workers correspond to patent applications. We find that firms with high levels of patenting also exhibit a high demand for skilled foreign workers. In the final section, we review the evidence for immigrant integration in the California tech sector, and propose a prospective avenue for future research, synthesizing the earlier findings.

Characteristics of the Innovation Economy: Knowledge Sharing and Agglomeration Effects

Understanding why foreign workers are integral to California's innovation economy requires some background on how this sector operates. A hallmark of innovation economies is the sharing of institutional knowledge between firms and employees. Increased competition for the best workers and most contemporary skills has created a culture of "job hopping" between firms to facilitate this exchange. The technical knowledge that drives the innovation economy can be scarce and expensive (Barley and Kunda 2006; Salzman, Kuehn, and Lowell 2013). In some technology and innovation hubs, movement between companies and technical roles is common, and workers will often take on a number of different roles in various projects—sometimes across firms at the same time. Allowing workers to navigate between companies not only helps to build worker experience and skills but also enables higher salaries (Barley and Kunda 2006). Job hopping allows the expertise held in firms to be transferred around and to be built upon, helping to propel the entire economy forward (Kuah 2002). California's refusal to enforce non-compete agreements (typically compelled by employers near the end of the hiring process, these restrict employees from leaving to work for competing firms) helped propel a culture of sharing knowledge between firms (Saxenian 1996; Gilson 1999). Compared to the rest of the country's workers, Californians have unusually high mobility among firms (Marx 2011; Nunn 2016).

Although job hopping allows some workers considerable autonomy (Shih 2006), it can also lead to a precarious work environment for all but the most highly qualified and sought-after workers. In response to the growing amount of job hopping and flexible work arrangements in the innovation economy, technology staffing firms have developed to facilitate a flexible workforce that can move between employers on a contract basis (Salzman 2016). The availability of these short-term contractors gives technology firms access to a workforce that may be brought on or dismissed depending on the project or company need, without having to make expensive, long-term commitments to individual workers as employees.

The flexibility of this workforce allows firms to keep core hiring levels low and to utilize specialized teams of contractors for projects or experimental tasks, where outcomes may be uncertain. This is sometimes called "the Hollywood [studio] model," whereby specialized workers come together for specific projects and may work on contracts rather than as salaried employees (Ayers et al. 2016). The project of high-tech companies is to create a new product or service, similar to the ways skilled workers in Hollywood come together to create a new film. The team disbands once the project is complete. Using contract work allows firms to be more agile when developing new technologies and practices and more responsive to fluctuations in customer demand. In addition, as these large contracting firms compete with one another, tech companies are able to access the best workers at the most competitive price.

Knowledge transfer becomes more effective when firms and talent are clustered closely together. Enabled by a relatively open institutional landscape, highly skilled workers and globally ambitious firms tend to attract one another and concentrate geographically. These concentrations of skilled workers and companies help to attract further talent and resources through agglomeration effects.

The Hollywood model works best in clusters such as those found in California, where the concentration of companies jostling for a global (rather than local) market enables related firms to collaborate rather than compete (Kerr et al. 2016; Porter 1998). These firms can then share a skilled workforce that has experience working for a number of different companies and different projects. As the region becomes a center for skills, it creates greater incentives for the further migration of skilled workers, either domestically or from abroad. The larger supply of workers spurs demand (because they make new tech developments possible) while giving employers the best choice of skills at a better price. Similar outcomes can be seen in many types of technology sectors (Addison 2006; Cheyre, Kowalski, and Veloso 2015; Porter 1998, 2000).

The effects of agglomeration create a demand for ever more specialized workers. In their Hollywood example, Kerr et al. (2016) argue that the growing concentration of actors and actresses in Hollywood furthers the in-migration of international aspiring talent. As the production capacity of the Hollywood studios has grown, it has demanded an ever more diverse set of skills and personnel. During the emergence of Hollywood's Golden Age, actors and actresses would play multiple roles in a single production, also doing their own makeup and stunts. Today, as production and markets have grown, unique personnel fill specialized roles and create demand for other types of work, such as craft services, special effects, and graphic imagery. These concentrations of talent enable individuals to specialize even further and become more productive (Cappelli 2012; Jones 2009).

Similar outcomes can be observed in California's other clusters of technological development, from Silicon Valley to San Diego. As the firms in innovation hubs across the state attract greater numbers of skilled workers, local companies can continue to specialize, build, and innovate, attracting new networks of skilled workers (Saxenian 2002; Scellato and Stephan 2012). Individual employees follow new technologies, services, and products and incorporate new learning into their work, rather than trying to maintain a broad foundation of skills that may be required for a more general position (Jones 2009).

How California Enables the Innovation Economy

The success of California's development of new technologies and products has not been an accident. Rather, it was enabled by key conditions that did not exist in the same configuration elsewhere in the United States (see Chapter 2). The first of these is a lack of a durable industrial legacy. The western United States was populated by newcomers disembedded from the industrial relations that characterized earlier-developed centers of industry on the East Coast and in the Midwest, creating an environment rich for experimentation and new forms of industry configuration (Saxenian 1996, 2006). Moreover, California metros have been able to adapt to change and seize opportunities; consider the case of San Diego, which transitioned from a pillar of the military and defense economy to a technology and innovation hub in the 1990s (Walshok and Shragge 2013). Migration to California from within the United States and abroad further contributed to this new landscape.

Saxenian (1996) describes those who helped build the conditions for California's technological foundation as pioneers of new kinds of industry in a new kind of region. Many who built California's innovation infrastructure during the 1970s and 1980s were newcomers, drawn to the state for higher education and for research opportunities in the state's burgeoning universities and research institutes. Saxenian describes the pioneer mentality of these early technologists as oppositional toward, and mistrustful of, East Coast attitudes and institutions. This mindset helped create the opportunity to build something completely new (also see Wadhwa et al. 2007; Kerr 2010; Porter 2000).

By the early twenty-first century, California-resident inventors regularly claimed the highest number of patents by state and surpassed expectations even after taking into account its large population (see figure 6.1). As late as 1997, California resident inventors claimed a 10.4% share of all patent documents issued worldwide (12,915 patents).[1] By 2015, Californians made up about 12% of the U.S. population,[2] but California-resident inventors were responsible for 28% of all resident-issued patents in the United States, followed by Texas, about 8% of the total U.S. population with 6.8% of the total patents.[3]

A more precise picture of California's output emerges when we look at the city level. When measured by the amount of patents issued, California cities are among the most innovative in the country, with four of the state's metropolitan areas represented among the top ten in the United States. Between 2000 and 2015, California metros were ranked first (San Jose–Sunnyvale–Santa Clara), third (San Francisco–Oakland–Fremont), fourth (Los Angeles–Long Beach–Santa Ana), and sixth (San Diego–Carlsbad–San Marcos) in the country for patenting output.[4] Although patents only tell part of the story, these rankings are suggestive of the innovative nature of the California economy.

Foreign Workers and Innovation

Human capital—skills and creativity—helps fuel the process of discovery for innovation industries. Foreign workers are a key source of this human capital. In 2016, the U.S. foreign-born workforce was 16.9% of the total (U.S. Bureau of Labor Statistics 2017), but in technology sectors, this share is much larger. According to estimates by the American Immigration Council, about 42% of California's STEM (science, technology, engineering and math) workforce is foreign born (American Immigration Council 2017). In the state's innovation-driven technology metros, this number is even greater (Wadhwa 2009; Wadhwa et al. 2007). One study suggests that as much as 74% of Silicon Valley's and San Francisco's technology workforce was born outside the United States (Silicon Valley Institute for Regional Studies 2016).

As the U.S. innovation economy grew in the late 1980s, employers demanded greater access to skilled workers. The result, the Immigration Act

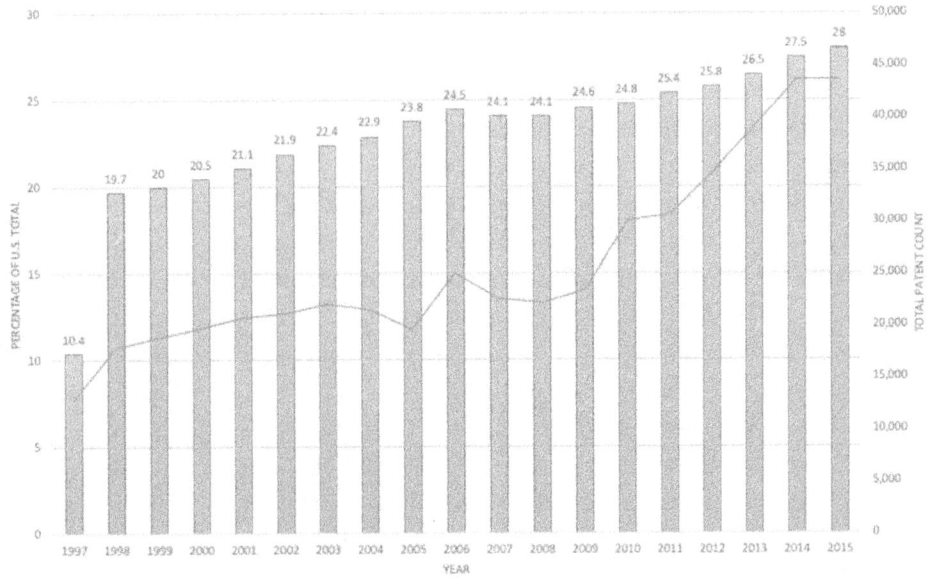

Figure 6.1. California patents, 1997–2017
Source: U.S. Patent and Trademark Office, "Calendar Year Patent Statistics (January 1 to December 31)," https://www.uspto.gov/web/offices/ac/ido/oeip/taf/reports_stco.htm.
Note: Line graph shows total patents awarded to California inventors; overlay on bar graph depicts percentage of U.S. total.

of 1990, made several employment-related changes to the U.S. system. Significantly, it established rules for the H-1B visa for nonimmigrant (that is, temporary) workers with at least a bachelor's degree. These visas, intended for workers in "specialty occupations," allowed foreigners to work in the United States for three years, extendable to six years, and also made them eligible for permanent residency if the employer elected to try to keep the worker. As the number of permanent residency visas is limited each year by nationality, and populous nations such as India and China do not receive more permanent visas than smaller nations, many successful "PERM applicants" could potentially wait for decades for permanent residency (and, eventually, citizenship; Chishti and Yale-Loehr 2016).

The H-1B visa ties residency rights to the issuing employer and position. Although changing employers is possible on an H-1B visa, it is not straightforward or guaranteed. In between jobs, H-1B visa holders cannot be self-employed or start their own businesses. These stipulations mean that job mobility for H-1B employees who desire sponsorship for a green card is limited (Hunt and Xie 2019).

The 1990 law established an annual cap of 65,000 for workers with a bachelor's degree, and in 2004 allocated an additional 20,000 visas for those with graduate degrees from U.S. universities. Congress has raised and lowered the cap at different times based on perceived demand, though it currently stands at the original 1990 level. Although some institutions (e.g., universities) are exempt from this cap, demand for these visas has long exceeded supply. Each year, visa applicants are approved on a first-come, first-served basis. If the program is oversubscribed, U.S. Citizen and Immigration Services issues visas through a lottery. The act further required employers to pay their H-1B workers at or above the prevailing wage for the position so that the visa would not become a back door to inexpensive foreign labor. Other visas also serve as vehicles for importing skilled permanent workers, such as the L-1 (for intracompany transfers) and the EB-1 and EB-2 (for advanced-degree STEM workers of "extraordinary" or "exceptional" ability), though in this chapter we concentrate on the more prevalent and easier-to-obtain H-1B.

H-1B visas provide employers access to a number of benefits. For example, research has shown that the H-1B visa program helped support the IT boom in the late 1990s (Bound, Khanna, and Morales 2016; Ghosh, Mayda, and Ortega 2015). Today, the H-1B visa remains the country's most significant source for international workers with specialty skills. Since its adoption, technology companies—and any firms hiring computer and information technology workers—have long been the largest beneficiaries of the H-1B visa. In 2015, more than 60% of all certified H-1B applicants were classified as working in computer-related occupations.[5]

Other studies have highlighted the contribution of migration flows toward American production and entrepreneurship (Hunt 2011; Wadhwa et al. 2007) and patenting (Akcigit, Grigsby, and Nicholas 2017). Both permanent and temporary migration, such as that facilitated by the H-1B visa, allows employers to access a greater talent pool than is available domestically, and to build teams able to utilize the most readily available skills from elsewhere. Studies of the U.S. foreign-born computer and engineering workforce find that migrants to the U.S. tend to be more highly skilled than their domestic counterparts, at a lower price (Hunt 2015). In addition, greater diversity and international talent in the workforce have been associated with a higher level of patenting by firms (Parrotta, Pozzoli, and

Pytlikova 2014) and less "groupthink" (Lyons 2017; National Economic Council 2011; Ozgen et al. 2014).

Business and technology leaders have also argued that migration allows firms to react and respond to the evolving pressures they face. Paul Camuti (2006), the former head of innovation at Siemens USA, maintains that the development of new methods, ideas, and products has become a "global, borderless process" from origins that were local or national, and puts a premium on not just the latest skills but on cross-cultural capabilities. The "borderless process" cited by Camuti also highlights the tension between this economy and its workers. Economies that require agility and movement between processes or projects require a flexible approach to skills and knowledge at the best value (Adams and Demaiter 2010; Case 2016).

The same prohibition of noncompete agreements that helps to facilitate brain circulation and knowledge transfer can also disincentivize employer investment in worker training, forcing employers to look outside the firm for fresh skills. Staffing firms, often utilizing H-1B workers, regularly fill the void. IT outsourcing companies have been found to receive a disproportionate number of H-1B visas. In 2016, the top five H-1B visa sponsors were the staffing companies Cognizant Tech Solutions, Infosys, Tata Consultancy Services, Accenture, and Wipro.[6]

In a competitive environment where skilled workers are in high demand, rapid mobility and poaching can be common (Cheyre et al. 2015; Whitley 2006). Firms desiring a low-cost and flexible labor force may be attracted to H-1B workers, especially the H-1B workers provided by staffing firms, precisely because contract workers provide some control in a volatile labor market. Workers who are tied to firms in the hopes of obtaining a green card or who can be hired and replaced at will (as contractors) provide a unique value for companies in part because they are so easily exploited.

The H-1B Application Process: Labor Condition Applications as Measures of Demand for Skilled Foreign Workers

Although we lack direct measures of demand for foreign workers, we do have indicators of employer desire for the *flexibility* to hire foreign workers for specific positions. For this, we analyze data from the Labor Condition Application (LCA) process. LCAs are an important part of the H-1B visa because companies seeking to hire workers in H-1B positions must first receive federal authorization to do so, and this requires filing an LCA with the Department of Labor's Employment and Training Administration.[7] A positive certification allows employers to *recruit* an international worker for the intended position if they choose to do so, but does not require that they pursue an actual visa. Actual *hiring* requires the successful receipt of the appropriate visa. Still, we believe it is a conservative assumption that firms that file LCAs at least are considering foreign workers, and want the flexibility to hire one if desired.

To be certified, positions must be compensated at or greater than the actual rate of pay for other employees in the same position, or above the prevailing wage for that specific occupation. The prevailing wage for these positions is determined by the National Prevailing Wage Center (NWPC), an office of the U.S. Department of Labor. The prevailing wage for each job description varies, depending on the worker location and intended duties.[8] In addition, firms are required to demonstrate that working conditions for visa holders are similar to those of other employees. Employers must file an LCA for each position they intend to staff with a foreign worker, and for each job site or work location where these workers will be employed.[9]

Determining the prevailing wage for international workers is not without controversy—especially due to the shifting nature of job descriptions, new types of employment enabled by technological progress, and alternative compensation structures (e.g., vested interests). When filing, employers have various strategies for setting the prevailing wage—among them, requesting a prevailing wage determination from the NPWC (which bases its decisions on Occupational Employment Statistics survey data) or using independent surveys of the labor market. In each case, however, the NPWC must certify the intended compensation as adequate. In 2015, the NPWC certified 208,689 H-1B positions in California, out of 217,456 requested. The average wage offered for these certified positions was $89,439.58.[10]

Despite the NPWC certification process, there have been numerous challenges to the wage determinations for H-1B visas, and the appropriate wage levels have long been subject to critique. *Computerworld*, a periodical focusing on the IT industry in the U.S., has highlighted a number of cases that appear inconsistent with the NPWC's own wage determination policies. For example, in 2017 the publication uncovered a successful H-1B visa application for Cupertino's Apple Computer that paid computer programmers a $52,229 yearly salary. This salary level is far below the industry average for the company's Silicon Valley location, where average wages in Santa Clara Country top over $90,000 yearly.[11] Political scientist Ron Hira has long highlighted instances where H-1B wages appear much lower than industry averages. In testimony to Congress in 2016, Hira discussed the case of Southern California Edison, where three hundred U.S. workers were replaced by H-1B workers making salaries 40%–50% less.[12] Hira described a Department of Labor investigation of the case, which found that no violations occurred and that H-1B workers could be paid less than domestic workers for the same positions. A similar finding was reached by judges in a civil suit filed by technology workers at Disney, who sued after they were laid off from their positions and told that if they did not train their foreign replacements, they would lose their severance packages.[13] Hira found that the replacement workers, from California IT staffing firm HCL Technologies, were paid 33%–39% less than the staff they replaced, who each earned over $100,000 a year plus benefits.

Employers and staffing firms have sought LCA filings for prospective employees in great numbers. In 2012, U.S. employers filed LCAs for 940,812 prospective H-1B positions. By 2015, the number of LCA filings had risen to 1,219,615. A majority of these positions were certified (847,959 and 1,173,149 respectively),[14] but ultimately only a small proportion of these were filled by H-1B visa recipients. Although some positions are exempt from the visa cap (such as educational institutions), the number of LCAs filed in California alone far exceeds the available new visas each year.

Despite the discrepancy between LCAs and actual hiring of foreign workers, we believe that LCAs can be used to examine employer desire for the flexibility to hire a foreign worker, and that the LCAs indicate employers' concern that the available supply of skilled native U.S. workers for anticipated roles may be inadequate. These approved filings give employers the opportunity to pursue hiring a foreign worker, should they choose to do so. Employers that file and are approved have a greater degree of hiring flexibility than those that do not.

An additional reason to focus on LCAs is that the data on filings can be very detailed. We can see the company name and the metro area, and analyze the relationship between the job positions anticipated for foreign labor and innovative output.

Finally, the actual hiring of H-1Bs workers, an alternative measure, has different problems—hiring of H-1Bs shows not just demand but firms' ability to win the lottery for the workers but also supply-side factors, such as foreign workers' desire for employment in particular firms, industries, and geographic regions. For these reasons, we use LCAs as a measure of the desire for the flexibility to hire foreign high-skilled workers.

Looking Closer at California's Demand
for High-Skilled Foreign Workers

Thus far, we have highlighted the unique characteristics that led California to become the country's leader in technological innovation, the role that highly skilled foreign workers play in sustaining levels of technical production, and some of the tensions that arise over this foreign workforce. We have also highlighted the growing role of the state's foreign workforce as a net contributor to the state's innovation economy. In this section, we examine two key measures: applications for foreign workers (through LCA filings) and patenting by firms, from 2008 to 2015. We chose these eight years due to data availability for these two key variables, but they also represent a unique period for California's innovation economy. The selected years capture the state's movement from the depths of the "Great Recession" of 2007–2012. During this time, the state's economic output moved from a state of decline toward one of growth.

The recession years indicate expected changes in both foreign talent demands and patenting, our key units of observation. We explore foreign-labor demand and patenting at the metro and also the firm level.

Labor Condition Application Filings
Table 6.2 represents all LCAs—all for H-1B workers—for California employers for California occupations.[15] With the exception of 2009, LCAs increased each year over the previous. These filings grew much faster than the state's GDP. It is important to note that because individual LCAs can be submitted for multiple positions under each job role, the actual number of foreign workers anticipated under these totals is likely higher than indicated here. A total of 57,631 California worksites filed LCAs for occupational roles across the time period of study (2008–2015).

We find that California's LCAs are concentrated in areas known for developing technological change. The highest level of anticipated flexibility to hire foreign workers is in the state's most innovation-rich metro area—the San Francisco–Silicon Valley corridor, and the greatest demand is in technology jobs (see table 6.3).

Patenting
Patenting is related to innovation, but we do not equate innovation with patents. All patents are measured equally, whether they be small technical changes to an existing product or a new data processing platform. Some

Table 6.2. H-1B LCAs filed by California firms and worksites

Year	LCAs
2008	60,548
2009	41,635
2010	50,899
2011	62,053
2012	68,927
2013	77,633
2014	86,562
2015	102,100

Sources: Office of Foreign Labor Certification disclosure data files and 2015 annual report, https://www.foreignlaborcert.doleta.gov/performancedata.cfm#dis; https://www.foreignlaborcert.doleta.gov/pdf/OFLC_Annual_Report_FY2015.pdf.

inventors choose not to patent their innovations, and others repeatedly issue patents for narrow changes that many may not consider true innovations. Filing costs and legal barriers may further prevent creators from patenting unique contributions, and still other applications take many years to be finally approved.

Innovation is extraordinarily difficult to measure, however, and patents—flawed as they are—can be the best available proxy. Although patenting is an imperfect measure, it can be illustrative when it comes to determining the economic impact of new technological developments. Patents can be valuable assets for firms and their inventors, and firms or individuals pursue them when there is an economic incentive to do so. For this reason, leading studies of regional innovation patterns rely on patent counts (e.g., Acs, Anselin, and Varga 2002; Bottazi and Peri 2003). The patent counts provide a consistent way to evaluate trends in innovative activity by year and by firm.

The data come from several public repositories released by the U.S. Patent and Trademark Office (USPTO). USPTO does not make complete records available on all issued patents. It releases isolated datasets related to patenting by metro/micropolitan area, firm, technology class, and year.[16] Here, we have brought these data together into a new, unique dataset from 2008 to 2015, coinciding with available LCAs. We matched the data on patenting by firm and firm year to our earlier dataset on anticipated labor demand.

Between 2008 and 2015, 12,757 California firms received 138,478 patents. As expected, these patents were unevenly distributed across the state. The

Table 6.3. California 2015 H-1B LCAs (by positions certified) by city and occupation

City name	Positions certified	Average wage offer (rounded to nearest $)
San Francisco	26,126	98,818
San Jose	23,397	95,308
Sunnyvale	14,124	93,197

Occupation	Positions certified	Average wage offer (rounded to nearest $)
Computer Systems Analysts	44,013	80,004
Software Developers, Applications	35,114	109,137
Computer Occupations, Other	21,988	79,144
Software Developers, Systems Software	18,644	115,361
Computer Programmers	17,985	68,643

Source: California 2015 state employment-based immigration profiles, U.S. Department of Labor, Office of Foreign Labor Certification, https://www.foreignlaborcert.doleta.gov/map/2015/ca.pdf.

greatest number of patents went to Silicon Valley and the wider Bay Area. The Sunnyvale–San Jose–Santa Clara metro area received 89,311 patents, with San Francisco–Oakland–Fremont receiving the next highest total, 57,543. After San Diego–Carlsbad–San Marcos's 29,825 patents, there is a sharp drop, and several other metros cluster around the 3,000–4,000 count. The main takeaway is that California innovation is not just a Silicon Valley story, even if that region is by far the most productive (see table 6.4).

Surprisingly, the California firms receiving the most patents were not in Silicon Valley but rather in Southern California. As shown in table 6.5, San Diego's Qualcomm received 9,930 patents across the time period, followed by Irvine's Broadcom Semiconductor. Apple, Intel, and Google round out the top five. Each of the top ten patent-receiving firms is found in California's computer or information technology sector rather than in other science and technology-based businesses, such as biotech, pharmaceuticals, or materials engineering.

Table 6.4. Top fifteen California metro areas by patents issued, 2008–2015

Metro area	Patents
San Jose–Sunnyvale–Santa Clara	89,311
San Francisco–Oakland–Fremont	57,543
Los Angeles–Long Beach–Santa Ana	42,793
San Diego–Carlsbad–San Marcos	29,825
Santa Cruz–Watsonville	4,406
Oxnard–Thousand Oaks–Ventura	4,119
Sacramento–Arden-Arcade–Roseville	3,999
Riverside–San Bernardino–Ontario	3,250
Santa Barbara–Santa Maria–Goleta	2,497
Santa Rosa–Petaluma	1,702
San Luis Obispo–Paso Robles	629
Salinas	530
Bakersfield–Delano	502
Stockton	500

Source: U.S. Patent and Trademark Office, "Patenting in U.S. Metropolitan and Micropolitan Areas, Breakout by Technology Class," https://www.uspto.gov/web/offices/ac/ido/oeip/taf/cbsa_cls/index.html.

LCAs and Patenting: How Are They Related?

When we combine both LCA and patenting data by firms, some relationships between demand for foreign workers and innovative output become clear. First, we find a strong correlation between LCAs and patents issued. The California data are consistent with existing U.S. research linking H-1B hiring to patenting (Hunt and Gauthier-Loiselle 2010; Kerr and Lincoln 2010). In a pooled dataset of all years of study and all firms, we find a correlation of .51 between patents and LCAs (as seen in table 6.6). The relationship between LCAs and patents is displayed in figure 6.2. Refining this further by taking the average of LCAs by year, the association becomes slightly stronger, at .53.

This relationship remains durable even when analyzing each year individually. Although the strength of the relationship varies yearly, the association between the variables is always above 40%, approaching 60% in 2013. When divided by yearly LCA filings, the correlation between patents and LCA per year is .46.

Although we claim no causal relationship (nor can we even specify which

Table 6.5. Top ten California firms by patents issued, 2008–2015 (all years)

Qualcomm Inc.	9,930
Broadcom Corp.	7,810
Apple Inc.	7,795
Intel Corp.	6,728
Google Inc.	6,352
Applied Materials Inc.	5,210
Sun Microsystems Inc.	4,291
Advanced Micro Devices Inc.	4,189
Xilinx Inc.	2,096
Altera Corp.	2,095

Source: U.S. Patent and Trademark Office, "Patenting in U.S. Metropolitan and Micropolitan Areas, Breakout by Technology Class," https://www.uspto.gov/web/offices/ac/ido/oeip/taf/cbsa_cls/index.html.

Table 6.6. Correlation table of LCAs and patenting by California firms

	Correlation of LCAs and patents							
Total	Avg/year	2008	2009	2010	2011	2012	2013	2014
0.51	0.52	0.51	0.47	0.52	0.52	0.57	0.43	0.40
	Correlation of LCAs and patents lagged one year							
		2008	2009	2010	2011	2012	2013	
		0.52	0.52	0.53	0.56	0.59	0.43	

way the causal arrow would point between LCAs and patents), we nevertheless argue that the relationship has importance. It suggests that employers utilize flexible talent pools provided by foreign labor to support the development of new projects and innovations. For instance, we might expect that patenting output could be an outcome of increased talent demands. That is, hiring behavior could influence later output. We investigate this by lagging patents by one year from the visas requested. Here, the correlation remains, but slightly weaker at .42 (see figure 6.3).

Characteristics of California's Top LCA-Filing Firms

Even when we don't make assumptions as to causation, the correlation between LCAs and patenting output indicates there might be more to the association between these two variables. To take a closer look, we limit our firm observations to the top fifty LCA filers and top fifty firms by patents, to

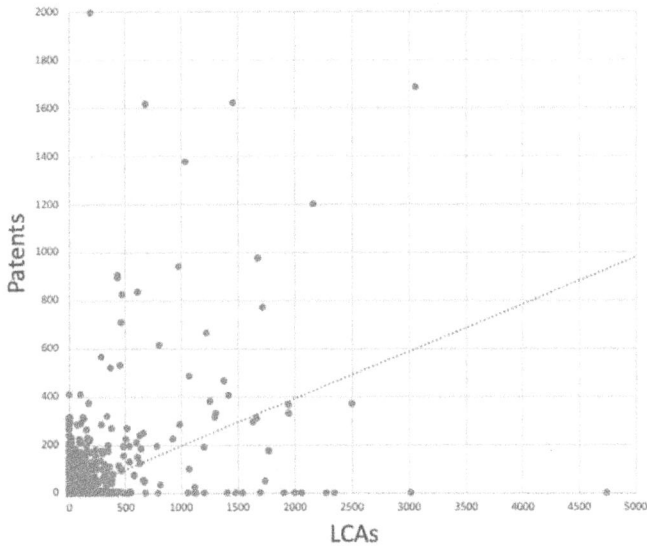

Figure 6.2. Correlation between LCAs and patents by firm, across
time series of study

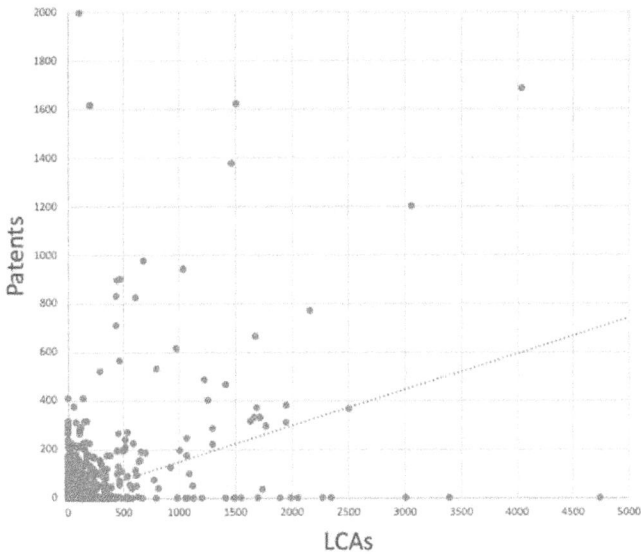

Figure 6.3. Correlation between LCAs and patents by firm, across time
series of study, lagged one year

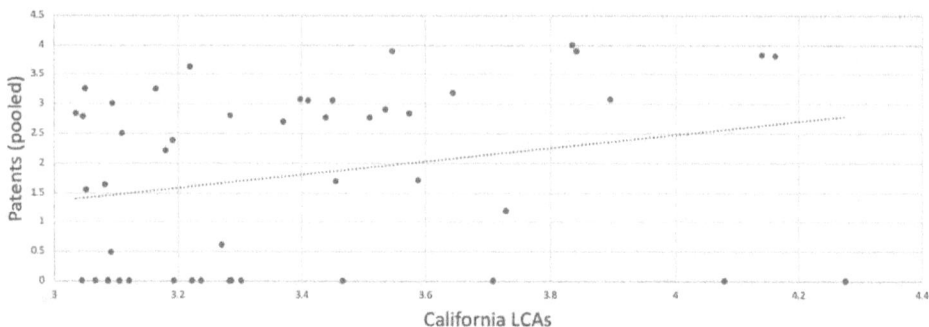

Figure 6.4. Correlation between yearly LCAs and patents received by firm, subset of top fifty requesting firms

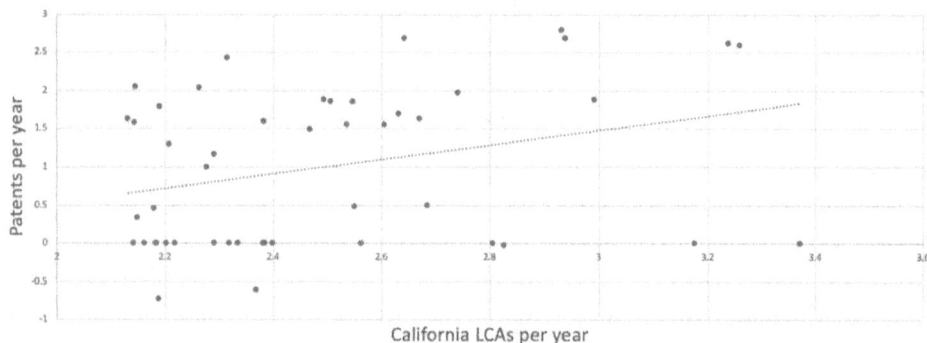

Figure 6.5. Correlation between yearly LCAs and patents received by firm, subset of top fifty requesting firms, lagged one year

see if the relationship still holds. In this subset, we find that in the years 2008–2015, California's top fifty LCA filers applied for nearly 170,000 positions, or nearly 30% of the total LCAs filed. The remaining 70% were requested by more than 57,000 firms. During the same time period, the top fifty firms filed nearly 60,000 patents, or about 43% of all California patents. In this narrower analysis, the correlation between LCAs and patenting remains (see figure 6.4). In an analysis not included here, this relationship is still maintained when logging both variables to reduce the impact of outliers (see figure 6.5). When accounting for LCAs by year, again, as we expect, the association remains.

Visualizing these data shows a clear linear relationship. However, there are several firms that cluster on the *x*-axis—firms that do not file *any* patents

Table 6.6a. Top fifty California companies by LCAs, 2008–2015

Employer	LCAs Avg/year	Patents Avg patent/LCA by year
HCL America Inc.	2,359.6	0.0
UST Global Inc.	1,498.9	0.0
iGate Technologies Inc.	638.9	0.0
Persistent Systems Inc.	366.3	0.0
University of California, Davis	250.9	0.0
RJT Compuquest Inc.	242.4	0.0
University of California, San Francisco	240.4	0.0
University of California, Los Angeles	216.4	0.0
Horizon Technologies Inc.	209.0	0.0
University of California, San Diego	195.9	0.0
Intelliswift Software Inc.	165.8	0.0
RS Software (India) Ltd.	159.8	0.0
Smartplay Inc.	152.9	0.0
University of California, Berkeley	152.8	0.0
Beta Soft Systems Inc.	145.4	0.0
Mindtree Ltd.	138.8	0.0
Lawrence Berkeley Laboratory	154.6	0.2
Marvell Semiconductor Inc.	233.5	0.3
Qualcomm Technologies Inc.	671.0	0.9
TIBCO Software Inc.	140.9	2.2
Adobe Systems Inc.	151.3	2.8
Cisco Systems Inc.	484.4	3.1
PayPal Inc.	356.5	3.1
LinkedIn Corp.	189.5	10.1
GlobalFoundries Inc.	195.1	14.8
Brocade Communications Systems Inc.	161.1	20.0
Salesforce.com Inc.	293.8	30.8
VMware Inc.	344.4	35.7
Facebook Inc.	404.1	36.5
KLA-Tencor Corp.	139.3	37.9
NetApp Inc.	241.3	39.8
Fujitsu Ltd.	468.6	43.3
Amgen Inc.	135.6	43.3

Table 6.6a. Top fifty California companies by LCAs, 2008–2015 (*continued*)

Employer	LCAs Avg/year	Patents Avg patent/LCA by year
eBay Inc.	429.0	50.4
Chevron U.S.A. Inc.	155.3	61.9
Hewlett-Packard Co.	352.9	70.8
Symantec Corp.	321.9	72.1
Oracle America Inc.	983.0	75.3
Oracle USA Inc.	312.3	75.3
Yahoo Inc.	552.3	94.6
Nvidia Corp.	183.0	109.6
Stanford University	140.1	111.4
Advanced Micro Devices Inc.	207.4	262.3
Google Inc.	1,815.0	397.4
Intel Corp.	1,728.0	421.0
Apple Inc.	868.4	487.9
Broadcom Corp.	439.8	488.6
Qualcomm Inc.	854.8	620.9

Source: California 2015 state employment-based immigration profiles, U.S. Department of Labor, Office of Foreign Labor Certification, https://www.foreignlaborcert.doleta.gov/map/2015/ca.pdf.

during the time period (see table 6.6a). What explains these cases that sit so far outside the expected range?

Within this list of top LCA filers, three main types of organizations are apparent: staffing and sourcing firms, universities, and technology companies. Staffing and sourcing firms filed 48,620 LCAs during this time, or 29% of the total LCAs filed across the state, and zero patents (see table 6.6b). Their staff usually work for other technology companies, supporting the development of new products, services, and processes at these firms.

Five public universities figure in the top fifty—UC-Berkeley, UC-Davis, UCLA, UC-San Diego, and UC-San Francisco. Together, they submitted 8,450 LCAs, or 5% of the LCA total for that time period.[17] The remaining top LCA filers were all high-technology companies, such as Qualcomm, Apple, and Google.

Although we do not claim that all or even most H-1Bs working at firms or universities are directly involved in patenting activity, these findings do fit our

Table 6.6b. California's top firms by LCAs and corresponding patenting by California worksites, 2008–2015

Employer	LCA Requests (2008–2015)		Patents (2008–2015)	
	Sum	Avg/year	Sum	Avg/year (firm type)
HCL America Inc.	18,877	2,360	0	0 (Contractor)
Google Inc.	14,520	1,815	6,352	397.4
Intel Corp.	13,824	1,728	6,728	421
UST Global Inc.	11,991	1,499	0	0 (Contractor)
Oracle America Inc.	7,864	983	1,202	75.3
Apple Inc.	6,947	868	7,795	487.9
Qualcomm Inc.	6,838	855	9,930	620.9
Qualcomm Technologies Inc.	5,368	671	15	0.9
iGate Technologies Inc.	5,111	639	0	0 (Contractor)
Yahoo Inc.	4,418	552	1,510	94.6
Cisco Systems Inc.	3,875	484	50	3.1
Fujitsu Ltd.	3,749	469	684	43.3
Broadcom Corp.	3,518	440	7,810	488.6
eBay Inc.	3,432	429	805	50.4
Facebook Inc.	3,233	404	584	36.5
Persistent Systems Inc.	2,930	366	0	0 (Contractor)
PayPal Inc.	2,852	357	49	3.1
Hewlett-Packard Co.	2,823	353	1,130	70.8
VMware Inc.	2,755	344	569	35.7
Symantec Corp.	2,575	322	1,147	72.1
Oracle USA Inc.	2,498	312	1,202	75.3
Salesforce.com Inc.	2,350	294	492	30.8
University of California, Davis	2,007	251	0	0 (University)
RJT Compuquest Inc.	1,939	242	0	0 (Contractor)
NetApp Inc.	1,930	241	633	39.8
University of California, San Francisco	1,923	240	0	0 (University)
Marvell Semiconductor Inc.	1,868	234	4	0.3
University of California, Los Angeles	1,731	216	0	0 (University)
Horizon Technologies Inc.	1,672	209	0	0 (Contractor)
Advanced Micro Devices Inc.	1,659	207	4,189	262.3

Table 6.6b. California's top firms by LCAs and corresponding patenting by California worksites, 2008–2015 (*continued*)

Employer	LCA Requests (2008–2015) Sum	Avg/year	Patents (2008–2015) Sum	Avg/year (firm type)
University of California, San Diego	1,567	196	0	0 (University)
GlobalFoundries Inc.	1,561	195	237	14.8
LinkedIn Corp.	1,516	190	161	10.1
Nvidia Corp.	1,464	183	1,747	109.6
Intelliswift Software Inc.	1,326	166	0	0 (Contractor)
Brocade Communications Systems Inc.	1,289	161	316	20
RS Software (India) Ltd.	1,278	160	0	0 (Contractor)
Chevron USA Inc.	1,242	155	991	61.9
Lawrence Berkeley Laboratory	1,237	155	3	0.2 (Research)
Smartplay Inc.	1,223	153	0	0 (Contractor)
University of California, Berkeley	1,222	153	0	0 (University)
Adobe Systems Inc.	1,210	151	43	2.8
Beta Soft Systems Inc.	1,163	145	0	0 (Contractor)
TIBCO Software Inc.	1,127	141	35	2.2
Stanford University	1,121	140	1,781	111.4 (University)
KLA-Tencor Corp.	1,114	139	600	37.9
Mindtree Ltd.	1,110	139	0	0 (Contractor)
Amgen Inc.	1,085	136	688	43.3

Sources: U.S. Patent and Trademark Office, "Patenting in U.S. Metropolitan and Micropolitan Areas, Breakout by Technology Class," https://www.uspto.gov/web/offices/ac/ido/oeip/taf/cbsa_cls/index.html; California 2015 state employment-based immigration profiles, U.S. Department of Labor, Office of Foreign Labor Certification, https://www.foreignlaborcert.doleta.gov/map/2015/ca.pdf.

earlier expectations about the role of skills in the innovation economy. Staffing firms provide a source of skilled, flexible labor for companies working on new technologies and products. Universities and research organizations contribute to the development of new innovations through basic research (for example, Google's initial search technology was developed at Stanford University funded by a National Science Foundation grant[18]) and, of course, workforce development. Finally, technology and science companies, beholden

Table 6.7. California's top firms by patenting and corresponding LCAs by California worksites, 2008–2015

Employer	Patents	Certified LCAs in public database
Qualcomm Inc.	9,930	6,838
Broadcom Corp.	7,810	3,518
Apple Inc.	7,795	6,947
Intel Corp.	6,728	13,824
Google Inc.	6,352	14,520
Applied Materials Inc.	5,210	1,018
Sun Microsystems Inc.	4,291	563
Advanced Micro Devices Inc.	4,189	1,659
Xilinx Inc.	2,096	403
Altera Corp.	2,095	432
Agilent Technologies Inc.	2,066	310
California Institute of Technology	1,803	1,073
National Semiconductor Corp.	1,788	206
Stanford University	1,781	1,121
Nvidia Corp.	1,747	1,464
Lam Research Corp.	1,685	446
Genentech Inc.	1,513	976
Juniper Networks Inc.	1,511	814
Yahoo Inc.	1,510	4,418
Western Digital Technologies Inc.	1,390	555
Pacesetter Inc.	1,247	1
Oracle America Inc. (Redwood City)	1,202	7864
Oracle America Inc.	1,202	2,498
LSI Logic Corp.	1,196	29
Symantec Corp.	1,147	2,575
Rambus Inc.	1,145	63
Hewlett-Packard Co.	1,130	2,823
Cypress Semiconductor Corp.	1,020	342
Sandisk Corp.	1,002	991
Chevron USA Inc.	991	1,242
Cadence Design Systems Inc.	933	564
Headway Technologies Inc.	879	106
LSI Corp.	839	822
eBay Inc.	805	3,432

Table 6.7. California's top firms by patenting and corresponding LCAs by
California worksites, 2008–2015 (*continued*)

Employer	Patents	Certified LCAs in public database
Isis Pharmaceuticals Inc.	787	32
Finisar Corp.	784	116
Synopsys Inc.	754	631
Amgen Inc.	688	1,085
Fujitsu Ltd.	684	3,749
Callaway Golf Company	660	52
International Rectifier Corp.	649	199
Honeywell International Inc.	636	68
NetApp Inc.	633	1,930
University of Southern California	613	378
KLA-Tencor Corp.	600	1,114
Intermolecular Inc.	595	45
Facebook Inc.	584	3,233
VMware Inc.	569	2,755
Power Integrations Inc.	562	59

Sources: U.S. Patent and Trademark Office, "Patenting in U.S. Metropolitan and Micropolitan Areas, Breakout by Technology Class," https://www.uspto.gov/web/offices/ac/ido/oeip/taf/cbsa_cls/index.html; California 2015 state employment-based immigration profiles, U.S. Department of Labor, Office of Foreign Labor Certification, https://www.foreignlaborcert.doleta.gov/map/2015/ca.pdf.

to the fast product cycles endemic to their industry, require a ready supply of workers with the latest skills to help build innovative products.

High Innovators with Low Demand for Foreign Workers
Many of California's largest patent-producing companies are also leading filers of LCAs. Table 6.7 shows that twenty-two of the state's leading patent innovators are also among the state's top fifty filers of LCAs. The top five firms by patent output are also among the top filers of LCAs. For the remainder of firms, a few outliers emerge that innovate at a high rate but do not file many LCAs, such as Pacesetter Systems. This medical device company filed only one LCA during the time period despite being granted more than twelve hundred patents.

What explains why a few companies are high innovators, but file few

LCAs? It is difficult to find a pattern or factor that explains all cases, high-lighting the need for further research. In several, the firms are older and have extensive existing technologies, among them Honeywell, LSI Logic, and Inter-molecular. Patenting may be partly explained by the legacies of these firms, their knowledge base, the use of staffing activities outside of California, and their business models. For example, the semiconductor firm Rambus did not need foreign workers because its business model was licensing its portfolio—and also litigating (Higginbotham 2015). Another case, Callaway Golf, is not generally considered to be a technology firm and may be working in an area where native workers are plentiful. Future work can explore in more detail which kinds of innovative firms are associated with desire for the flexibility to hire H-1B workers and which kinds of firms patent, but do not request H-1Bs.

Conclusion: What Is the Future Role of Foreign Workers in California's Economy?

Both temporary and permanent resident foreign workers play significant roles in California's innovation economy. This chapter has shown that highly skilled H-1B workers—or at least the desire for the flexibility to hire them—appear related to the output of many of the state's leading technical compa-nies and in the staffing and sourcing firms that support them. Firms filing LCAs to authorize the hiring of foreign workers enjoy more flexible hiring for their positions relative to firms that do not. Relatedly, we've shown how the largest filers of LCAs are the technology staffing and sourcing firms. Although little information is available about the work done by contractors and where and for whom they work, the demand for these workers as indicated by LCA filings has only grown over time. It is these workers who help staff and enable California's innovation firms with the flexibility and skills to continue to do the work they do.

But what are the potential costs of this reliance? As indicated in work by Hira and others, many questions remain about the reliability of the wage determination process. Highly visible examples of companies exploiting the H-1B visa loopholes to shed more expensive, and generally older, native work-ers continue to raise alarms. There is a darker side, then, to the use of tem-porary visa workers in California's dynamic labor markets. Will native work-ers become casualties of the fast-paced technical environment demanded by today's technology—with H-1B workers victims of an immigration regime that ties them to employers (many of them contractors) for considerable stretches of time, with little control over their autonomy?

Although not covering the staffing and sourcing companies included in our study of California, Hira (2010) shows the dual uses of H-1Bs—they are both a bridge to permanent immigration and a source of cheap, temporary labor. When examining staffing firms that concentrate their business model on sourcing jobs to India, Hira finds that these firms very rarely sponsor their H-1B workers for green cards (with several between 0 and 5% sponsorship).

This relates to the subject of this chapter, which is the integration of immigrants in California's tech sector. There is some reason to believe that these patterns are changing, and the integration of foreign-born tech workers seen in the California data is actually higher than that seen in Hira's national data. He focuses on firms that bring workers from India to learn American jobs while on H-1B visas and then return to India, where they can perform the same job for a fraction of the price of workers based in the United States. In Hira's national data, an outlier among the staffing and sourcing companies is Cognizant, which sponsored 71% of its H-1Bs for permanent residence. At the time of publication, Hira surmised that Cognizant was different from the others due to its base in the U.S. Similarly, the staffing and sourcing firms in the California data are based in California, and thus may be more likely to also sponsor H-1Bs for permanent residence.

In addition, recognizing the scarce skills needed to utilize the latest technologies, tech firms frequently sponsor the green cards of applicants, which makes them permanent (and more integrated) residents. For example, Qualcomm, as we show, is one of the leading patenting companies in California, and has sponsored nearly all of its H-1Bs for permanent residence. Oracle's record was similar. Google sponsored about half of its H-1Bs for permanent residence—a far lower percentage than Qualcomm, but still much higher than most staffing firms.

An additional point about the economic integration of migrants in the tech sector involves wages. Table 6.3 showed the wages that H-1B workers would make while employed in California. With a few exceptions, these wages are six figures, or nearly so. Although we lack the data to directly compare native and foreign workers in similar jobs, these salaries suggest that middle-class lifestyles—and some basic level of economic integration—are within reach for foreign workers in the heart of California's tech sector.

The H-1B foreign labor certification program has been subject to continual scrutiny—and controversy—as the demand for these positions by employers far outstrips their availability. On May 1, 2018, the U.S. Department of Labor found Cloudwick Technologies, a Bay Area technology and IT services firm, in violation of the federal H-1B foreign labor certification program.[19] Cloudwick was found to be paying IT professionals from India net salaries of around $800 per month, despite promising expected monthly earnings of $8,300.[20] In October 2018, a Silicon Valley–based owner of four staffing companies received a twenty-count indictment for fraud, accused of using his multiple staffing agencies to subvert the H-1B program and using fraudulent documents for illegitimate work assignments.[21] Further scrutiny of the program under the Trump administration's overall immigration agenda may limit its future use by companies,[22] potentially inhibiting California firms access to the human capital that may be playing key roles in creative and technical outputs.

Questions about the future viability of the H-1B program are added to problems raised by increasing costs in the state's innovation clusters and levels of inequality across the state, which may prevent future native-worker mobility into the technology clusters. Although the state continues to attract the country's largest share of international migrants, for the past two decades, the state similarly leads the country in outbound moves (see Chapter 2). Rising costs and out-migration may threaten the sustainability of the state's innovation economy. How California manages to navigate this changed landscape remains to be seen.

Ten years after Steve Jobs announced the iPhone to a rapturous audience, Apple topped the Fortune 500 list for most valuable companies in 2017 with a market value approaching $1 trillion. California technology companies claimed three of the list's top five spots, highlighting the increasing role that their innovations have in people's everyday lives, and the leading role California plays in producing them. Today, California remains the country's most innovative state and the world's fifth-largest economy, following only the United States (as a whole), China, Japan, and Germany.[23] The state continues to serve as a magnet for the world's most innovative minds and talents, who have gone on to contribute to the state's innovation clusters in technology, medicine, energy, entertainment, and more.

Although the state may have been most successful at combining the ingredients of an innovation economy, it does not have the exclusive rights to them. As we have shown, California's innovation economy is linked to the state's openness to the world's most highly skilled, productive, and innovative people. However, uncertainty over visas for foreign workers and growing costs can limit the opportunities for experimentation, creativity, and entrepreneurship that helped create the state's innovative legacy. Employers who once were happy to employ workers in California may look increasingly to offshoring, especially as new technologies have made it increasingly easy for firms to work across borders and employ nonlocal skilled talent. To maintain the state's innovation capacity, California must continue to attract the world's most skilled and talented while ensuring the training and hiring of its native workforce.

Notes

1. In 1997, the number of patents issued by the U.S. Patent and Trademark office totaled 124,147. California resident inventors claimed a 10.4% share of the total. For further details and state breakdowns, please see https://www.uspto.gov/web/offices/ac/ido/oeip/taf/pat_tr97.htm. For further details, please see U.S. Department of Commerce, *1997 Population Profile of the United States*, 12, https://www.census.gov/prod/3/98pubs/p23-194.pdf.

2. Please see U.S. Bureau of the Census, "QuickFacts: California," https://www.census.gov/quickfacts/fact/table/CA,US/PST045217.

3. U.S. Patent and Trademark Office, "Patenting Trends Calendar Year 2015," https://www.uspto.gov/web/offices/ac/ido/oeip/taf/pat_tr15.htm.

4. U.S. Patent and Trademark Office, "Patenting in Technology Classes Breakout by Origin, U.S. Metropolitan and Micropolitan Areas: Count of 2000–2015 Utility Patent Grants," https://www.uspto.gov/web/offices/ac/ido/oeip/taf/cls_cbsa/allcbsa_gd.htm

5. For more detailed occupational information, please see occupational tables 8 and 9 at https://www.uscis.gov/sites/default/files/USCIS/Resources/Reports%20and%20Studies/H-1B/H-1B-FY15.pdf. Complete information on occupations by visa category can be found in U.S. Department of Labor, Employment and Training Division, *Office of Foreign Labor Certification: Annual Report 2015*, https://www.foreign-laborcert.doleta.gov/pdf/OFLC_Annual_Report_FY2015.pdf.

6. Please see U.S. Citizenship and Immigration Services, *Approved H 1B Petitions (Number, Salary, and Degree/Diploma) by Employer Fiscal Year 2016*, https://www.uscis.gov/sites/default/files/USCIS/Resources/Reports%20and%20Studies/Immigration%20Forms%20Data/BAHA/h-1b-2016-employers.pdf.

7. LCAs are also required for two smaller visa programs—the H-1B1, for use by workers from Chile and Singapore, and the E-3, for Australian workers. We focus later on the far more numerous H-1B demand, though statistics also include H-1B1 and E-3 demand.

8. Prevailing wages depend on a worker's job title, the geographic area where the work will be done, and the worker's skill level. For the H-1B, H-1B1, and E-3 visas, employers have the option of using one of three wage sources to obtain the prevailing wage: (1) requesting a prevailing wage from the NPWC; (2) using a survey conducted by an independent authoritative source; or (3) using another legitimate source of information. For more detail, see https://www.foreignlabor-cert.doleta.gov/pwscreens.cfm.

9. For more detail, see https://www.dol.gov/whd/regs/compliance/FactSheet62/whdfs62J.pdf.

10. Although California's average salary of just under $90,000 appears high, it is by no means the highest average salary reported in the Department of Labor's statistics. West Virginia, while requesting significantly fewer H-1Bs, offers an average salary of over $100,000, with North Dakota offering the second highest, of just over $94,000. For more detail, see https://www.foreignlaborcert.doleta.gov/map.cfm?year=2015 and https://www.foreignlaborcert.doleta.gov/pdf/OFLC_Annual_Report_FY2015.pdf.

11. For more detail, see Patrick Thibodeau and Sharon Machilis, "U.S. Law Allows Low H-1B Wages; Just Look at Apple," *Computerworld*, May 15, 2017, https://www.computerworld.com/article/3195957/it-careers/us-law-allows-low-h-1b-wages-just-look-at-apple.html.

12. Ron Hira, testimony before the U.S. Senate Subcommittee on Immigration and the National Interest of the Judiciary Committee hearing on "The Impact of High-Skilled Immigration on U.S. Workers," Dirksen Senate Office Building, February 25, 2016, http://www.epi.org/publication/congressional-testimony-the-impact-of-high-skilled-immigration-on-u-s-workers-4/.

13. For more, see Julia Preston, "Judge Says Disney Didn't Violate Visa Laws in Layoffs," *New York Times*, October 13, 2016, https://www.nytimes.com/2016/10/14/us/judge-says-disney-didnt-violate-visa-laws-in-layoffs.html.

14. For more detail, please see U.S. Department of Labor, Employment and Training Division, *Office of Foreign Labor Certification: Annual Report 2015*, https://www.foreignlaborcert.doleta.gov/pdf/OFLC_Annual_Report_FY2015.pdf.

15. In 2008, the Office of Foreign Labor Certification began disclosing its program data, providing access to data that had largely been inaccessible. Although data on pre 2008 LCAs exist, they are restricted to only forms that were e-filed, and thus are not a complete sample and do not distinguish the intended use of the certified worker. Although several immigration categories require certification by the Department of Labor, for the purposes of this study, only labor certifications filed in support of temporary skilled immigration pathways—overwhelmingly H-1B visas—are analyzed. The Office of Foreign Labor Certification warns, "Each data set is cumulative, containing unique records identified by the applicable OFLC case number, and any noticeable typographical or other data anomalies may be due to internal data entry or other external customer errors in completing the application form. The data provided by the public disclosures is not exhaustive, but is representative of the total certified positions. https://www.foreignlaborcert.doleta.gov/performancedata.cfm#dis. Errors

were checked, and listings were harmonized to ensure the correct employer spelling. Any subsequent errors are the responsibility of the authors.

16. Data on U.S. patenting come from USPTO's Technology Assessment and Forecast database. When referring to patent location, it is important to highlight that regional patent counts are based on the residence locations of the first-named inventors at the time of grant. For an explanation of the available data releases, please see "Patenting in U.S. Metropolitan and Micropolitan Areas, Breakout by Technology Class Count of 2000–2015 Utility Patent Grants, https://www.uspto.gov/web/offices/ac/ido/oeip/taf/cbsa_cls/explan_cbsa_cls.htm; for an example of the data used in this chapter, see https://www.uspto.gov/web/offices/ac/ido/oeip/taf/cbsa_cls/index.html.

17. Although these universities are particularly innovative and receive billions of dollars in research grants, they do not account for any patents during this time period because University of California patents are first filed under either the personal name of the inventor or collectively under the California Board of Regents in the filing database. By comparison, Stanford, which has a different patent protocol for its professors, filed for an average of 111 patents a year and 1,121 positions during the time period.

18. For more detail, see https://www.nsf.gov/discoveries/disc_summ.jsp?cntn_id=100660.

19. Ethan Baron, "H-1B Abuse: Bay Area Tech Workers from India Paid a Pittance, Feds Say," *Mercury News*, May 8, 2018, https://www.mercurynews.com/2018/05/01/h-1b-abuse-bay-area-tech-workers-from-india-paid-a-pittance-feds-say/.

20. See U.S. Department of Labor, "U.S. Department of Labor Investigation Recovers $173,044 in Wages For 12 Technology Employees Due to Violations of the H-1B Visa Program," news release, May 1, 2018, https://www.dol.gov/newsroom/releases/whd/whd20180501–2.

21. For an example, see U.S. Attorney's Office, Northern District of California, "South Bay Resident Charged with Visa Fraud and Mail Fraud," news release, November 2, 2018, https://www.justice.gov/usao-ndca/pr/south-bay-resident-charged-visa-fraud-and-mail-fraud.

22. Ananya Bhattacharya, "H-1B: All the Obstacles Standing between Indian Techies and Their Prized Visa," *Quartz India*, April 2, 2018, https://qz.com/1242265/the-us-opens-the-h-1b-season-but-itll-be-tougher-than-ever-before/.

23. Lisa Marie Segarra, "California's Economy Is Now Bigger Than All of the U.K.," *Fortune*, May 3, 2018, http://fortune.com/2018/05/05/california-fifth-biggest-economy-passes-united-kingdom/.

7   English Language Learners

Marisa Abrajano, Lisa García Bedolla,
and Liesel I. Spangler

Since the Americanization programs of the late nineteenth and early twentieth centuries, states and schools have served as important sites of immigrant integration (King 2000). The 1911 Dillingham Commission report deemed eastern and southern European immigrants a threat to U.S. society and urged that the new public school system be used to teach literacy to these new immigrants. Since then, states have used their education systems to facilitate students' social, cultural, economic, and linguistic acculturation in order to advance the integration of immigrants as productive members of U.S. society. As the U.S. state with the largest foreign-born population, California and its public schools have been tasked with the responsibility of the linguistic instruction of more English language learners (ELs) than any other state in the United States. Thus the educational policy choices made in the state capitol affect the achievement of the millions of ELs being educated within the California public education system. Given California's preeminent status as an educator of EL students in the United States, it is important to analyze the impact its policies and practices have on the educational trajectories of EL students.

In this chapter, we focus on the role of education in its ability to help support immigrant linguistic integration in California. Mastering the English language is crucial for immigrants' and their children's long-term engagement in U.S. society. Public education, by way of K–12 schooling, plays the largest role in English language instruction in the United States. Although immigrants to California are seventeen years older on average than the native born (see the introduction to this volume), half of the state's children have at least one immigrant parent. California leads the nation in having the largest number of ELs in their student population, with just over 1.3 million (or just over 20% of the total) students classified as ELs during the 2017–18 academic year.[1] The state therefore offers the ideal case study to examine the education policies and processes used by school districts in the state to determine which students should be classified as ELs. In particular, we are interested in examining the consequences of such policies on classification outcomes for incoming kindergarten students (as measured by California's EL assessment exam CELDT, now English Language Proficiency Assessments for California).

We do so by compiling historical data on English language proficiency exams in California's public schools from 2002 to 2016, supplemented with a survey of these districts to understand how school districts identify potential ELs among incoming kindergartners. Our findings offer important insights on this process, one of which is the lack of uniformity across school districts in terms of whom they choose to test and therefore classify as ELs. That is, some districts exercise more discretion than others. Discretion is important because these exams' extremely low passage rates mean that being triggered to take these exams almost always means that a student will be classified as an EL.

We argue that how school districts interpret parents' answers to the home language survey about languages present in the home suggests that the framing of English language acquisition as necessitating the loss of the home language remains embedded within the practice of how California schools classify ELs. It is evident in the assumption on the part of many school districts that the presence of any language other than English in the home (as reported in the home language survey) by definition means that the child must be deficient in English and therefore must be evaluated via testing.

The Role of Education in the Immigrant Integration Process

There are many residents of the United States who do not speak English well. According to Ryan's analysis of the 2011 American Community Survey shown

Table 7.1. Language spoken at home, by English speaking ability and nativity status

| Nativity status | Population 5 years and over | Spoke a language other than English at home (%) | Spoke a language other than English at home | | | | | |
| | | | Spoke Spanish | | | Spoke a language other than Spanish | | |
			Population 5 years and over (number)	Spoke English "very well" (%)	Spoke English less than "very well" (%)	Population 5 years and over (number)	Spoke English "very well" (%)	Spoke English less than "very well" (%)
Native	251,380,737	10.6	19,487,953	80.9	19.1	7,185,626	84.8	15.2
Foreign born: naturalized Citizen	18,094,967	79.0	5,431,946	44.8	55.2	8,856,595	54.4	45.6
Foreign born: not a citizen	22,048,387	89.0	12,659,888	23.4	76.6	6,955,012	45.9	54.01

Source: Excerpt from Ryan (2013), using the 2011 American Community Survey.

in table 7.1, more than half of the foreign-born residents who speak languages other than English at home stated that they speak English less than very well (Ryan 2013). In a more extreme case, there are households, labeled by the U.S. Census as "linguistically isolated," where no members over the age of fourteen speak English well or at all (Siegel, Martin, and Bruno 2001). According to the 2015 National Academies of Sciences, Engineering and Medicine report (Waters and Pineau 2015), approximately 4.5% of U.S. households were classified as linguistically isolated in 2013, and of the linguistically isolated households, households that speak Asian/Pacific Islander languages and Spanish made up the largest shares (26% and 23%, respectively).

Further, the share of families in the United States that do not speak English at home has been increasing over time. Ryan (2013) finds that in 2010, 59.5 million residents spoke a language other than English at home, which represents almost 20% of the American population at the time. She finds that between 1980 and 2010, the number of residents who spoke a language other than English at home increased by 36.5 million, representing a 158% increase. In 2011, 22% of school-age children (ages five to nineteen) spoke a language other than English at home; however, 78.5% of those students also spoke English very well (Ryan 2013). Thus one should not assume that because a student speaks a language other than English at home, the student is not proficient in English.

These trends also are apparent in data from school districts. According to the National Center for Education Statistics (NCES), in 2016, 9.6% of the students enrolled in school in the United States were classified as ELs, for a total of 4.9 million.[2] The largest EL populations in terms of raw numbers were in Los Angeles Unified (152,592 EL students) and the New York City schools across the five boroughs (142,572 EL students). In terms of the proportion of the overall student population, 56.2% of the students in Santa Ana Unified School District in Southern California were ELs (Ruiz Soto, Hooker, and Batalova 2015). When examining the state-level populations of ELs, the western states had the largest EL populations—California (24.5%), Nevada (17.4%), Texas (15.2%) and Colorado (13.3%) (Ruiz Soto, Hooker, and Batalova 2015). On the East Coast, Florida has the largest population of EL students (10.3%), followed by New York State (8.8%) and Virginia (7.9%). With almost 10% of the American student population being classified as ELs, the role of English language learning programs in U.S. schools becomes even more critical for students who are non-English-speaking immigrants or children of non-English-speaking parents.

Education plays a large role in immigrant integration by facilitating other forms of immigrant acculturation, such as linguistic, civic, and economic integration. For young migrants and the children of immigrants, schools often are the primary vehicle for learning English. And in the context of the United States, learning the English language is arguably the most important task for an immigrant because it supports the other domains of acculturation and integration outcomes. The relationship between education and English proficiency can be expressed by a causal circle. Immigrant students go to school to learn English; however, the research suggests that when entering school, students with limited English proficiency (LEP) tend to be slower to acquire academic skills compared to students who are more proficient in English (Kieffer 2008).

The ability of an LEP student to learn English in schools carries crucial downstream effects. English proficiency is positively associated with wages and job placement (Bleakley and Chin 2004; Borjas 2015; Chiswick and Miller 2009). English proficiency is also associated with civic and political outcomes, such as naturalization and participation in civic organizations (Bloemraad 2006; Stoll and Wong 2007; Waldinger, Chapter 5 of this volume). Lower levels of English proficiency are associated with higher levels of residential segregation and being subject to housing discrimination (Iceland and Scopilliti

2008; Purnell, Idsardi, and Baugh 1999; Toussaint-Comeau and Rhine 2004). Considering health outcomes, lower English proficiency has been found to be associated with lower levels of socioemotional well-being and higher levels of chronic health conditions and psychological distress (Kang et al. 2014; Yoo, Gee, and Takeuchi 2009; Zhang et al. 2012). Among students specifically, lower English proficiency increases psychological pressures due to bullying at school and alienation from peers (Yu et al. 2003).

In addition to teaching the English language, education plays a crucial role in providing civic and political education. Individuals generally receive the bulk of their political education from their parents (Beaumont 2011; Campbell et al. 1960; Jennings and Niemi 1968; Jennings, Stoker, and Bowers 2009; Miller and Shanks 1996). Young immigrants or children of immigrants may not be as likely to receive the same level of political knowledge about the American political system from their parents as are U.S.-born children with U.S.-born parents (Waters and Pineau 2015). Furthermore, political and civic interest has declined for U.S. youth since the mid-twentieth century (Galston 2001), and there appears to be a racialization of political knowledge (Delli Carpini and Keeter 1996), both of which can further complicate the political engagement of immigrants and the children of immigrants. Thus schools can play a crucial role in educating these youth.

Civic education may not be a panacea for immigrant integration, however. As Junn (2004) points out, there is no guarantee that equalizing civic and political knowledge and participation will translate into equal levels of political agency. However, we do know that improved civic knowledge can have positive consequences. Civic knowledge has been found to foster immigrant integration by providing information about individual and group-level interests (Delli Carpini and Keeter 1996; Galston 2001; Zaller 1992), supplying the requisite knowledge to participate politically (Delli Carpini and Keeter 1996; Galston 2001; Popkin and Dimock 1999) and to appropriately interpret current political events and their consequences (Galston 2001; Popkin and Dimock 1999). Thus a lack of civic knowledge among immigrants and their children can have important negative consequences for their levels of civic engagement.

The existing research suggests that certain educational practices, such as encouraging the development of skills related to political action, have the power to increase political efficacy, as well as reduce the gaps in efficacy that stem from socioeconomic status (SES) and disparate levels of home discussion

(Beaumont 2011). Furthermore, increasing fluency in English can help support political participation and integration (Ramakrishnan 2005; Wong et al. 2011). Encouraging first- or second-generation students to embark on academically rigorous course work can positively impact future political participation (Humphries, Muller, and Schiller 2013). Student engagement with school-related activities may foster the behaviors and values necessary for political participation (Callahan and Muller 2013; Youniss, McLellan, and Yates 1997).

The benefits of educating school-age children are not limited to just the students; education can also positively affect their parents. Parents who engage with their children's schools can help foster their own civic engagement (Terriquez 2012). The students themselves also have been found to transfer their own political knowledge and resources to their parents (Bloemraad and Trost 2008; Callahan and Mueller 2013; Wong and Tseng 2007).

Finally, education can provide the skills and access to resources necessary for successful economic and labor-market integration for first- and second-generation immigrants, which is particularly important given labor-market discrimination on the basis of race, ethnicity, and skin color (Bertrand and Mullainathan 2004; Frank, Redstone Akresh, and Lu 2010; Hersch 2008, 2011). Learning English is a critical part of labor-market integration in the United States, as the vast majority of jobs require some level of English fluency, and English fluency has been linked to higher wages (Bleakley and Chin 2004). One study found that interested teachers and counselors play an important role in motivating immigrant students to pursue appropriate educational and occupational opportunities and in providing resources for them to do so (Portes and Fernández-Kelly 2008). It is important to note that education received within the United States is important, not just years of education overall. The economic returns of education are larger for education gained postmigration than premigration, particularly for individuals coming from countries with lower-quality education systems than that of the United States (Betts and Lofstrom 2000).

The Role of Education in English Language Proficiency

As the review of the literature has shown, education plays a critical role in the integration of immigrants in the United States across a variety of domains. Educational outcomes tend to be higher for the second generation than for the first generation. The 2015 National Academies of Sciences, Engineering, and Medicine report (Waters and Pineau 2015) demonstrates that, on average, the years of education increase from 12.1 years among first-generation men and 12.3 years among first-generation women to 13.9 years among second-generation men and 14.0 years among second-generation women.

Clearly, the U.S. education system can greatly improve immigrant outcomes. Unsurprisingly, there are differential educational outcomes for immigrant children and children of color when compared to their peers. Children of immigrants who identify as black or Latinx tend to have lower grades than children of immigrants who identify as white/Anglo (Pong and Hao 2007). Foreign-born Latinx students experience higher dropout rates than their U.S.-born Latinx peers (Laird et al. 2007; White and Kaufman 1997). It is important to note that country of origin can affect the relationship between immigration status and educational outcomes; Asian immigrants of school age tend to fare better in terms of GPAs, high school graduation rates, and college attendance than their Latinx counterparts (Pong and Hao 2007; Portes and Hao 2004). Much of this effect, however, can be explained by the selection process in U.S. immigration policy and the social capital that immigrants bring from their countries of origin (Feliciano 2006). For example, China and Vietnam send a larger proportion of individuals with above-average education levels relative to their nonimmigrant populations than does Mexico (Lee and Zhou 2015). As mentioned before, the children of immigrants tend to do better across multiple scholastic measures than do first-generation school-age immigrants (Kao and Tienda 1995; Waters and Pineau 2015).

Various explanations have been proposed for why these differential outcomes occur between immigrant children and their native peers: student language acquisition (Kao and Tienda 1995); family and neighborhood SES (Entwisle and Alexander 1993; Pong and Hao 2007); school quality (Entwisle and Alexander 1993; Pong and Hao 2007); parental involvement, attitudes, and expectations (Hao and Bonstead-Bruns 1998; Kao and Tienda 1995; Perreira, Harris, and Lee 2006; White and Kaufman 1997); and parents' education and English proficiency (Bleakley and Chin 2008; Glick, Walker, and Luz 2014; Terriquez 2012).

English proficiency remains central to much of this discussion. In other words, English proficiency and immigration are often intersectional. Parents having limited English proficiency can lead to their children having less English proficiency. Yet it is important to keep in mind that not all immigrants are ELs. When we look at the interaction of students and parents, immigrant parents simultaneously benefit from their children's linguistic abilities in navigating the host country (Tseng 2004; Valenzuela 1999), but can also make it more difficult for their children to learn English and do well in school (Bleakley and Chin 2008; Glick, Walker, and Luz 2014).

Supporting proficiency in English is arguably one of the most important functions of schools with regard to the education of LEP immigrant students. The federal government provides mandates for educational outcomes, but states and school districts implement the policy to achieve these mandates, which leads to some state-level variation. Federally, the Every Student Succeeds Act (ESSA—formerly No Child Left Behind) outlines very basic requirements for the instruction of LEP students. First, it requires schools to provide English language education to LEP students. Second, it requires LEP students to receive subject-area instruction in accordance with relevant state standards. Historically, these state educational standards have varied quite significantly. However, since 2010, there has been a push to create a common set of educational standards across all states, called the Common Core State Standards (CCSS) Initiative. Currently, forty-two U.S. states have adopted the CCSS. ESSA also requires states to implement standardized testing of all students, including ELs. If certain benchmarks (e.g., adequate yearly progress) are not met, schools risk losing federal funding or having the state intervene.

Since ESSA and the CCSS Initiative, a major source of variation among states is the identification of ELs and the state-level examinations to assess student progress in accordance with federal law. When it comes to the identification of ELs, each state is responsible for testing the potential students to determine the students' level of English proficiency. States such as California, New York, Texas, and Arizona maintain their own placement examinations. The majority of U.S. states have joined the WIDA consortium,[3] which maintains both standards for instruction as well as a placement exam for potential ELs.

This chapter seeks to understand how ELs in California are identified and the consequences of the classification process. Ineffectively identifying and assessing potential ELs can create problems for how schools use their scarce language support resources. California has the largest number of ELs in the United States in terms of raw count and as a percentage of the overall enrolled student population: over 1.3 million students and 20% overall. The sheer numbers of ELs can strain the state and federal resources available to schools, so maintaining effective EL identification schemes is particularly important in California. In the next section, we show the flaws in the application of California's process to identify potential ELs, which can result in the misclassification of students.

Identifying English Language Learners

Given the important support and resources that language learners need to be successful in school, it is imperative that students' classification as ELs be accurate. A previous study showed that EL classification in California, particularly at the kindergarten level, was too broad and was likely to be including students who should not have been classified as ELs (García Bedolla and Rodríguez 2011). García Bedolla and Rodríguez argued that the wide net being cast by California's EL classification system could in some ways render the classification itself meaningless, given its application to such a wide range of students with very different levels of English language ability. Part of the problem was that there was no clear definition of what constitutes "an English language learner" (Abedi 2008, Abedi and Gándara 2006). That definition was found to be left to district interpretation, resulting in significant variability in classification criteria and rates across the state. This study updates that analysis by looking historically at California English Language Development Test (CELDT) passage rates from 2002 to 2016 and analyzing school districts' use of the home language survey as a tool for triggering CELDT testing.[4]

The EL identification process begins in California when parents fill out a home language survey (HLS), which usually is included as part of the paperwork required by districts in order to register a child for school. Even though districts are allowed to use their own surveys, almost all California districts use the template provided by the California Department of Education, which includes the following four questions:

1. Which language did your child learn when he/she first began to talk?
2. Which language does your child most frequently speak at home?
3. Which language do you (the parents or guardians) most frequently use when speaking with your child?
4. Which language is most often spoken by adults in the home? (parents, guardians, grandparents, or any other adults)

The use of the HLS for these purposes is a problem for a number of reasons

(Bailey and Kelley 2010). On the parent side, some parents may not understand the questions because of the vagueness of the question wording. For example, if a grandparent lives in the home and speaks another language, the parent may write that language down in response to question 4 (Q4), regardless of whether or not the child speaks that language. Only about half of the districts provide any sort of instruction to parents about the purpose of the questions or the implications of their answers (García Bedolla and Rodríguez 2011), which increases the probability of parental confusion. One also can imagine a situation where a home is bilingual, but the child is English dominant. If the other language is mentioned in the answers to questions 1, 3, or 4, the child will be tested, even if the parent answered only "English" to question 2.

Typically, any non-English answers to these HLS questions triggers the CELDT (now English Language Proficiency Assessments for California, or ELPAC, as of the 2018–19 school year; we refer to the CELDT throughout this chapter because that was the test in place during the years we analyze in our data). These tests are used to (1) identify LEP students; (2) determine the level of English language proficiency of those students; and (3) assess the progress of LEP students in acquiring the skills of listening, speaking, reading, and writing in English. In this study, we focus exclusively on item number one—the use of the CELDT to accurately identify LEP students in California's public schools.

Districts have a certain amount of discretion over how they use the answers to this survey to trigger CELDT testing to determine a student's English proficiency. In many districts, the inclusion of any language other than English (or, in some cases, any language in addition to English) in one of the answers triggers administration of the CELDT to that child. We found that all districts used any non-English answer to questions 1–3 as a trigger. The place where they had discretion was in their interpretation of Q4, regarding which language is most often spoken by adults in the home. That is why district-level usage of that question is the focus of this chapter.

Part of the goal of this analysis is to see whether the nature of the trigger affects proficiency rates. In other words, does the assessment process itself inadvertently hold back some children from learning English as well as they otherwise would have? In a previous study, 6% of kindergartners identified to take the CELDT were found to be English proficient (García Bedolla and Rodríguez 2011). In the California Department of Education's own evaluation of the CELDT, 75% of native English speakers who were administered the test were not found to be English proficient. The quality of the testing trigger is important because parents cannot opt out of having their child take the CELDT. In other words, if the district determines that the child must be tested, parents have no choice. Kindergartners identified as EL cannot be reclassified as English language proficient until the end of second grade because it is at that point that they are able to take the statewide standardized test in language arts (now the California Assessment of Student Performance and Progress, formerly the California Standardized Testing and Reporting exam). Thus, a misclassification in kindergarten could lead to the student receiving three years of inappropriate language education and services if the student was actually proficient in English all along.

Figure 7.1 shows that CELDT passage rates remain quite low throughout the state, supporting previous research which found that passage rates are so low that being triggered to take the test is almost a guarantee of EL classification.[5] The small number of students taking the CELDT who achieve a score of "English proficient" may be due to the length and content of the exam, difficulties with assessing young students' English language abilities using standardized tests, and who administers the exam (Goldenberg and Quach 2010; Wright 2010; Stokes-Guinan and Goldenberg 2011). It should be noted that the reduction in scores shown in figure 7.1 including and following the 2006–07 academic year is due to a rescaling of the CELDT scores that makes the proficiency scores comparable across exam administrations and grades; as part of this rescaling effort, the skill requirements for English language proficiency increased (California Department of Education 2007, 29).

The length and content of the exam are concerning, and both affect the CELDT's validity as an English language assessment tool. The CELDT (and the new ELPAC) assesses the four domains of listening, speaking, reading, and writing in English and is aligned to the English-language development standards adopted by the California State Board of Education. In 2007, California's Education Code Section 60810 was amended to authorize early literacy assessment of ELs in kindergarten and first grade starting with the 2009–10 school year. Entering kindergartners and first graders are given the same test, which includes reading and writing requirements. As an example, the 2010–11 test required students to read and write the word *apple*, among others. As of 2009–10, the test was also expanded, now taking up to one and a half hours for children to complete. As can be imagined, taking such a long test administered by a stranger is challenging for four- and five-year-old

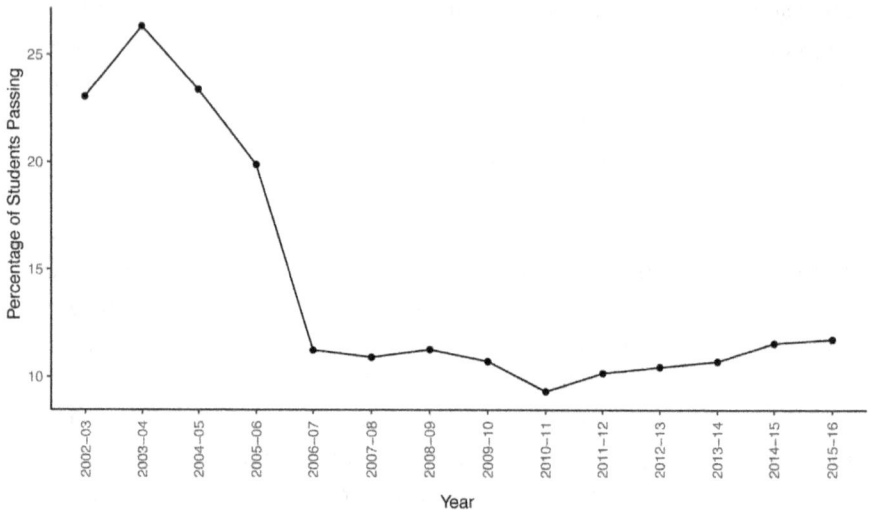

Figure 7.1. Mean CELDT passage rates for all unified (noncharter) school districts, 2002–2016

children about to enter kindergarten. Parents are not allowed to be in the room with children while they take the test, likely increasing the children's overall anxiety and making it difficult for them to effectively complete the assessment (Epstein et al. 2004).

Further, the test is administered almost entirely in English, instead of in the student's first language. Rumberger and Gándara (2004) cite several research reports and professional organization studies to argue that "testing students in a language in which they are not yet proficient is both invalid and unethical" (2041). The ESSA requires that states "make every effort" to assess students in their first language. There have long been questions about the appropriateness of standardized assessments for English learners in general. However, an exam of this length, administered in English, seems especially inappropriate for students in this young age group who are still developing their language skills and who have not yet been in school, and therefore are inexperienced in the routines and expectations of school (Abedi 2004, 2008; Abedi and Gándara 2006, Rumberger and Gándara 2014).

Overview of Kindergarten English Language Learner Classification in California

As of the 2015–16 school year, 34% of California's kindergartners are classified as ELs. Figure 7.1 shows the mean CELDT passage rate for kindergartners in all of California's school districts serving kindergarten students (i.e., elementary and unified school districts) from 2002 to 2016. We see that over this time period, proficiency among earlier cohorts of kindergartners declines rapidly and then slowly begins to increase with more recent cohorts. One should also notice that even at the peak year (2003–04), the mean proficiency of the 2003–04 cohort is only 26.3%.

Figure 7.2 summarizes the percentage of kindergarten students classified as ELs in California's elementary and unified school districts statewide. Figure 7.3 summarizes that same information for the school districts in our sample. We see from this analysis that the districts that responded to our survey had a higher percentage of kindergartners classified as ELs than California districts overall. This is in part due to our data collection process. In addition to directly contacting school district representatives, we gathered information from EL Master Plans on district websites. EL Master Plans are required only for school districts with a certain number of EL students. In addition, the larger the district's EL population, the more likely it is to have EL-related information on its website. (See the next section for more details on how we surveyed.)

Our Survey

As noted earlier, school districts in California have discretion in how they use the HLS to trigger testing. Much of the discretion they have relates to whether or not they use Q4 to automatically trigger testing. For this reason, we analyzed whether the use of discretion, particularly on Q4, affects the percentage of EL students in a district. Q4 is controversial as to whether it should trigger language proficiency testing because it is the only question on the state's recommended list of questions that does not involve the student; instead, it asks what language the adults speak at home. A student may only speak English and thus have English for the answer to the first three questions. However, if the parents or grandparents speak another language, it would potentially trigger testing for the English-only student. Given the difficulty of the CELDT

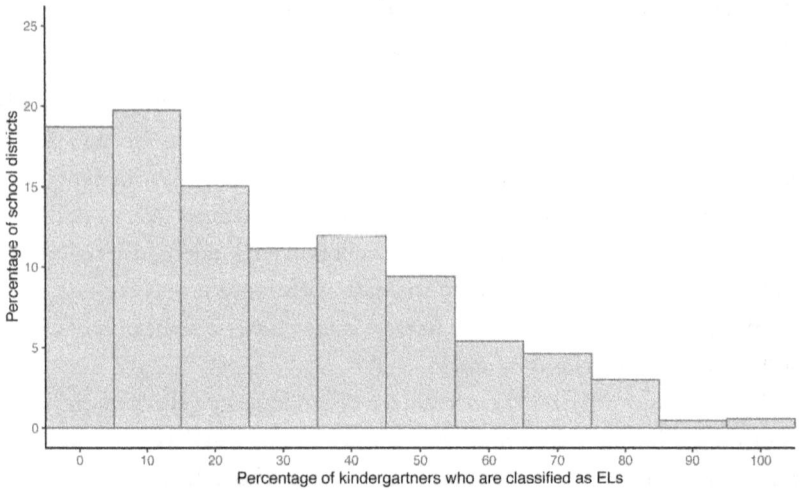

Figure 7.2. Breakdown of schools by percentage of ELs in kindergarten in all California elementary and unified school districts

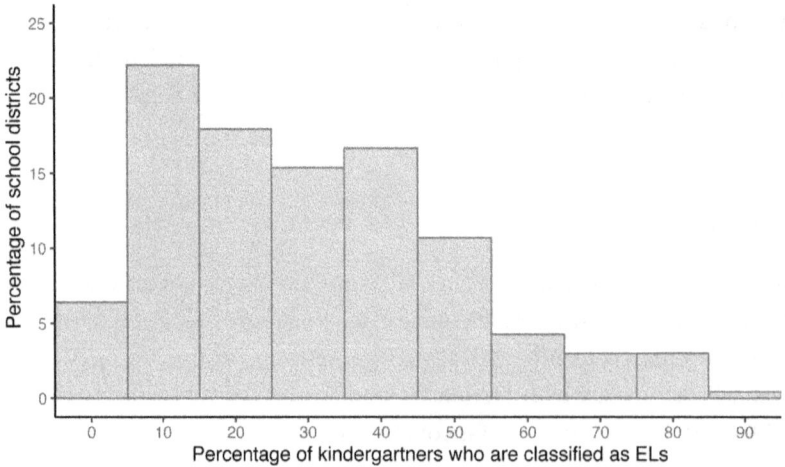

Figure 7.3. Breakdown of schools by percentage of ELs in kindergarten in responding districts

exam, that student may very well end up identified as an EL even though English is the student's native language.

We began by surveying the information provided on the district websites of the 868 elementary school districts and unified school districts in California. We looked for a description of how they use the HLS to initiate CELDT/ELPAC testing. This information was generally found in the EL Master Plan. An EL Master Plan is maintained by every district that has a number of ELs that falls above a certain threshold. For the schools that did not have information on their websites, we contacted the most proximate person to the English Language Development (ELD) program (e.g., the ELD coordinator) via email as to how the school uses the HLS, specifically Q4. In some cases, an email address was not available, in which case the school was not contacted personally.

Our survey revealed that school districts fall into one of three groups with regard to how they use Q4. For some, it never triggers testing—either the question is omitted from their district's HLS or it is included, but the answers are used for purposes other than testing (e.g., parental communications). By contrast, some schools always use non-English responses to Q4 to prompt testing of the student. Some schools fall somewhere in the middle and use staff discretion; usually, a non-English answer prompts an interview with the parents and student(s) to determine whether testing is warranted.

We acquired the information from 237 school districts, or 27.3% of the 868 elementary and unified districts in California. Of those for which we have information, all of the school districts used non-English responses to questions 1–3 of the HLS to initiate testing (as mandated by the California Department of Education). Districts used discretion in terms of whether to use Q4 to initiate testing. As shown in figure 7.4, of the 237 school districts, about two-thirds ($N = 157$) did not use Q4 to initiate testing. One in five districts ($N - 48$) used discretion when receiving non-English responses on Q4 to initiate testing, and about 14% ($N = 32$) districts always initiated testing with a non-English response on Q4.

Figure 7.5 shows the distribution of the survey responses by county. The counties are ordered by their population size, with the smallest counties on the left and the largest counties on the right. We see in figure 7.5 that the districts that always test with non-English responses on Q4 seem to be concentrated in particular counties (e.g., Santa Clara and San Bernardino). We will see later that this cannot be completely explained by the percentage of foreign-born or non-English speakers within the particular school district.

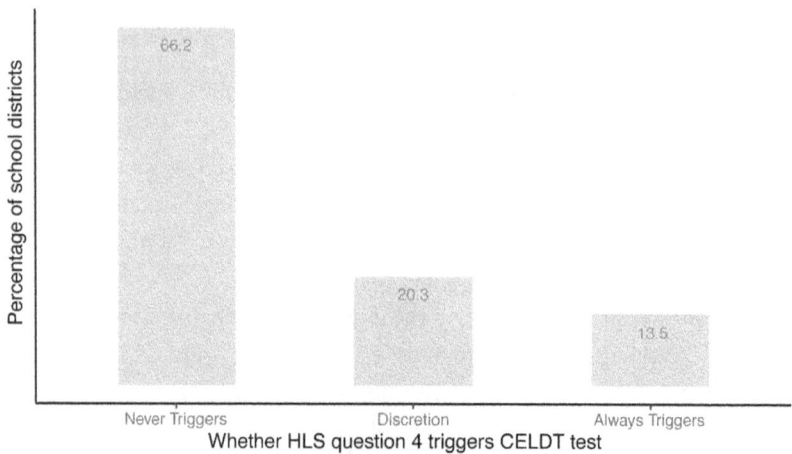

Figure 7.4. Breakdown of home language survey use among public kindergarten-serving school districts in California

Some of our analysis suggests that schools feel able to exercise more discretion around EL classification when they have fewer EL students. Figure 7.6 shows that school districts that use discretion with Q4 (and thus do not take a hard stance on whether to use the question or not) on average have fewer EL students as a proportion of the school's population.

We decided to look at other types of correlations between survey use and (1) English proficiency in the district, (2) region/county size, (3) immigration and language variables, (4) race/ethnicity, and (5) SES. We find that only the immigration and language variables seem to have an impact on whether school districts used discretion on the HLS. Figure 7.7 shows a seemingly contradictory correlation. School districts that use the HLS more stringently have, on average, fewer noncitizens in the district, but conversely, more foreign born in the district. There does not seem to be any correlation between how a school uses the HLS and the percentage of immigrants in the district.

Figure 7.8 shows that school districts that use discretion on the HLS on average have fewer households who speak a foreign language at home. When breaking the home language down into Asian languages and Spanish, the trends are not as clear. The analysis suggests that school districts that use Q4 to require testing seem to have slightly more households that speak Asian

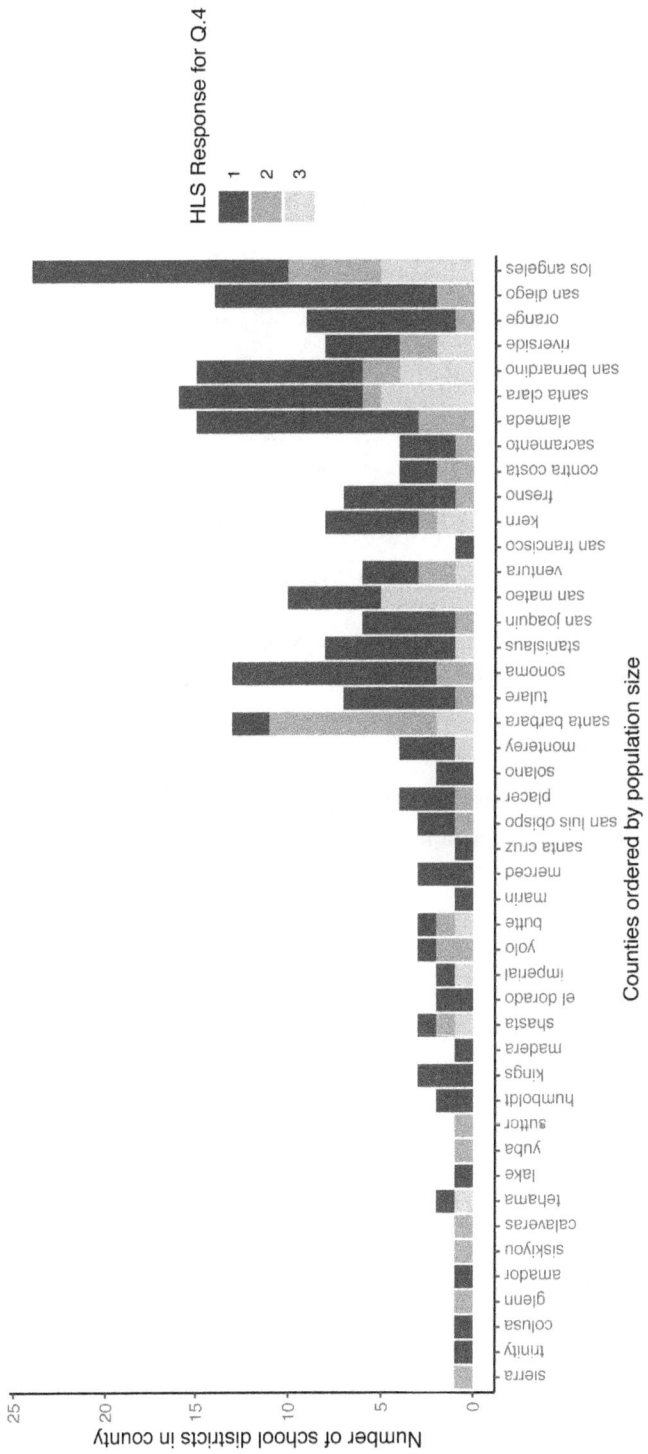

Figure 7.5. Distribution of responses by county, with columns ordered by county population

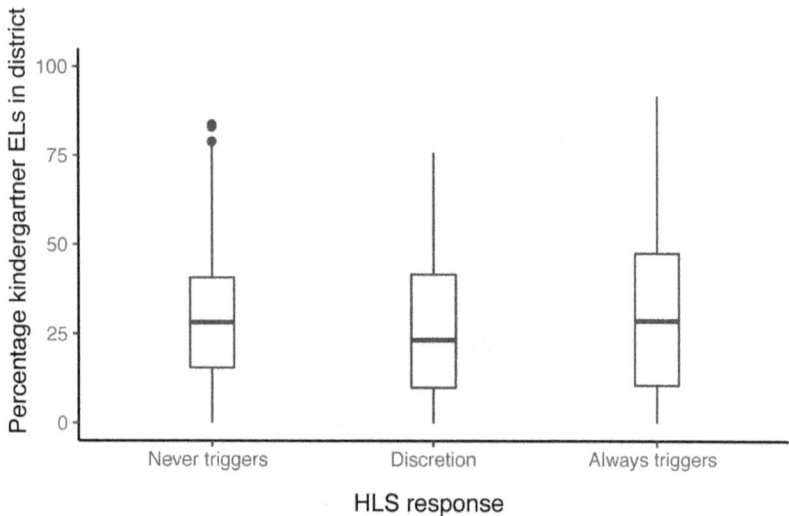

Figure 7.6. Percentage of EL kindergartners in school districts, broken down by survey responses

languages at home, whereas districts that do not use Q4 in the decision to test have a slightly higher proportion of Spanish-speaking families.

The history of Americanization programs and national English Only efforts suggests that language policies often have more to do with ideas about U.S. national identity than about language learning per se (Schmidt 2000). Scholarship looking at racialization processes in the United States has shown that Asian Americans and Latinos have been racialized differently over the course of U.S. history (DeGenova 2006). FitzGerald and Cook-Martín (2014) argue that domestic racialized responses to immigration policy are affected by internal pressures and the international context. For all these reasons, it is not surprising that school districts with large numbers of Asian-origin immigrants and those with Latin American–origin immigrants approach the classification process differently. This is likely due to contextual differences, such as geography and SES, and also differences in how these different immigrant-origin groups, and by extension their languages, have been constructed within the U.S. racial hierarchy.

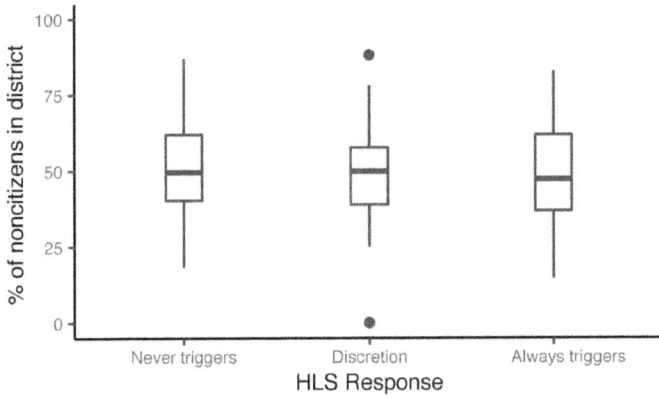

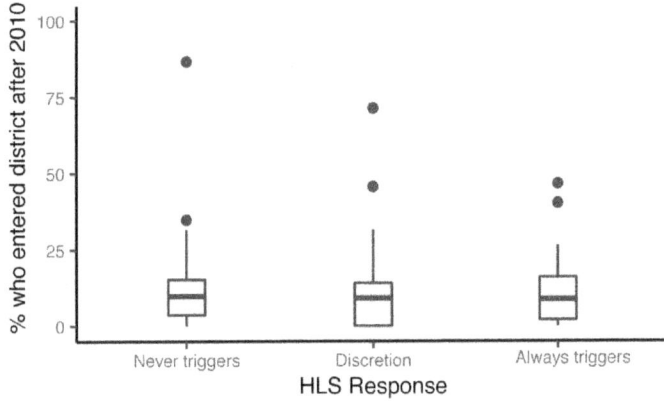

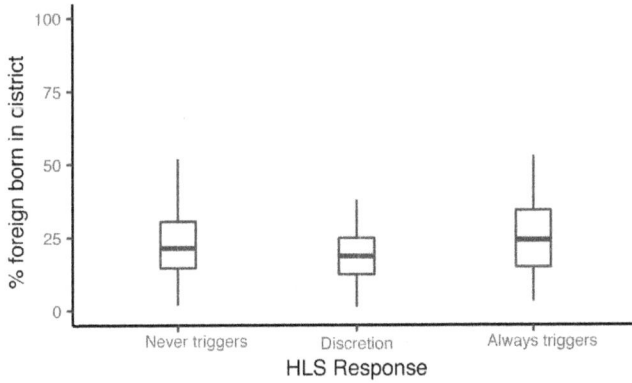

Figure 7.7. Immigration correlations.

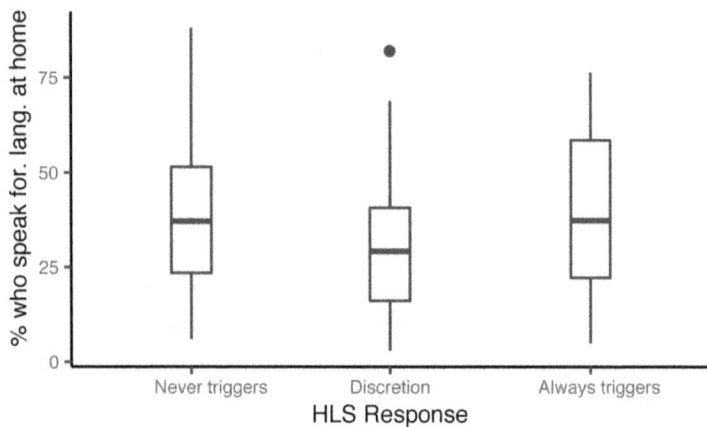

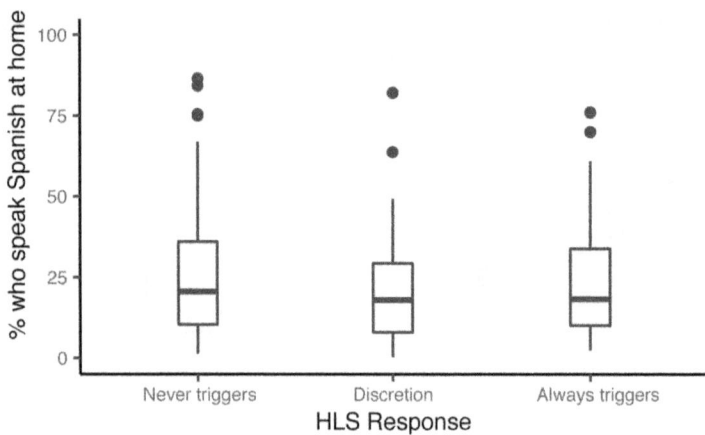

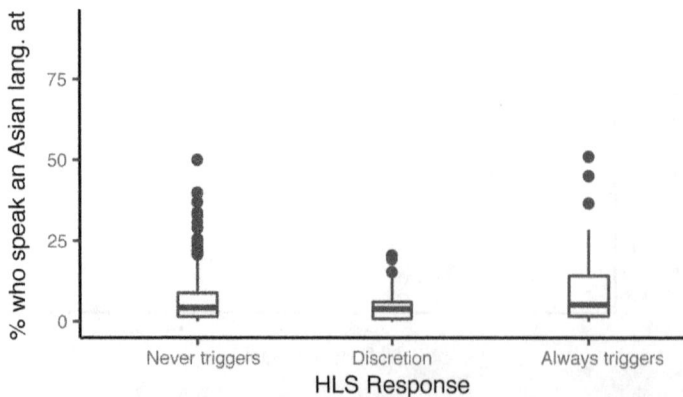

Figure 7.8. Language correlations

Predicting the English Proficiency of Kindergartners in California

Table 7.2 summarizes our modeling of English proficiency while controlling for district use of the HLS and other demographic and district-level variables. The models are based on school-level data from schools in elementary and unified school districts in California. The analyses only include kindergarten students in those schools. The first two models are ordinary least squares (OLS) models with school district fixed effects and standard errors clustered by school district. Models 3 and 4 are hierarchical linear models where the intercepts are grouped by school district.[6] In all of the models, the reference group for the Q4 variables are schools that do not trigger testing using Q4.

In the fixed effects models, schools in districts that use discretion in testing have a lower percentage of proficiency among EL students than schools in districts that do not trigger testing, all else being equal. Interestingly, in these same models, schools in districts that always trigger testing have a higher percentage of proficiency among EL students than schools in districts that do not trigger testing as easily, all else being equal. Neither of these variables have statistically significant relationships with our dependent variable in the multilevel models.

The only two variables that are robust across the two sets of models are the percentage of EL students in the school and the interaction of the use of discretion in the school district with the percentage of ELs in the school. For every 1% increase in the number of EL students in the school, the percentage of proficiency of EL students decreases by anywhere between 28% and 33%, all else being equal. In regard to the interaction, for schools that are in districts that use discretion with Q4, for every 1% increase in the percentage of the EL population, the percentage of proficiency drops an additional 9%–11% compared to schools where Q4 does not trigger testing. Figure 7.9 indicates that the schools with the largest EL populations are the most at risk for the decrease in proficiency associated with the use of discretion on Q4.

Conclusion

California is home to ten million immigrants, which constitutes about one-quarter of the foreign-born population in the United States (Johnson and Sanchez n.d.). Half of California's children have at least one immigrant parent (Johnson and Sanchez n.d.). Clearly, it is important that California schools be

Table 7.2. Predicting the English proficiency of kindergartners

| | Dependent variable: Percentage of school proficient in English | | | |
| | Fixed effects models | | Hierarchical linear models | |
	(1)	(2)	(3)	(4)
Q4: Discretion * Percentage of ELs		0.11***		0.09***
		(0.04)		(0.03)
Q4: Always triggers * Percentage of ELs		0.05		0.02
		(0.07)		(0.05)
Q4: Discretion	0.14***	0.10***	0.001	0.03
	(0.02)	(0.02)	(0.01)	(0.02)
Q4: Always triggers	0.23***	0.23***	0.02	0.02
	(0.04)	(0.04)	(0.02)	(0.02)
Percentage of ELs in school	−0.33***	−0.29***	−0.32***	−0.28***
	(0.02)	(0.02)	(0.01)	(0.02)
School met adequate yearly progress (NCLB)	0.02	0.02	0.02	0.02
	(0.02)	(0.02)	(0.02)	(0.02)
Percentage who speak foreign language at home in SD	−1.86	−2.03	0.36*	0.38*
	(1.31)	(1.32)	(0.21)	(0.22)
Percentage white in SD	−2.56**	−2.78***	0.06	0.05
	(1.04)	(1.06)	(0.07)	(0.07)
Percentage Hispanic in SD	1.34***	1.31***	0.15	0.16
	(0.49)	(0.50)	(0.12)	(0.12)
Percentage Asian American in SD	−1.63***	−1.83***	−0.25*	−0.26*
	(0.41)	(0.43)	(0.14)	(0.14)
Percentage bachelor's degree or higher in SD	3.07***	2.94***	0.30***	0.30***
	(0.72)	(0.73)	(0.07)	(0.08)
Percentage moved to U.S. after 2010 in SD	0.65***	0.71***	0.02	0.01
	(0.18)	(0.19)	(0.06)	(0.06)
Percentage of noncitizens in SD	1.23***	1.21***	0.17**	0.17**
	(0.33)	(0.34)	(0.07)	(0.07)

Table 7.2. Predicting the English proficiency of kindergartners (*continued*)

	Dependent variable: Percentage of school proficient in English			
	Fixed effects models		Hierarchical linear models	
	(1)	(2)	(3)	(4)
	(0.33)	(0.34)	(0.07)	(0.07)
Percentage of foreign born in SD	0.94	1.11	0.09	0.05
	(1.00)	(1.02)	(0.25)	(0.26)
Population of SD	0.0000***	0.0000***		
	(0.0000)	(0.0000)		
Scaled population of SD			0.002	0.01
			(0.06)	(0.06)
Percentage below poverty level in SD	0.51	0.68	0.41***	0.40***
	(1.09)	(1.10)	(0.14)	(0.14)
Median household income in SD	−0.0000***	−0.0000***		
	(0.0000)	(0.0000)		
Scaled median household income in SD			0.30***	0.32***
			(0.07)	(0.08)
Constant	2.52**	2.74**	0.03	0.02
	(1.13)	(1.15)	(0.07)	(0.07)
Observations			2,454	2,454

$*p < 0.1; **p < 0.05; ***p < 0.01.$

effective in serving the needs of immigrant-origin students, particularly in terms of language acquisition. The first step in serving those students is accurate classification (or not) as an English language learner. Some might argue that misclassification is a trivial matter, with little harm to students. However, the potential negative effects are multiple:

> Inappropriate classification decisions may place students who are at a higher level of English proficiency into remedial or special education programs and may deprive less-proficient students of appropriate curriculum and assessment. Poor placement decisions may affect promotion and graduation, which consequently affects students' academic progress and self-esteem. Misclassification of ELLs may also impact school, district and state accountability

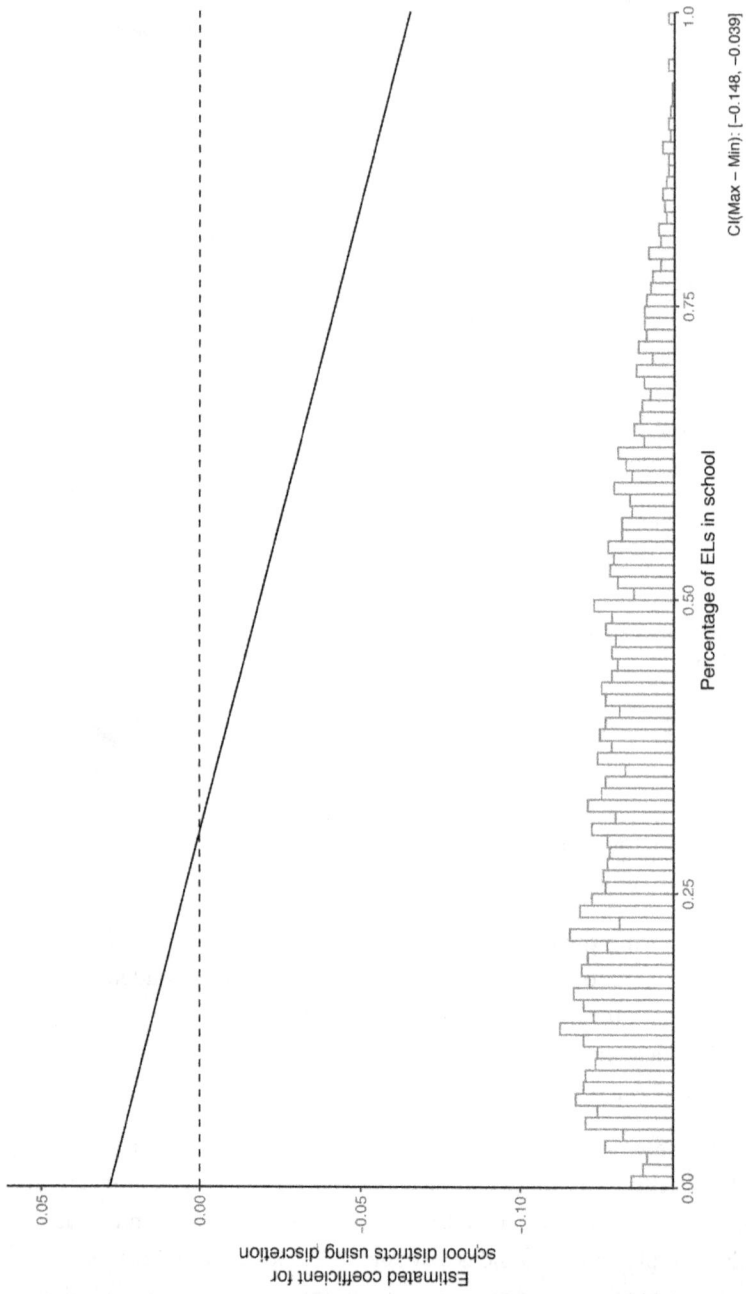

Figure 7.9. HLM's estimated coefficient of a school district using discretion, by percentage of ELs of school

systems resulting in negative repercussions. Delay in the reclassification of students who have reached English proficiency may deny them the opportunity to achieve and may reduce access to courses needed for post-secondary education, while premature reclassification may cause ELL students to lose needed specialized academic language instructional services and be placed at greater risk for educational failure. (Abedi 2008, 28)

Our findings suggest that EL classification rates depend largely on the policies school districts use in reference to the HLS and when it triggers the CELDT (now the ELPAC). The remarkably low passage rates for students taking that test, passage rates that were extremely low (25%) for U.S. born English speakers in the California Department of Education's own assessment, mean that triggering for the test almost guarantees a student's EL classification. Clearly, this system does not seem to be classifying students appropriately. At a minimum, it seems the test as it is currently constructed is more geared toward assessing language development and school readiness than simply English language ability. That seems the only logical explanation for why students who were known to be native English speakers could be classified as not English proficient. We would suggest that the testing instrument be more narrowly tailored to focus specifically on English language ability.

But, even more important, classification should not depend solely on a student's performance on one test. Abedi (2008) recommends a new classification system that uses multiple data points from different tests in order to obtain a more holistic view of the student's academic performance. This would be an important step forward. But we would suggest that parental input and teacher evaluation should be considered as well. In terms of the role of parents, no immigrant parent wants his or her child not to learn English. Yet under the current system there is no mechanism through which parents can have input as to the school's assessment of their child's English proficiency. Such a system of parental input would help in cases where a standardized assessment might have misclassified a student. Similarly, teachers are often better able to assess students' language abilities than one-time standardized tests. With the caveat that few teachers in California have adequate training on how best to serve ELs (Rumberger and Gándara 2004), it is still the case that teachers have much more interaction with students and are a good source for identifying a case of misclassification. The current system offers no role for teachers to provide information to the district when they believe an error has been made. A more holistic process that incorporates multiple pieces of information about a student from different sources is much more likely to result in an accurate classification than a one-time test.

Properly identifying students as ELs is important so that they may receive the linguistic and academic support they need to effectively acquire English while still learning the subject-matter content appropriate to their grade level. We know that this skill development is key to academic success. California's current classification system, however, seems too broad and likely includes many students who should not be in remedial language programs. This not only may harm their academic trajectory but also takes scarce resources away from those students who are most in need of these academic supports.

The current flawed system remains in place, we would argue, because of the contentious politics around bilingual education and immigration in the United States. It is impossible to separate English language learning in schools from the broader debates about immigration and U.S. national identity (Schmidt 2000). Many advocates of bilingual education fear that expressing concerns about the classification system will undermine support for bilingual education in general, particularly during a time of increased nativism. Well-meaning district personnel, by contrast, often still maintain many of the nativist assumptions that were the foundation of twentieth-century Americanization programs. As an example, using Q4 as an automatic trigger assumes that the presence of another language in the home, even with no evidence that the language is spoken by the child, means that the child is likely to be deficient in English. Similarly, this automatic triggering does not leave open the possibility of a fully bilingual child, proficient in English and another home language. Given that California is no longer a top immigrant destination, it is likely that our schools will have to incorporate more students whose parents are perhaps one step removed from the immigration experience, but who want to preserve their family language in the third generation and beyond. Our current classification system is not designed to consider the needs and experiences of those students.

California's experience with EL classification is a cautionary tale for other states. It is important for school districts to remain focused on the key purpose of classification—to accurately determine the linguistic needs of its students—rather than on the politics surrounding the issue. We realize that this is often easier said than done, particularly with regard to immigration and language policy. But the fact that even in "blue" and "pro-immigrant" California (see Colbern, Chapter 3 of this volume), our schools still have difficulty classifying and serving EL students demonstrates the difficulty of carrying out effective language classification policies in the current political climate and given the connections that remain to the Americanization programs that were begun in our nation's schools over a century ago. Only by facing this history will we be able to move toward more effectively serving the needs of EL students.

Notes

1. *Source:* California Department of Education, *CalEdFacts*, https://www.cde.ca.gov/ds/sd/cb/cefelfacts.asp.

2. "English Language Learners in Public Schools," https://nces.ed.gov/programs/coe/indicator_cgf.asp.

3. For more information on the WIDA consortium, visit https://www.wida.us/aboutus/mission.aspx.

4. As of the 2017–18 academic year, California schools began to phase in use of the English Language Proficiency Assessments for California (ELPAC) exam. Even though the ELPAC is a new test, many of its components are exactly the same as the CELDT, making analysis of the CELDT still relevant to EL classification processes in the future. See www.elpac.org/about/.

5. The missing data for this file should be noted. For example, 2,365 district-years are missing information for the percentage of students who take the CELDT exam as an initial assessment in kindergarten and pass. There are also no data for Alpine County.

6. Please note that the coefficients of interest in the random intercept models 3 and 4 are interpretable in the same manner as a single-level OLS model.

8 How Californians See Immigration

Zoltan Hajnal, Taeku Lee, and Kristy M. Pathakis

In this chapter, we seek to illustrate and understand the views of Californians on immigration. As much as any other state in the nation, California has been grappling with immigration-related questions for decades. California borders Mexico—until recently the major immigrant-sending nation. California has the largest immigrant population in the nation. Fully 27% of the state's population is foreign born, roughly double the figure for the rest of the nation. California also has by far the largest undocumented immigrant population in the country. Roughly one in five undocumented immigrants lives within California's borders (Pew Research Center 2016). Largely as a result of immigration, California is now a majority-minority state. All of this makes immigration visible and central in the minds of the state's residents. All of this also means that California could be a bellwether for the nation as a whole as the country becomes more diverse and we move onward toward a majority-minority nation. How Californians feel about immigrants and immigration policy today could be an indication of how Americans writ large are likely to feel in the future.

We examine views on immigration because they are important. There are weighty questions to consider. Is immigration, at its heart, a beneficial or burdensome phenomenon? Should we endeavor to increase or decrease the immigrant population? Should we try to cut off undocumented immigration and in so doing alter the nature and source of our immigrant population? And how should we treat the immigrants who are already here? Should we expand services and provide a welcoming environment that helps immigrants prosper, or should we restrict access in the hopes of reducing the immigrant population?

How the public feels about these questions will almost certainly have an impact on the policies that the state pursues going forward. When Californians expressed considerable anger and fear about the immigrant population in the mid-1990s, policies in the state shifted sharply against the immigrant population. But as those views have become more positive, the state government has embraced an array of more progressive and more welcoming policies. What we think and say about immigration has mattered in the past and will likely matter in the future.

The views of Californians on immigration cannot be summarized simply or succinctly. A deep dive into attitudes on immigration points to several, sometimes contradictory patterns. Californians are at once increasingly liberal and yet still divided on immigration. A solid and growing majority of Californians holds positive views of immigrants and favors more inclusive and permissive policies. At the same time, a shrinking yet sizeable share of the state's residents is both anxious about immigration and eager to clamp down on services and opportunities for immigrants. Most Californians think unauthorized immigration is a major problem in the state, but most also reject the idea of mass deportations, and favor citizenship for the undocumented. Californians are also divided in simultaneously feeling warmly toward the immigrant population yet concerned about immigration's broader impacts.

This equivocal nature of public opinion about immigration and immigrants is, however, fading over time. The one very clear trend is that California residents are becoming more sympathetic to the immigrant community and more willing to offer that community tangible policy benefits. By many measures, the shift toward a more welcoming stance on some questions is remarkable. And this shift is not only real but also meaningful in its impact on policymaking in the state, leading to sharp reversals in policy. California, a state that was at the forefront of the anti-immigrant backlash in the 1990s, is now at the forefront of the "resistance" movement at the state level to harsh anti-immigrant federal policymaking and policy implementation in the Trump administration (see Chapter 3).

In all of this, California is both like and unlike the rest of the nation. California mirrors the nation in its ambivalence about immigration and its division over immigration-related policy. But California stands out from the rest of the nation in terms of the balance of those positive and negative sentiments. On almost every question we examined, residents of this state tend to hold considerably more favorable views toward immigrants and more optimistic assessments of their role in society. California also parallels the country as a whole in terms of the shift to more accepting attitudes. But California's movement to being a more welcoming state has been more swift and more dramatic than the country's as a whole. As a result, California has increasingly become a liberal outlier in the immigration debate.

Lest Californians become too self-congratulatory, it is worth highlighting the main source of the shift to being a more welcoming state. Increasing support for immigrants and policies that might benefit immigrants may be less about individual opinions shifting and much more about some of the changing demographics discussed in Chapter 2. California has become more hospitable to immigration largely because immigrants themselves constitute a larger and larger share of the state's population. White views have not shifted all that much, and large segments of the white population remain wholeheartedly antagonistic on the subject of immigration. In terms of their views on immigration, whites in California are not that different from whites around the nation. Being Californian or living in California does not automatically lead to more liberal attitudes on immigration.

As a result, there is a sharp racial divide in California on matters of immigration. Moreover, in California (as in the rest of the United States), this racial divide is mirrored by a partisan divide. Our analysis suggests, however, that although partisan identity is now clearly the biggest factor shaping public views on immigration, the core, underlying source of division on immigration in California is race.

In this chapter, we introduce this complex terrain of public opinion on immigrants and immigration among Californians. We first briefly describe the data we draw on for our findings. Then we walk readers through a description of how salient immigration is as an issue to Californians, whether Californians are generally positive or negative in their views of immigrants, and what they prefer on a range of policies relating to immigration. We then dig a bit deeper into this background account by examining how Californians' views have changed over time and the roots of some of their attitudes on immigrants and immigration policy.

Data

As immigrants and immigration policy have become increasingly salient, there has been a steady, growing interest in public opinion on the topic, and with that interest, polling on immigrants and immigration (see, e.g., Lee and Kim 2018). To assess the attitudes of Californians, we drew on data from several surveys that are well recognized for the quality of their sample and measurement. Specifically, we present data primarily from three sources: the 2016 American National Election Study (ANES), the 2016 Cooperative Congressional Election Study (CCES), and several editions from 2016 to 2018 of the Public Policy Institute of California Statewide Survey (PPIC). When offering more in-depth analysis of divisions within the California population, we lean more heavily on the larger sample sizes in the CCES and ANES. As immigration has not always been a prominent issue in the minds of pollsters, data on long-term trends in opinions are more limited. But we are able to assess midterm trends using data from the 2006 to 2016 CCES and longer-range trends for a smaller number of questions in the ANES (1976–2016) and PPIC (1988–2018) surveys.

Californians' Views Today

We begin by assessing how salient immigration is as an issue to Californians. How important is immigration, and how does its salience rank alongside other critical issues of the day? The 2016 CCES asked respondents how important a variety of issues was to them, ranging from "very high" to "no importance at all." As figure 8.1 shows, immigration landed roughly in the middle in terms of the importance of the fifteen issues the CCES asked about. A vast majority (73%) of Californians view immigration as "very" or "somewhat" high in importance, with almost none (2%) who felt that immigration was of "no importance." To note a few select comparisons, as an issue in 2016, immigration was not as critical as health care, government corruption, or jobs; it was similar to gun control, taxes, and crime, and more important than abortion or same-sex marriage.[1]

It is clear from this and other surveys that, in general, immigration is not *the* most important problem in the minds of the state's residents. When asked the ubiquitous open-ended "most important problem" issue salience item, in survey after survey, relatively few Californians pinpoint immigration as deserving of being singled out.[2] In the 2016 ANES, only 5% of Californians

Health care	59.4%
Social Security	57.4%
Government corruption	57.2%
National security	56.6%
Jobs	51.0%
Gun control	49.3%
Immigration	45.7%
Taxes	44.3%
Crime	43.0%
Environment	42.0%
Race relations	39.7%
Budget deficit	39.6%
Defense spending	35.2%
Abortion	30.8%
Gay marriage	19.7%

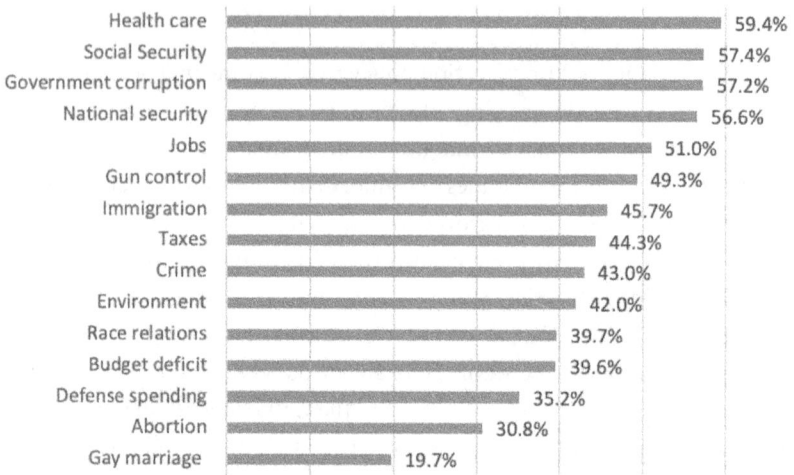

Figure 8.1. Issue importance: Very high
Source: 2016 Cooperative Congressional Election Study.

felt that immigration was the most important problem in the country. For comparison, when asked about "the most important issue facing people in California today"—a question that PPIC Statewide Surveys asked occasionally, in October 2016 only 6% of adult residents cited immigration, with 28% mentioning jobs and the economy, and 14% identifying the drought as most important.[3]

Yet the salience of issues also varies, sometimes even dramatically, as circumstances change—for example, a refugee crisis; a new law, court ruling, or ballot initiative; or partisan candidates who seek to politicize the issue for their electoral gain. The PPIC Statewide Survey has regularly asked this "most important problem facing the people of California today" question, and, in general, immigration is a moderately salient issue for Californians—important enough that it is regularly one of the top five issues mentioned, but not so important that it exceeds the salience of jobs and the economy. Yet, as we see in figure 8.2 (which shows the top five responses to this question between January 2016 to mid-2018), the policies and rhetoric of the Trump campaign and now the Trump administration have propelled the issue much closer to the forefront of Californians' minds. Since the November 2016 election, immigration has been the first or second most commonly mentioned most important problem for Californians, with a range of 11%–20% of respondents

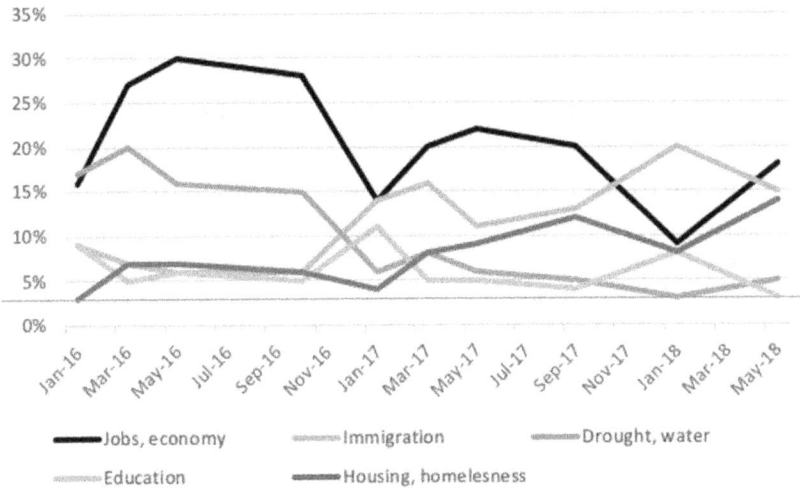

Figure 8.2. Most important problem facing Californians
Source: Public Policy Institute of California, Statewide Surveys.

mentioning immigration in a PPIC Statewide Survey between January 2017 and May 2018.

This high and growing salience of immigration as an issue for Californians sets the backdrop to our overview of public opinion, but how do California residents view immigrants generally? On that broad question, the answer is relatively clear. Although the importance of immigration may respond to the Trump era's nativist rhetoric and restrictionist policies, there is no denying that overall, Californians are welcoming and warm toward immigrants.

The overwhelming majority of adults in California believe that immigrants are a benefit to the state. When asked about whether immigrants represent primarily a burden to the state "because they use public services" or a benefit "because of their hard work and job skills," roughly three-quarters of respondents to the September 2017 PPIC Statewide Survey indicated that they felt that immigrants as a whole were more of a benefit than a burden to the state. Only 20% answered that immigrants are a burden. These figures for 2017 represent a high-water mark for positive views toward immigrants in the PPIC time series since 1988, and other surveys in recent years point equally clearly to positive views on immigrants as a group. When survey participants were asked in the 2016 ANES to report how warmly they feel toward

Hispanics on a temperature scale ranging from 0 degrees ("cold," negative affect) to 100 degrees ("warm," positive affect), the mean feeling thermometer score among Californians was a warmish 71 degrees.[4] Not all Latinos, of course, are foreign born, and conversely not all foreign-born Californians are Latino. Yet Latinos still comprise one out of every two foreign-born Californians, and much of the vituperative and nativist rhetoric on immigration bears a distinct anti-Latino cast. In this context, Californians' warmth toward Latinos is notable.

That generally positive sentiment is echoed in other assessments of immigrants. When asked about the overall economic impact of immigrants, fully 65% of Californians agree that "immigrants are generally good for the economy" (ANES). Only 11% disagree with that statement, and a further 24% aren't sure one way or the other. Residents of the state also hold largely favorable views about the cultural impact of immigrants. When asked whether "America's culture is generally harmed by immigrants," two-thirds of adults in the state either disagreed strongly or disagreed somewhat. A relatively small fraction agreed that immigrants have a net negative impact on culture, and some 22% expressed ambivalence.

When the focus shifts to undocumented immigrants, however, that largely positive sentiment breaks down relatively quickly. For an overall assessment of views toward the undocumented, we turned again to the 2016 ANES feeling thermometer, this time with the reference group "illegal immigrants." Figure 8.3 displays a histogram distribution of answers to the question, and on this aspect of attitudes toward immigrants, Californians fall squarely between cold and warm, with a mean thermometer rating of 50 degrees toward "illegal immigrants." Although there is some debate over the reliability of feeling thermometers as an individual measure of affect, the mean score of 50 suggests clearly that Californians' views of undocumented immigrants are not particularly favorable. As a point of reference, Californians profess to hold significantly more positive views for most racial groups. Mean thermometer scores for blacks (71 degrees), Asian Americans (71 degrees), and whites (70 degrees) are all significantly higher than the 50 degree mean for undocumented immigrants.[5]

When we dig deeper into the figure, several significant patterns emerge. First, many Californians fall toward the center of the thermometer scale, with roughly a third somewhere between 40 and 60 degrees on the 100 degree scale. This ambivalence is a theme that recurs in our analysis. At the same

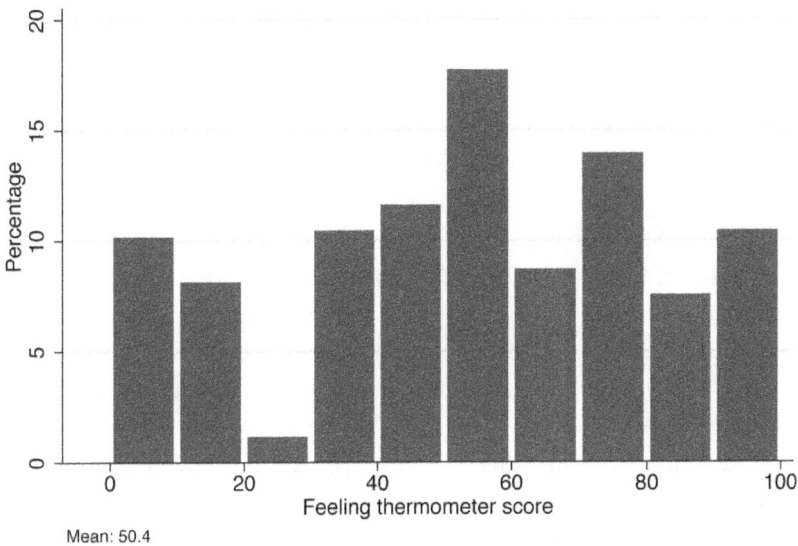

Figure 8.3: Feelings toward "illegal immigrants"
Source: 2016 American National Election Study.

time, the tails of this distribution are heavy: nearly one in five Californians feel very warmly toward undocumented immigrants (rating them above 80 degrees or higher), and roughly the same proportion are very cold toward this group (rating them 20 degrees or lower). Whereas Californians hold decidedly more mixed views toward undocumented immigrants, the views of non-Californians in the 2016 ANES are a full 10 degrees colder, with a mean thermometer rating of 40.5 degrees.

It is important to note that further analysis reveals that how residents feel about the undocumented is in many ways closely connected to how they feel about immigrants more broadly or about racial and ethnic groups that are linked to immigration. In particular, feelings about the undocumented are highly correlated with feelings about Hispanics ($r = .49$, $p < .01$), feelings about Asian Americans ($r = .38$, $p < .01$), and feelings about Muslims ($r = .42$, $p < .01$). Views of the undocumented are largely uncorrelated with views of whites. This muddling together of views of the undocumented and views of immigrants in general as well as racial groups closely linked to immigration is far from unique. A range of studies suggests that many Americans fall prey to the misperception that most immigrants are here illegally, and often harbor images of undocumented Latinos when they think about immigration (Brader, Valentino, and Suhay 2008; Valentino, Brader, and Jardina 2013; Perez 2016).

Californians also held equally mixed or divided views about Muslim Americans, a group that is majority foreign born and often the target of nativism and narratives of threat. Until recently, few surveys have asked about attitudes toward Muslims, but those that have reveal relatively negative attitudes. In 2016, the ANES measured the extent of anti-Muslim stereotypes as violent and unpatriotic. On a scale of 1 to 7 (peaceful to violent; patriotic to unpatriotic), the mean score for Californian respondents was 3.8 on the stereotype of Muslims as violent and 4.1 on the stereotype of Muslims as unpatriotic. By contrast, Californians rated "Christians" much more positively at 2.9 (more "peaceful" than "violent") and 2.6 (more "patriotic" than "unpatriotic") on these scales.

At the same time, a large share of the state's residents recognize and sympathize with the challenges and animus facing Muslims in America. Almost all Californians feel that Muslims face considerable discrimination, with 88% reporting that Muslims face at least a moderate amount of discrimination. Californians are also less likely than the nation as a whole to support restrictionist policies aimed at Muslims. A March 2017 PPIC poll found that six in ten adults in the state opposed the president's revised travel ban involving six predominantly Muslim countries. In the 2016 CCES, when asked, "What do you think the U.S. government should do about immigration?" and given the option "ban Muslims from immigrating to the U.S.," less than one in five Californians selected this extreme measure.[6] Nationally, almost a quarter of Americans favored a Muslim ban.

Division reemerges when Californians are asked about different aspects of what has come to be known as the immigrant threat narrative (Abrajano and Hajnal 2015). Perhaps chief among the concerns raised by that narrative is the belief that immigrants take jobs away from Americans. Californians are far from immune to that narrative. In a recent poll, fully 69% of residents believe that immigrants are "extremely likely," "very likely," or "somewhat likely" to take away jobs from native-born Americans. At the same time, most of this sentiment is with the view that immigrants are "somewhat likely" to compete for jobs (43%), and only 12% see this possibility as "extremely likely." Nearly a third (31%) believe that it is "not at all likely" that immigration would result in job losses for the native born.

Other aspects of disagreement are visible in Californians' views on crime and American identity. On crime, President Trump's now infamous statement about Mexicans bringing drugs and crime and sending rapists to the U.S. appears to resonate with at least a nontrivial minority of Californians. In the 2016 ANES, almost half of California's residents did not think that immigrants increase crime, but 28% weren't sure, and a further 23% of California's residents agreed that immigrants do increase crime.

Views on American culture and identity are also a source of some dispute. Although the clear majority of Californians believe that it is not important to "have American ancestry" to be "truly American," a far from insignificant minority—33%—believe that such ancestry is "very important" or "fairly important." On a similar register, Californians are roughly split on the statement that to be truly American, it is important to be born in the U.S. (47% agreed; 53% disagreed). In addition, two-thirds of Californians felt that to be truly American, it is important to follow American customs and traditions, while only a third did not think it was important at all. On the question of language and American identity, however, there was close to a consensus: 83% of Californian respondents in the ANES felt that it was either very important or fairly important to speak English to be considered truly American.

Overall, Californians hold liberal and inclusive views toward immigrants—but not all Californians and not toward all immigrant or immigrant-based groups. There remain real divisions over the impact of the immigrant population and real ongoing concerns related to jobs, crime, and national identity.

Views on Policy

Valenced questions about immigrants are instructive, but they may represent an oversimplified portrayal. Positive and negative assessments of groups are, after all, susceptible to "political correctness" (or what survey researchers term "social desirability" effects), and beliefs about policies and the allocation of finite resources are often a tougher test of public opinion than overall sentiments of favorability. Moreover, there is a long-standing finding that Americans appear far more tolerant and egalitarian when their views are given as general statements of principle than when those same views are tethered to policies.[7] For example, the tip of the iceberg is the general assessment of the immigration policy status quo. In a 2000 PPIC survey, Californians were asked how satisfied they were with that status quo. Only 7% felt that immigration policy was "fine the way it is," while a whopping 69% of Californians responded that they thought it needed "major changes," and a further 22% recommended "minor changes."

Note, however, that dissatisfaction with the policy status quo is a catch-all that includes both those Californians who would prefer a shift toward more restrictionist policies *and* those who would prefer the opposite, a shift toward more liberal policies. In this section, we examine some of this heterogeneity of opinion over a range of immigration-related policies. Is the warmth of Californians toward immigrants matched by their generosity on policies that require expenditure of resources? To this question there are two overarching patterns. First, Californians are far from unanimous in their policy views. On the policy questions we examined, there is a diversity of views among Californians: Some value the inclusion of immigrants and investments fully integrating them; others favor limits to migration and curbs on spending; and there is often a sizeable group in the middle that is unsure of its views. Second, notwithstanding this mix of views, the balance is discernibly positive and welcoming. Where Californians are not split in their policy views, they favor incorporation and inclusion. More often than not, the inclusive view outnumbers the exclusionary view by two to one.

We start with the most basic of policy questions about immigration—whether levels of in-migration should be increased, decreased, or kept at about the same level. Californians are relatively evenly split, and for this question there is no clear consensus. Data from the 2016 ANES indicate that 23% of the state would like to see immigration increased, 45% are fine with current levels of immigration, and 31% favor a decrease in immigration.

Levels of migration, of course, are just one of many aspects of immigration. By contrast, Californians largely agree on several other specific aspects of immigration reform. Notable among these is the question of whether unauthorized migrants should be allowed to remain and under what status. Regardless of the question wording, upward of two-thirds of the population favor allowing the undocumented to stay, and a majority typically favors creating a pathway to citizenship. For example, in response to a March 2017 PPIC question, 68% of adults believed that undocumented immigrants living in the U.S. "should be allowed to stay in the U.S. and eventually apply for citizenship." A further 12% felt that the undocumented should be allowed to stay, but without a pathway to citizenship. Only 15% of Californians thought that undocumented immigrants should be required to leave the U.S. Those figures almost perfectly match a similar question from a 2016 USC Dornsife/*Los Angeles Times* poll. That 2016 poll found that 65% of voters favored a pathway to citizenship, 14 chose an option that allowed the undocumented to stay in the country without citizenship, and 16% favored deportation.[8]

This very favorable support for pro-immigrant reforms is also evident on the question of border walls and the debate over "Dreamers" (undocumented immigrant youth). The overwhelming majority of Californians oppose building a wall along the border with Mexico: A September 2017 PPIC survey found that 73% oppose, and the 2016 USC Dornsife/*Los Angeles Times* poll found similar numbers who dislike this policy idea. Similarly, three-quarters of adult Californians indicate that they are concerned that federal efforts will negatively "impact undocumented college and university students" (November 2017 PPIC). Fully 85% favor "protections given by DACA which includes protection from deportation and a work permit" (January 2018 PPIC).

At the same time, just around the corner from these liberal views are some decidedly more mixed views on immigration policies involving enhanced enforcement and deportation powers and extending public goods benefits to undocumented immigrants. First, support for California's undocumented immigrants thins out on policies that entail the expenditure of resources. Only 46% of likely voters in the state would allow undocumented students to qualify for student loans at state universities (March 2016 USC Dornsife/*Los Angeles Times* poll). And according to the same poll, even fewer (43%) would extend Medi-Cal, the state's health care program for low-income families, to all immigrants regardless of status.

Dissensus is also more visible on the question of federal enforcement and deportation efforts and how California should respond to them. Roughly half of all Californians say they worry "a lot" (30%) or "somewhat" (21%) "that someone that you know could be deported" as a result of stepped-up federal immigration efforts (PPIC May 2017). About half of adult residents also believe that "increased federal immigration enforcement" will have "a negative impact on business, jobs, and the economy," while 24% believe that the impact would be positive, and 27% are unsure about the policy's likely impact (PPIC May 2017).

Opinion is also diverse on the question of whether California should combat federal action. Roughly equal numbers of voters supported and opposed a ban on sanctuary cities—places that refuse to hand over immigrants suspected of being in the United States without permission (March 2016 USC Dornsife/ *Los Angeles Times* poll). When the target of federal action is students, however, Californians are more supportive of state and local resistance. Seven in ten residents are concerned (46% "very concerned" and 24% "somewhat concerned") that increased federal enforcement may negatively impact undocumented students in their local schools. And roughly two-thirds of adults favor designating their local school district as a "sanctuary safe zone" to protect undocumented students from federal immigration enforcement (PPIC April 2017).

The lack of a consensus in the state is perhaps most evident when pollsters give residents a range of different policy options to choose from. Asked to recommend one or more policies (among a range of nine options), the two most popular policies fell on either end of the political spectrum. Californians were almost as likely to recommend "identifying and deporting the undocumented" (32%) as they were to offer legal status to Dreamers (35%) (CCES 2016). Likewise, the share that chose increased border patrols (6%) was not all that different from the share that wanted to "grant legal status" to undocumented immigrants if they paid their taxes and had no felonies.

To sum up, on some dimensions of policy, the warmth that Californians express toward immigrants extends into generosity in support of building bridges to citizenship and not walls of exclusion. On other dimensions, however, such as interposition of state and local resistance to aggressive federal policies against undocumented immigrants and eligibility for resources such as education loans and health care benefits, that generosity is less manifest.

Trends over Time

California, by almost every conceivable measure, is becoming more and more diverse. Over the last half century, immigration has swelled the state's population. The share of the state that is foreign born has increased from just 9% in 1970 to 27% today, or roughly twice the national average. Furthermore, an additional 24% of California's population are second-generation children of immigrants, putting the immigrant-based (first and second generations combined) population as a majority of the state's population. Because a disproportionate share of this post-1965 wave of migration to California has been immigrants of color from Asia and Central and South America, over the same time period, California has also transformed from a predominantly white state to a majority-minority state.

Those shifts could easily have sparked a negative reaction on the part of native-born whites, and at least for a period they did. But a look at how Californians' opinions on immigration have changed over time indicates, first and foremost, a remarkably positive shift in views. Although an actual empirical analysis of the question is beyond the scope of this chapter, it is at least reasonable to speculate that the anti-immigrant ballot initiatives that won popular majorities in the California of the 1990s (Propositions 187 and 227, and perhaps even 209), would not survive the changes in attitudes and composition in present-day California. There are only a limited number of items on immigration that have been asked consistently over time, but on almost every question for which we have data, there has been a notable softening of attitudes.

We begin by revisiting the "feeling thermometer" items, for which there is a significant time series. Recall that the items ask respondents to rate how they feel about a reference group on a temperature scale ranging from 0 to 100 degrees. This item was asked in regard to Latinos in the ANES from 1976 to 2016.[9] Figure 8.4 plots mean responses by year over these years, adding a trend or regression line to help highlight the over-time change.

Californians have clearly warmed toward Hispanics over time. In the 1970s, respondents were somewhat lukewarm, with a mean rating of 55 degrees on the 100 degree scale in 1976. But almost every year after that, mean opinion toward Hispanics has warmed. By 2016, the residents of the state express substantially warmer feelings about Hispanics, with a mean thermometer score of 71 degrees. This shift is not only visible but also statistically significant. A fitted regression estimates an increase in warmth of 0.35 degrees each year over this time series.

As we noted before, "immigrant" is far from synonymous with "Latino." Asking the feeling thermometer item of other immigration-related reference groups might result in markedly different trends. The reality is that they do not. By every measure that we could find, California has become more welcoming toward immigrants over time.

Perhaps the strong test of this is how Californians feel toward "illegal immigrants." We have already noted that Californians are concerned about and, on some aspects, divided in their views about undocumented migration. The ANES asked the feeling thermometer item about "illegal immigrants" from 1988 to 2016. Here again, we see in figure 8.5 a conspicuous upward slope. In 1988, the first year for which data are available, Californians felt

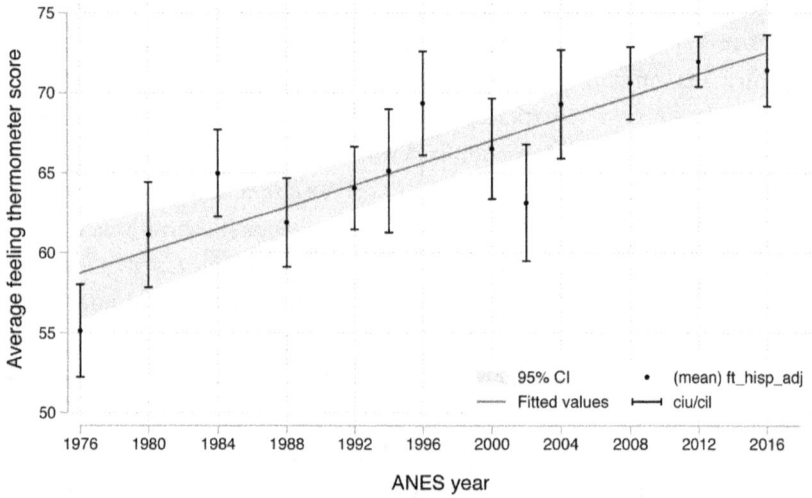

Figure 8.4. Feelings toward Latinos, 1976–2016
Source: American National Election Study.

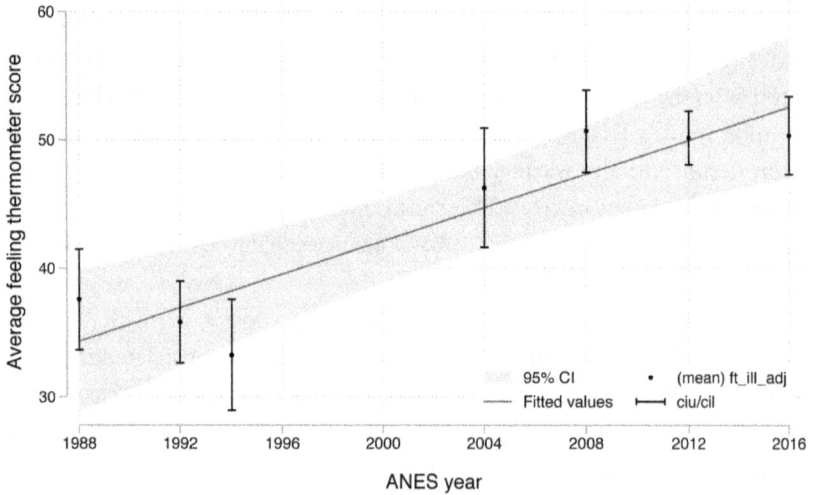

Figure 8.5. Feelings toward illegal immigrants, 1988–2016
Source: American National Election Study.

largely cold, with a mean temperature score of 37.5. By 2016, affect even toward undocumented immigrants thaws to a middle-of-the-road average of 50 degrees. That is far from a warm embrace, but it is nonetheless a far cry from what was seen in the 1980s and 1990s.[10]

Similar shifts over time can be found on other questions about immigrants and immigration. For instance, in Field Polls, the share of adults who see illegal immigration as a very serious problem declined from a high of 65% in 1982 to just 50% in 1998. We also see significantly more positive views on the question of whether immigrants are on net a benefit or a burden. The time series here only starts in 2000, but even within the last two decades there is a real uptick in views. Figure 8.6 shows that the share of Californians who believe that immigrants are a benefit has grown from 55% in 2000 to 76% in 2017.[11]

The few questions on immigration *policy* that have been repeated over time reveal a similarly positive trend. Recall that we earlier noted that Californians today are roughly evenly split on the question of whether current levels of immigration should be increased or decreased, with a plurality satisfied with the status quo. Viewed over time, this is a dramatic shift in opinion toward support for greater levels of immigration. As shown in figure 8.7, in 1994 (the height of the Proposition 187 campaign), nearly two-thirds of Californians (63%) favored decreased levels of immigration, while only one in twenty supported increased levels. Today, only about a third favor reduced levels. At the other end of the spectrum, the share of Californians who favor expanded immigration levels has climbed to nearly one in four.[12] And to round out the choice set, the proportion of Californians who are just fine with levels as they are has increased from a low of about 30% in 1994 to majorities or near majorities in more recent years.

Thus, despite the dramatic increases in California's foreign-born population over the last several decades, its residents appear more and more comfortable with the prospect of continued population growth through migration into the future. Evidence of that increasing comfort is also visible on policy questions related to undocumented immigration. On whether undocumented immigrants should be barred from access to public services, Californians spoke loudly and clearly in 1994 when the state passed Proposition 187, a measure designed to prevent undocumented immigrants from gaining access to public services in education, health, and welfare. Then, nearly three

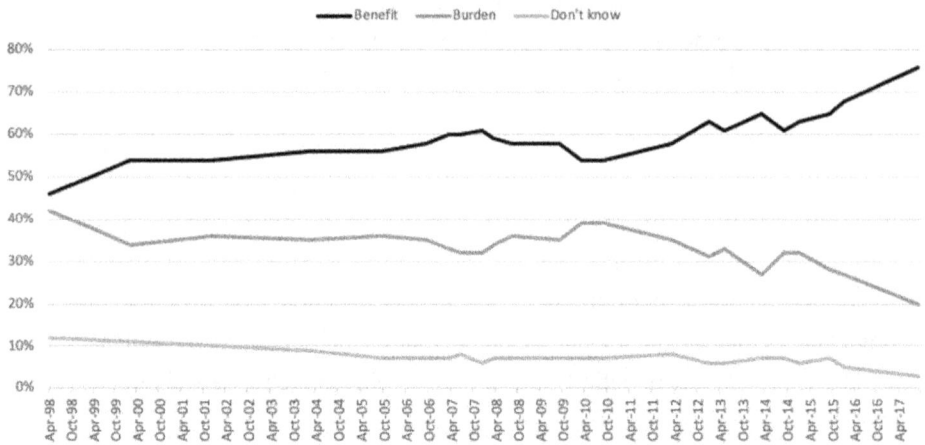

Figure 8.6. Are immigrants a benefit to California because of their hard work and job skills, or are they a burden because they use public services?
Source: Field Poll, 1998–2017.

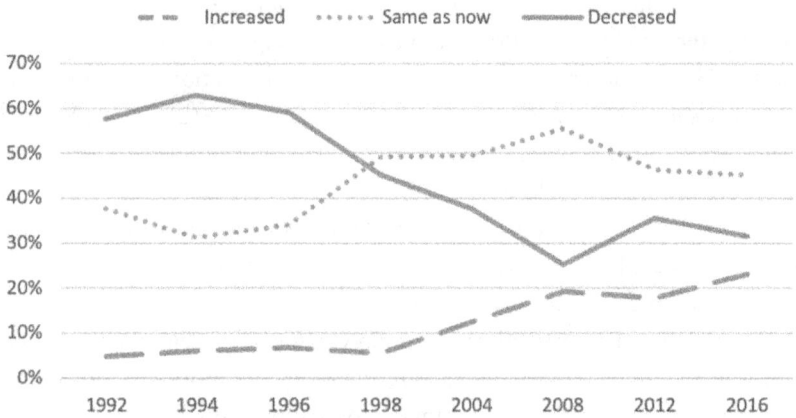

Figure 8.7. What should immigration levels be?
Source: American National Election Study.

out of every five of the state's voters supported the so-called Save Our State measure.

More recently, polls show a greater sense of care and generosity when Californians are asked about sharing the state's public coffers to help its undocumented population. By 2002, a slim majority of the state's residents (53%) was on the other side of the debate, indicating that undocumented immigrants should not be denied public services such as education and health care. A few years later in 2008, fully 66% of the state maintained that undocumented immigrants should be allowed to apply for work permits. And by 2017, the overwhelming majority of the state's residents seemed to be in favor of fully incorporating the undocumented population. In March 2017, 80% of respondents to a PPIC poll indicated that undocumented immigrants should be allowed to stay in the U.S. And in early 2018, further polling data show that 85% of the state now favors continuing protections for the undocumented Dreamers. In just the last seven years, the share of the public favoring deportation for the undocumented fell from 25% to 15%.[13]

Uncovering the Sources of Immigration Attitudes

In this final section, we aim to get to the root of some of the patterns of public opinion on immigration that we have thus far presented. What factors help to shape views on immigration in the state? What is the source of California's welcoming attitude? To answer those questions, we examined a range of demographic and political characteristics and their ties to immigration views. The results suggest a dominant role of four factors: partisanship, ideology, race, and religion. Other factors that typically shape public opinion, such as age, education, income, and gender, play a role, but not nearly to the same extent as these four.[14] In short, when it comes to immigration, the state is divided politically, racially, and religiously more than anything else.[15]

To provide a visual illustration of the relative roles of partisanship, ideology, race, and other demographic factors in shaping immigration views, figures 8.8, 8.9, and 8.10 display mean preferences by group for three core questions about immigration: feelings toward the undocumented population, a general assessment of current immigration levels, and the border wall initiative favored by President Trump. In each of these figures, the marginals for partisanship, ideology, and race are compared to select background factors that commonly differentiate public opinion: nativity, education, income, age,

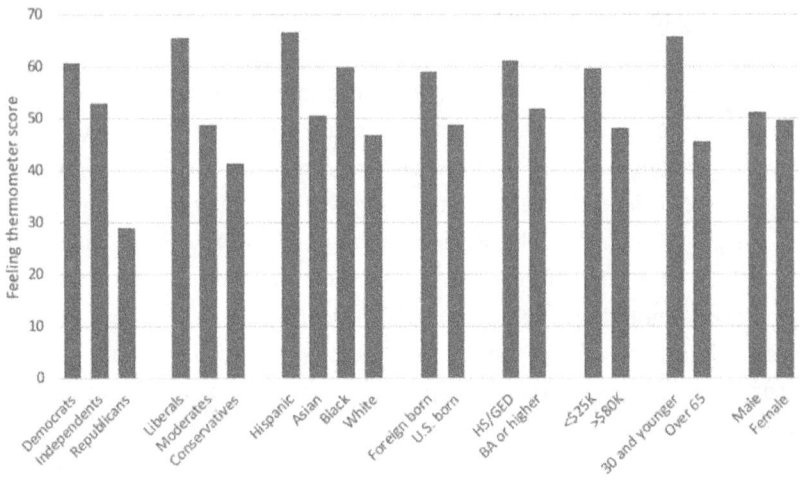

Figure 8.8. Warmth toward illegal immigrants
Source: American National Election Study.

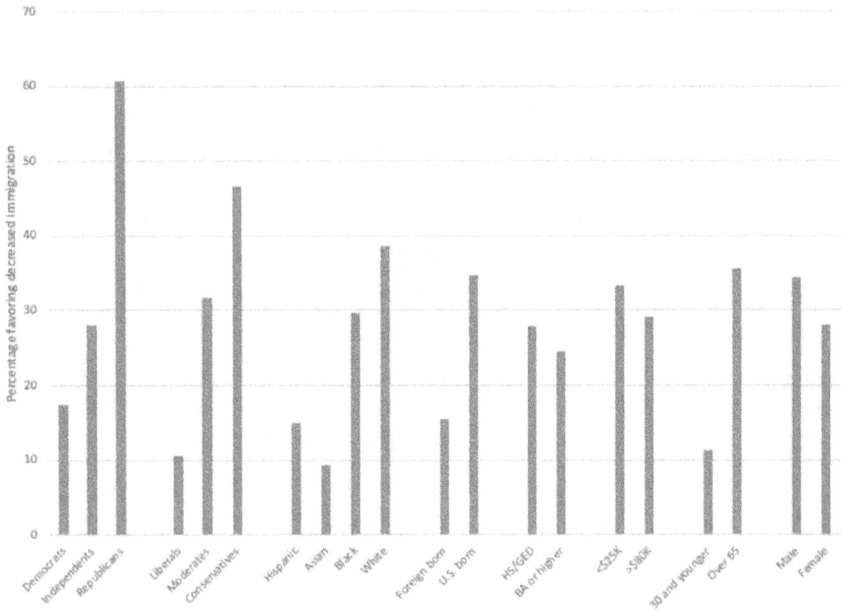

Figure 8.9. Support for decreased immigration levels
Source: American National Election Study.

and gender. The next sections describe these figures and add other, more specific findings for each group.

Party Identification

By far the biggest factor shaping views on immigration in California today is party identification. On just about every measure we looked at, Democrats tend to be substantially more favorable toward immigrants than Republicans. Sometimes that division is massive. Democrats, for example, offer twice as warm ratings of the undocumented population as Republicans. The average feeling thermometer scores are 29 degrees for Republicans and 61 degrees for Democrats.

The partisan division is as large or even larger on policy. Whereas only 17% of Democrats in the state would like to see current immigration levels decreased, a clear majority (61%) of Republicans favor decreasing immigration. More recent policy debates that involve President Trump seem to spark even larger partisan gaps. Democrats in the state are almost unanimously opposed to an extended wall along the southern border with Mexico, while Republicans are overwhelmingly in favor of the policy. All told, 92% of self-identified Democrats oppose the wall, while only 28% of Republicans do (PPIC March 2017). The reverse is true when it comes to protecting the undocumented. Here recent PPIC polls indicate that 80% of Democrats favor state and local government acting "to protect the legal rights of undocumented immigrants in California," while only 27% of Republicans favor such action (PPIC January 2017).

There are, however some cases where the partisan divide is more moderate. For example, clear majorities of both Democrats and Republicans in the state think there should be a way for undocumented immigrants to stay in the country legally. The difference here is that Democrats are more overwhelmingly in favor of allowing the undocumented to stay than are Republicans (93% in favor vs. 68% in favor). Generally, partisan differences are more muted on nonpolicy questions that get at feelings toward immigrants more broadly.

Interestingly, over-time analysis reveals that the partisan divide is relatively new. Before California's Republican governor Pete Wilson campaigned on Prop 187, the so-called Save Our State initiative, in 1994, large partisan divides on immigration were relatively rare. Since that time, partisan division on immigration has been growing sharply—both within and outside the state (Hajnal and Rivera 2014). One explanation is the increasingly divergent

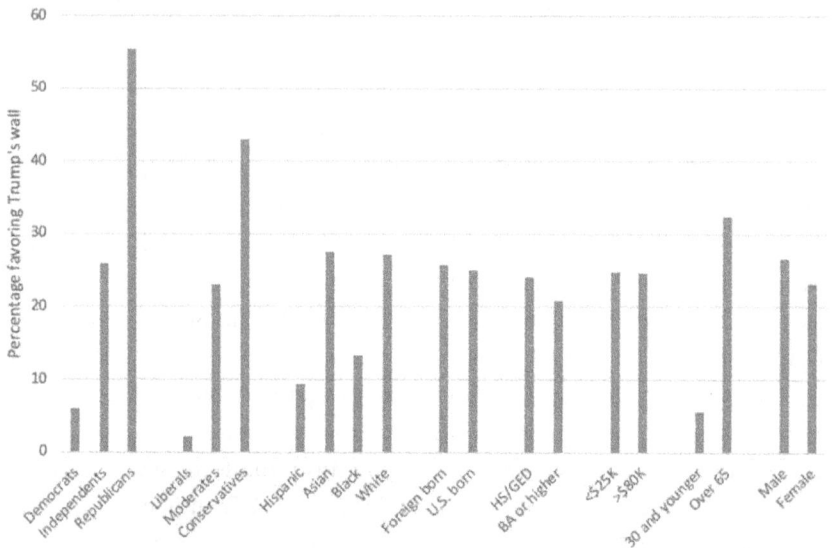

Figure 8.10. Support for building Trump's wall
Source: American National Election Study.

stands of Republican and Democratic leaders on the issue of immigration. Over time, Republican elites have shifted noticeably to the right on immigration, while Democratic elected officials have moved to the left (Abrajano and Hajnal 2015; Wong 2016).

Ideology

Views on immigration are shaped almost as much by the ideological positions of California's residents. Self-described liberals tend to express overwhelmingly positive views of immigrants, and they tend to favor more inclusive and welcoming policies, while conservatives hold nearly the opposite views.

On the feeling thermometer, the average rating of undocumented immigrants differs sharply between liberals (66 degrees) and conservatives (41 degrees). Likewise, only 10% of liberals favor a decrease in immigration, while almost half of conservatives (47%) do. The contrast is even starker on attitudes toward a border wall. A tiny fraction of liberals in the state favor the wall (2%), while almost half (43%) of conservatives do. Liberals and conservatives significantly differ on almost every question we looked at.

Race

There is a relatively clear racial pattern to views on immigration. Latinos in the state tend to express overwhelmingly positive views toward immigrants—be they documented or not—and Latinos generally favor policies that provide immigrants with services and resources. Whites in the state tend to fall on the other end of the racial spectrum. Whites are often divided over immigrants and immigration policy, but their views as a whole are much less positive than those of Latinos in the state. Asian Americans and African Americans often end up somewhere in the middle. As the following figures indicate, Asian Americans tend to be particularly negative on questions related to undocumented immigration and somewhat more positive on questions related to documented immigration.

For example, on feelings toward the undocumented, the average rating by Latinos is 67 degrees compared to only 47 degrees from whites, 51 degrees from Asian Americans, and 60 degrees from African Americans. Policy divides by race are often even larger. Only 15% of Hispanics in California think immigration should be decreased. A little less than half of whites (41%) hold that opinion. On this question, Asian Americans are the least negative, with only 7% saying that current immigration levels should be decreased. Blacks fall near the middle (22% favoring decreased immigration). No racial group in California favors extending the wall along the entire southern border, but again sharp racial differences do emerge: 9% of Hispanics, 32% of whites, 32% of Asian Americans, and 12% of blacks agree that the wall should be extended.

In large part reflecting these racial differences, nativity also plays a significant role. Foreign-born Californians are more likely to feel warmly toward the undocumented (59 degrees on average), less likely to support decreased immigration (15% support reductions), and less likely to favor a border wall (25% favor the wall) than are their native-born counterparts (49 degrees on average; 35% support reductions; 31% favor the wall). Where one is born matters, but race matters even more.

Other Factors

Although observers of California politics often point to background factors such as class, age, and gender as primary drivers of politics in the state, our analysis suggests that these factors are of secondary importance when it comes to immigration. That is not to say that divisions do not exist by income, education, age, gender, and, in regard to immigration, differences between the native born and the foreign born. Indeed, on every one of these dimensions, significant differences of opinion did emerge for most of the immigration questions we looked at. But those differences tended to be relatively small—generally less than 10 percentage points and often less than 5 percentage points. Despite attention to the gender gap in the media in recent elections, the gender gap on most questions related to immigration was negligible, ranging between 0 and 6 percentage points. Likewise, being married or single and having children or not generally made little appreciable difference to views on immigration.

Most measures of class or socioeconomic status revealed relatively limited division on immigration. The most educated Californians rarely differed from the least educated Californians by more than 10 points across the range of questions, and the richest Californians differed from the poorest Californians by even smaller margins. It is also worth noting that the effects of class tend to be mixed. On many of the measures of socioeconomic status that we looked at, higher status in California tends to be linked with colder views of the undocumented and generally more negative views of the immigrant population, but on other measures the opposite is true. Thus the net impact of class is often quite limited. The one exception was unemployment, where there was a 22-point gap between the unemployed and other Californians on the question of whether or not immigration levels should be decreased. The unemployed—perhaps reflecting their precarious economic position and a belief that immigrants pose competition for jobs—were more likely to favor reductions in immigration and also somewhat more likely to support a border wall.[16]

Of the background characteristics examined, age and nativity were most prominent. Older Californians—those over sixty-five years—were 25% more likely to support declines in immigration than were younger Californians, those thirty and younger. Equally large generational gaps emerged in regard to the wall and feelings toward the undocumented. Similarly, we found that native-born Californians were significantly more likely to be cold toward undocumented immigrants (by 10 thermometer scale points) and more likely to support decreased immigration levels (by almost 20%). There were no differences by nativity in support for building a wall, however.

More important, as we will see, much of this divide by age and nativity in regard to immigration is really just a function of racial demographics. Whites tend to be older and U.S. born, and Hispanics and Asian Americans tend to be younger and foreign born. All told, these demographic characteristics tend to pale in comparison to the partisan, ideological, and racial divides we outlined earlier.

Combining Factors

To see which *demographic* factors really are driving attitudes on immigration, we undertook a series of regression analyses that incorporated all of the different demographic characteristics in one model.[17] The results of those analyses differ from immigration question to immigration question, but a fairly clear pattern does emerge. As figures 8.11, 8.12, and 8.13 reveal, only two factors consistently shape immigration attitudes when we control for a range of other demographic characteristics. Those figures show the predicted effects of each significant factor on feelings toward the undocumented, attitudes on current immigration levels, and support for Trump's border wall, respectively.

These figures reveal that race retains a central position in helping us understand how Californians think about immigration. And very clearly on the race front, Latinos stand out. On every question, net controls for socioeconomic status, gender, religion, and other factors, Latinos in the state hold much more positive views of immigrants and favor more inclusive policies. For example, Latinos feel, all else being equal, 23 degrees warmer toward the undocumented than do whites. What is less clear is where Asian Americans and African Americans fall on the racial spectrum. Blacks hold substantially more positive views of the undocumented than do whites of a similar status, but they are not significantly different from similar whites on the border wall or attitudes about immigration levels. Asian Americans do not stand out from whites on any of the three questions.

The other dominant factor in these models is religion. Keeping in mind that the number of respondents for some religious denominations is low for many of the questions we analyzed, the discussion is nonetheless insightful. Even after incorporating all of the different demographic factors, the divide between atheists and Evangelicals persists. In fact, religion rivals race. The predicted undocumented immigrant thermometer score is 34 degrees lower for Evangelicals than it is for atheists, all else being equal. It is important to note that all of the other Californians whom we lumped together in the "other religion" category for simplification stand out from atheists almost as much. Controlling for other factors, there is a sharp divide between the religious

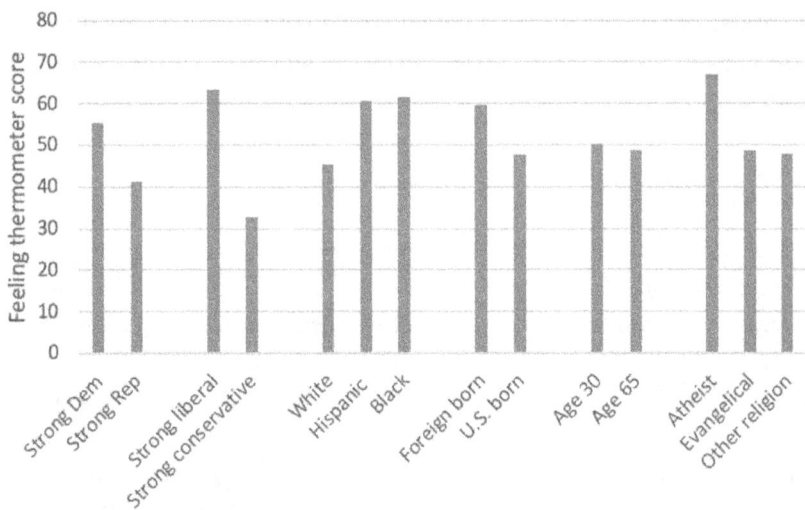

Figure 8.11. Predicted warmth toward illegal immigrants
Source: American National Election Study.

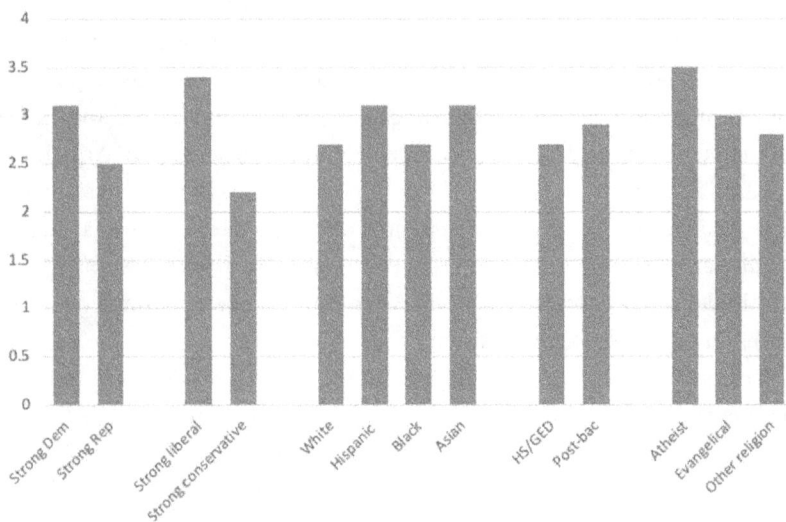

Figure 8.12. Predicted support for increasing immigration (4–5 = increase; 3 = leave the same; 1–2 = decrease)
Source: American National Election Study.

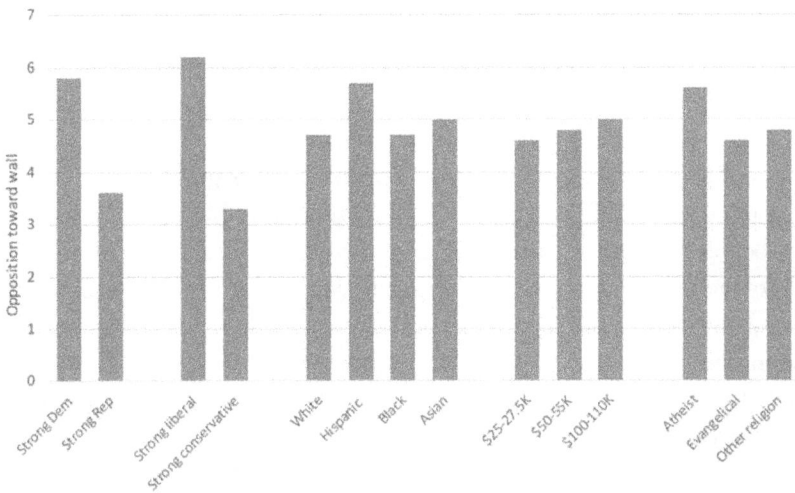

Figure 8.13. Predicted opposition toward Trump's wall (1–3 = favor; 4 = neither favor nor oppose; 5–7 = oppose)
Source: American National Election Study.

and the nonreligious on immigration, with the nonreligious exhibiting much more positive views of immigration.

By contrast, most measures of class or socioeconomic status are insignificant in most of these models. Income generally does not play an independent role. Education is sometimes significant, and when it is, Californians who are more well educated tend to hold more favorable views of immigrants. But even here the predicated gap is typically less than half the size of the racial or religious divides. Once again, gender appears to matter little.[18]

How California Compares to the Rest of the Country on Immigration

We have only looked at California in isolation to this point. But when considering views in the state, it is instructive to compare California to the rest of the nation. Is California more welcoming to immigrants than the rest of the nation? And is any difference between California and the country driven by factors we have looked at, or is California unique in some deeper sense when it comes to immigration?

The answer to the first question is clear. On almost every measure that we have examined, the state's residents hold significantly more welcoming views toward immigrants and significantly more generous policy preferences than the rest of the nation. Typically, the difference between California and the rest of the country is about 5–10 percentage points.

Californians express significantly warmer feelings toward both Latinos and undocumented immigrants. An overall feeling thermometer toward undocumented immigrants shows an 11-point gap between the state and the rest of the nation—a 50-degree average rating in California versus a 39-degree rating outside California. And that difference has existed for some time. The mean feeling thermometer scores for the rest of the United States (California excluded) are lower than the averages in figures 8.3 and 8.4 for every year in which the questions were asked.

California also tends to be substantially more liberal on immigration policy than the rest of the country. Californians are a lot less likely to favor reductions in the numbers of immigrants. Whereas only about a third of state residents want immigration reduced, fully 45% of respondents in the rest of the country support reducing immigration (Pew Research Center 2019). Nationwide, according to Pew Research Center data, 60% of the population opposes "substantially expanding the wall along the US border with Mexico." In California, almost three-quarters of the population (73%) oppose Trump's wall. Likewise, the share of Californians who favor an extended border wall (24%) is significantly smaller than the share of Americans who favor a wall (33%). Residents of California are also less likely to believe that immigrants take jobs away from Americans. Almost a third of Californians (30%) believe that immigrants are not at all likely to take away jobs from Americans. That figure is 23% for the rest of the states. About the same 10-point gap exists for a range of other questions on immigrants and immigration policy. By almost all measures, California is an increasingly and uniquely welcoming state.

Moreover, the shift toward more positive views toward immigrants appears to be happening in California at a faster pace than it is elsewhere. The trend lines that we saw in figures 8.3 and 8.4, which examined feelings toward the undocumented and feelings toward Hispanics, are visibly steeper than they are for the rest of the country. (Figures for the nation as a whole are not shown.) Regression analysis further reveals that the time trend in California is significantly more positive than it is for the rest of the nation on both questions.

Finally, at least some of the differences between California and the rest of the nation persist after we control for race and other demographics. And on rare occasion, differences between the state and the nation endure when we control for party identification and ideology. In some ways, California really is different and more welcoming.

But in some respects, California is not that unique. On a minority of immigration-related questions, we uncovered no significant differences between the state and the nation. Particularly on questions that asked about stereotypes of Latinos and a few much more specific policy debates, views in California mirrored views in the nation as a whole.

And on many questions that we looked at—very roughly about half of the questions—the significant difference between those inside and those outside California faded away after we controlled for race, nativity, and other demographic characteristics. On these questions, California is only different because the mix of people is different.

It is also difficult to know whether the more positive trend over time in California is due to a greater shift in views by individual Californians over time or is due to population changes in the state. In other words, we could be growing more positive relative to the rest of the nation because residents are getting to know and be more comfortable with immigrants or because we have more and more new residents who bring with them positive views of immigrants (e.g., more foreign born; more Hispanics; and more liberal, Democratic whites).

Lastly on this point, it is important to note that whites in California are not that different from whites in the rest of the nation when it comes to immigration. Once we control for basic demographic factors such as age, education, and income, white Californians are not statistically significantly different from other white Americans on most of the immigration questions we examine.[19] Living in the state doesn't seem to lead to a shift in white views. Once again, this suggests that California is different largely because it is a majority-minority state. Put another way, simply being Californian or living in California doesn't appear to make its residents different.

The Impact of Public Opinion on Policy in the State

California's increasingly welcoming attitudes on immigration are important not simply because they reflect a softening of views on immigration but even more so because they have impacted policy in the state. The trends that we see in attitudes over time closely mirror changes in policy that the state has experienced over time.[20]

California's policy response to immigration has changed dramatically over the last few decades. It is perhaps not surprising that as one of the first states to face large-scale immigration in the twentieth century, California was one of the first states to actively target undocumented immigrants. With Proposition 187, the "Save Our State" initiative of 1994, the voters of California passed a measure that sought to exclude undocumented immigrants from access to a range of public services. Many other states followed suit. But California was the first. Soon thereafter, the state also passed Prop. 227, a measure that outlawed bilingual education.

As the issue of immigration became more and more central, state policy shifted more and more to the right, not only on measures explicitly about immigration but also on a host of other policy areas where the immigrant population could be beneficiaries. During this period, California fell from among the top half of all states in per-pupil education funding in 1980, when whites represented the overwhelming majority of schoolchildren, to near the bottom (forty-fourth place) in 2009, when Latinos were the single largest racial/ethnic group among school-age children (California Budget Project 2010). Likewise, corrections funding more than tripled as a proportion of the budget from only about 2.9% in 1980 to well over 10% in 2005 (California Budget Project 2012). Driving this growth in prison spending was a series of stricter sentencing laws such as California's famous 1994 "Three Strikes Law," which imposed mandatory life sentences for all three-time felons.

But as the state has become more diverse, as attitudes on immigration have shifted, and perhaps not coincidentally as the Democratic Party has amassed more and more power in the state, policy has once again shifted back to the left. With the active support of Latinos, who now account for 38% of the population, and with the strong backing of Latino legislators, who now hold 23% of the seats in the state legislature, a series of pro-immigrant measures has passed the legislature. This includes measures offering undocumented immigrants in-state tuition, driver's licenses, and the opportunity to practice law (see Chapter 3). Education and corrections funding is also now slowly following suit. In the last few years, state education funding has already seen a slight but noticeable uptick. With voters passing Prop. 30, a tax measure that is expected to raise billions for K–12 education, the state is likely to see even more growth in education spending. On the other end of the spectrum, corrections funding has dropped markedly, and the state has initiated a number of steps to gain early release of prisoners. Further, it has shifted resources from imprisonment to rehabilitation. As many have noted, over the last three decades, California has transformed itself from a leader in anti-immigrant policymaking to a leader in providing creative, forward-thinking policies on immigration and an array of other important policy areas (California Immigrant Center 2018).[21] A range of different factors has contributed to these policy changes in California, but the increasingly positive views of California's residents on the topic of immigration have certainly made a difference. And they could make a difference in the future as well. Given that there is little reason to think that the trend toward greater acceptance of immigration has ended, there may also be little reason to expect policy not to continue to shift to the left.

It is interesting to speculate about whether the rest of the nation will follow the same path as California: an anti-immigrant backlash followed by a shift to more welcoming views and policies. If demographics are destiny, there is reason to believe that it could. The anti-immigrant backlash that occurred first in California has clearly already spread to the rest of the country. One might then predict that as the country becomes more diverse and moves toward a majority-minority nation, it too will shift markedly to the left on immigration.

Notes

1. As a more narrowly focused item, the March 2016 USC Dornsife/*Los Angeles Times* poll asked Californians whether they viewed the issue of "illegal immigration" as a "crisis, a major problem but not a crisis, a minor problem, or not a problem at all." To this question, 23 percent saw unauthorized migration as a crisis; another 39 percent viewed it as a major problem; and only 37 percent saw it as either minor or no problem at all.

2. The "most important problem" facing the state or nation, or to the respondent personally is a time-tested means of measuring issue salience in opinion surveys. For a good critical discussion of this measure, see Wlezien (2005).

3. There are, however, some signs that immigration is growing in importance for state residents. A January 2018 PPIC survey found that Californians were more likely to see immigration as the most important issue for the governor and the legislature to work on this year than any other issue. Twenty percent of adults ranked immigration as the most pressing issue, more than double the number citing any other single issue.

4. Respondents are asked, specifically, "How would you rate Hispanics? Ratings between 50 degrees and 100 degrees mean that you feel favorable and warm toward the group. Ratings between 0 degrees and 50 degrees mean that you don't feel favorable toward the group and that you don't care too much for that group. You would rate the group at the 50 degree mark if you don't feel particularly warm or cold toward the group."

5. However, views toward Muslims (mean of 56 degrees) do roughly mirror views toward the undocumented. On the measurement reliability of feeling thermometer scales, see Lupton and Jacoby (2016) and Wilcox, Sigelman, and Cook (1989).

6. Respondents were instructed to "select all that apply" from a choice set that also included "grant legal status to all illegal immigrants who have held jobs and paid taxes for at least 3 years, and not been convicted of any felony crimes"; "increase the number of border patrols on the U.S.-Mexican border"; "grant legal status to people who were brought to the U.S. illegally as children, but who have graduated from a U.S. high school"; "fine U.S. businesses that hire illegal immigrants"; "admit no refugees from Syria"; "increase the number of visas for overseas workers to work in the U.S."; "identify and deport illegal immigrants"; "ban Muslims from immigrating to the U.S."; and "none of these." The "ban Muslims" response category (and three others listed here) was only asked of a randomly selected fifth of the sample.

7. On social desirability and survey response, see Tourangeau, Rips, and Rasinski (2000) and Blinder, Ford, and Ivarsflaten (2013); on the "principle-policy paradox" in public opinion, see Schuman et al. (1988).

8. They also mirror results of a 2016 ANES survey question that, using a different set of options, found that a clear majority (59 percent) favored a pathway to citizenship if the undocumented "meet certain requirements"; 14 percent would support citizenship "without penalties"; 12 percent would "[m]ake all unauthorized immigrants felons and send them back to their home country"; the remaining 15 percent favored a guestworker program.

9. Depending on the year, the terms used were *Chicanos, Hispanics, Hispanic-Americans*, or *Latinos*.

10. Note that the trend shows a dramatic dip in the mean affect in 1994, corresponding to the passage of Proposition 187. In most of the available measures, there is a turn against illegal immigrants during that time.

11. Interestingly, the change in Californians' views is evident not only in their growing levels of support but also in their diminishing uncertainty of opinion. When the PPIC time series on this item began, just over 10 percent of respondents were unsure what they thought about the impact of immigrants; this proportion has declined to 3 percent today. This suggests that fewer Californians hold weak or uncertain views on immigration.

12. Data from the Field Poll reveal a similar pattern. In that study, the share of Californians who favor a reduction in immigration fell from 62 percent in 1987 to 39 percent in 1998.

13. All polling figures here are from PPIC surveys.

14. However, due to low sample sizes for some religious categories, we forgo a detailed analysis of religion's role in immigration views.

15. At first glance, age looks like a major factor, but as we will see, much of the age gap in opinion is driven by race, ethnicity, and nativity. Younger Californians are much more likely than older Californians to be foreign born and not non-Hispanic white.

16. Of course, a relatively small share of the state population was unemployed at the time.

17. We also incorporate partisanship and political ideology in these regression models. Party identification and ideology are strongly correlated with immigration views, but it is likely that both partisanship and ideology are themselves a function of different demographic factors such as race and class, so we do not interpret their effects as causal. When party and ideology are excluded from the models, the impact of the different demographic factors tends to increase, but the overall importance of race and religion persist.

18. Alternative specifications of our regression model that take into account marital status, employment status, home ownership, and children in the household do not appreciably change the results. Moreover, these additional factors do not significantly contribute to the explanatory power of the models.

19. White Californians are different from whites around the country in one important way. The views of white Californians toward Hispanics as a group have improved significantly more rapidly over time since 1976 than have the views of other whites around the country. That could be because the views of individual whites have shifted more in California than elsewhere, or it could be because many whites with more negative views of immigrants have migrated out of the state over this period.

20. Of course, more liberal policymaking on immigration could also be leading to more support for those policies—especially if they are effective.

21. "The California Blueprint: Two Decades of Pro-Immigrant Transformation (2015)," http://www.caimmigrant.org/research-and-analysis/the-california-blueprint/.

Afterword: Immigrant Integration and the Law

Hiroshi Motomura

What is the role of law in the integration of immigrants in California? The question is central to this book. The path to an answer is daunting and easily lost if we confine ourselves to an intuitive focus on the laws that directly enhance or retard integration in different domains. Integration occurs in a context defined by law, but this means more than the laws directly bearing on integration. This afterword explores more broadly how law influences integration. My goal is to offer a framework for understanding this book as a whole. My argument is that assessing immigrant integration—including integration into state and local communities in California—requires close attention to federal engagement with immigration and immigrants, including but not limited to federal enforcement.

Part I sets the stage by explaining how the role of law in immigrant integration has four key dimensions. Part II explores the interaction between two of those dimensions—the federal versus the state and local—and the relationship between enforcement and integration. Building on Part II, Part III examines more closely why analysis of immigrant integration in California is incomplete unless it considers the effects of the federal climate on all immigrants. Federal context can dampen what state and local integration measures in California can achieve. Part IV closes by reflecting on what is at stake. Immigrant integration in California is not a path to *state* citizenship. Instead, the struggle is over the meaning of U.S. national citizenship, with immigrant integration as an arena for contesting how Californians can be *Americans* in waiting.

I. Four Dimensions of Immigrant Integration

The role of law in immigrant integration has four key dimensions. All are essential for a full understanding of any integration measure. Especially important is seeing how these four dimensions are nested in such a way that each dimension implicates the others. My goal in mapping this terrain is to suggest a framework for analysis, especially for seeing how various issues are connected to each other. I further want to suggest ways of understanding how different aspects of the large question of immigrant integration can benefit from empirical research, including the findings presented in this volume.

A. Levels of Government

The first dimension asks about the level of government that generates measures addressing immigrant integration. Measures can come from supranational, national, regional, and local governments. In this dimension, the competent level of government will depend on structural arrangements in any given country based on its constitution or a similar framework. In the European Union, for example, national law addresses many aspects of integration (such as naturalization), and EU law addresses other aspects (such as recognition of professional qualifications).

In the United States, immigration law—defined as questions of admission and expulsion from the national territory—has been a matter of exclusive federal regulation since the 1870s (Motomura 2014, 65–69). But immigrant integration is often a matter of state or local competence—for example, through public education. That said, federal law may directly influence integration, depending on the type of migrant and on the type of integration. For example, federal immigration law limits the ability of states and localities to integrate unauthorized migrants by offering public benefits (including access to education).[1]

B. Integration and Enforcement

A second dimension asks how the integration of immigrants is related to immigration law enforcement. In some situations, a government decision to foster or dampen the integration of immigrants is also, in practical terms, a decision to foster or dampen the enforcement of immigration law. This is especially true in the case of unauthorized migrants. For example, some state and local laws in the United States have tried to make it impossible for the unauthorized to find work or housing. The political origins of these measures suggest that they are best understood as state and local efforts to make life difficult enough for the unauthorized that they will leave or "self-deport," or not come to that state or locality in the first place. In this way, a law or policy that seems to retard integration is functionally a law or policy that promotes immigration enforcement.

In political contrast, California and some other states—and localities in California and elsewhere—have adopted measures that both foster the integration of some unauthorized migrants and neutralize federal immigration enforcement against these migrants. In some states, including California, unauthorized migrants are eligible for driver's licenses.[2] From one perspective, driver's licenses have the purpose and effect of integrating unauthorized noncitizens into local communities. Their ability to drive to work broadens their access to the labor market without constant fear of detection as unlicensed drivers. But more than integration is at stake. Traffic stops followed by charges of driving without a license often lead local police to arrest drivers who are unauthorized migrants, and then to detain and transfer them into federal immigration custody. In this context, a driver's license is not just an integration measure. It also insulates the unauthorized from immigration enforcement (Motomura 2018, 440–42, 466–67).

C. Types of Immigrants

A third dimension of the role of law brings out the distinctions among different groups of immigrants. Does an immigrant integration measure focus on unauthorized migrants, refugees, or lawful permanent residents? The example of driver's license eligibility has acquired particular political relevance as a way to foster or retard the integration of the unauthorized. But of course many laws and policies address the integration of other noncitizens. Examples include financial support for the resettlement of refugees, and government measures that make it easier or harder for lawful permanent residents to become citizens through naturalization. These are government decisions about the integration of refugees and permanent residents, respectively.

Within broad categories of noncitizens such as the unauthorized, refugees, and lawful permanent residents, it is also analytically helpful to consider subcategories. Unauthorized migrants who are students may be the beneficiaries of integration measures and favored in legal and political debates over integration, whereas manual laborers may be disfavored. Lawful permanent residents may be the beneficiaries of some integration measures, but only if they have lived in the United States in that status for a certain number of years.[3] Veterans of the U.S. military are often favored.[4] In all categories of noncitizens, those with criminal convictions are generally disfavored.

D. Government and Private Enterprise

A fourth dimension of the role of law in immigrant integration tries to acknowledge the relationship between government agencies and private enterprise. Some integration measures are entirely governmental in their implementation, but many call for the involvement of private enterprise. Here I use the term *private enterprise* to reach beyond for-profit entities to include any nongovernmental actor—nonprofit agencies, labor unions, political parties, and other nongovernmental organizations. Governments often rely on private-enterprise actors for a variety of purposes. Examples include outreach to affected communities to convey information or to attract participation in government programs; delivery of services that range from language instruction to application processing; and supply of information to government agencies to use in integration or enforcement initiatives.

The key question in this fourth dimension is whether and how a government enlists—or requires—the participation of a nongovernmental actor to reach its immigrant integration aims. Does the government outsource some immigrant integration functions? In turn, questions of delegation and accountability arise. One concern is that any delegation of authority or implementation to nongovernmental entities—just like delegation to different levels of government—increases risks of opaqueness, waste, ossification, and discrimination or other unlawful practices. The same questions arise when nongovernmental entities have a role in immigration enforcement functions that affect immigrant integration.

E. Applying the Four Dimensions

All four dimensions are essential to drawing an accurate picture of any integration measure. Consider, for example, a local law that requires private companies to use a government computer database to verify that each of its employees is in the country lawfully and has permission to work. Applying the four dimensions, this is a law that (1) is local; (2) resists workplace integration in order to enforce immigration law indirectly; (3) focuses on unauthorized migrants; and (4) requires private enterprise to cooperate with government enforcement. As a second example, the federal government might offer funding to community organizations that provide language instruction to permanent residents who wish to naturalize. This is a law that (1) is federal; (2) addresses integration but not enforcement; (3) focuses on lawful permanent residents; and (4) incentivizes but does not require private involvement in providing integrative services. A third example is a proposal to provide federal financial assistance for college tuition for recently arrived refugees. This is an integration measure that (1) is federal; (2) focuses on integration; (3) addresses refugees only; (4) mobilizes public and private institutions of higher education as sites of immigrant integration. In all three of these examples, overlooking any of the four dimensions would leave the analysis incomplete.

This framework allows comparison of a wide range of integration measures regardless of the arena for integration. These three examples range from the labor market, to language integration and naturalization, to education. I recognize that this framework is not a complete listing of all that matters for integration. Other, more basic factors shape the entire body of measures that foster or limit an immigrant's membership in a new society. These factors include values fundamental in the receiving society, including the social welfare system and concepts of national belonging and citizenship. Also pertinent are anxieties about immigrants, including national security, economics, language policy, religion, race, and more. Other factors include other aspects of the receiving society that shape its reception of immigrants. Relevant here may be an aging population as well as labor shortages or surpluses. My purpose in setting out these four dimensions in Part I is not to diminish the importance of any of these other factors, which are both crucial and fundamental. Rather, this framework should illuminate *how* these and other attributes of any society might influence immigrant integration. To pursue this inquiry, Part II looks more closely at the legal framework for immigrant integration in California.

II. Law and Immigrant Integration in California

A. Levels of Government and Immigrant Integration in California

This closer look at law and immigrant integration in California starts with my first dimension: levels of government. Laws in California that affect immigrants in some way may be adopted by government entities, such as the state of California, or smaller units such as counties, cities, and school districts. Sometimes these measures are formalized in texts such as statutes, municipal ordinances, and the like. Or these measures might be less formal, such as city or school district budget decisions that affect immigrants in one way or another; these measures still operate as forms of law.

All of these state and local laws operate under a basic constraint in U.S. constitutional law. Immigration law has been exclusively a federal domain since the last quarter of the nineteenth century, when federal immigration statutes emerged (Motomura 2014, 65–69). Since then, federal law has both displaced and precluded any state or local laws that might have regulated immigration. But this federal exclusivity is confined to "immigration law," traditionally defined as the law regulating the admission of noncitizens to the United States and the terms under which they may remain (Motomura 2006). For example, state and local governments may not operate inspection stations on the U.S. border or physically deport noncitizens.[5] This principle still leaves states and localities—including the state of California and numerous localities in California—ample room to affect immigrants and influence immigration, in spite of the apparent exclusivity of federal immigration regulation.

B. State and Local Laws and Integration

How have states and localities acted in the space left to them to address immigration and immigrants? Two types of measures have drawn attention in California over the past generation. Some touch on the integration of immigrants, and others on immigration law enforcement. As for integration, prominent are rules that enhance integration by expanding eligibility for public benefits. Shimkhada and Ponce address this topic earlier in this volume by analyzing health care coverage rules (see Chapter 4). Education is another key area. The U.S. Supreme Court established in its 1982 decision in *Plyler v. Doe* that the U.S. Constitution requires states and localities to enroll resident children in K–12 public schools regardless of their immigration status.[6] But this requirement does not address the aspects of K–12 public education that may directly affect immigrant integration, such as identifying and supporting immigrant children with limited English proficiency. In Chapter 7, Abrajano, García Bedolla, and Spangler elucidate this topic. *Plyler* also does not guarantee access to higher education, where state and local responses have varied widely across the United States (Aleinikoff et al. 2016, 503–10).

For its part, California has adopted several statewide measures that enhance unauthorized migrants' access to higher education (Motomura 2014,

145–50). These include AB 540, which allows unauthorized migrants and others, including a large number of U.S. citizens, to pay lower resident tuition rates based on prior attendance at a high school in California.[7] Another significant measure to enhance access—and thus to enhance integration—is the so-called California DREAM Act.[8] It makes students eligible for important forms of college and university financial aid that had been unavailable to them because they lack lawful immigration status.

Another arena for state and local measures to enhance integration is driver's licenses and identity documents (see Chapter 3 of this volume). Driver's licenses foster access to the job market, and employment is a crucial vehicle for integration, both economically and socially. Municipal ID cards allow unauthorized migrants to participate more fully in the regular economy—for example, by facilitating commercial transactions such as purchases of real and personal property, money transfers, and savings deposits (Motomura 2014, 84–85).

The integration-enhancing effects of health care, education, driver's licenses, and identity documents go beyond the practical effects of eliminating disadvantage in these arenas. Those practical effects are momentous, to be sure, but the additional effects of enhancing a sense of belonging and self-worth also deserve mention (Abrego 2008, 723–31). The integration fostered by a combination of these measures is often far greater than the sum of their parts.

C. Integration and State and Local Involvement in Immigration Enforcement

As I suggested in the introduction to this afterword and now explain more fully, integration into state and local communities takes place against the backdrop of immigration law enforcement. Although immigration enforcement—like immigration law itself—is officially a matter of federal law and implementation, states and localities play a substantial role. A state or local government that engages in immigration enforcement will undercut much of what it might seem to be attempting with other measures that appear to enhance integration. So it is important to examine state and local engagement with federal immigration enforcement—and then in Part III to examine federal immigration enforcement itself.

In California as elsewhere, state and local engagement with immigration enforcement has covered a wide political spectrum. At one end, some state and local measures supplement federal enforcement of laws affecting immigration and immigrants—for example, by helping identify noncitizens who may be removable from the United States, and by detaining them until federal personnel can take them into custody. This state and local cooperation is the express goal of federal programs that include Secure Communities and 287(g) agreements, named after the Immigration and Nationality Act provision that authorizes them (Aleinikoff et al. 2016, 1213–24).[9] The targets of these measures include not only the unauthorized but also lawful permanent residents who may have become removable due to certain criminal convictions.

What if state and local governments decide unilaterally—without federal government authorization or delegation—to involve themselves directly in immigration enforcement by applying the coercive power of government through arrest, detention, transfer of detainees to federal custody, and the like (Motomura 2014, 125–31)? The U.S. Supreme Court limited this unilateral state and local authority in its 2012 decision in *Arizona v. United States*—a ruling consistent with the idea that only the federal government may regulate the admission and expulsion of noncitizens.[10] Thus states and localities may play a role in direct immigration enforcement only when the federal government explicitly or implicitly delegates such power to them. This limit on state and local authority led the court in *Arizona* to invalidate three provisions of Arizona Senate Bill 1070 and to limit implementation of a fourth. A crucial constitutional defect was that this state law—authorizing and even requiring state and local personnel to arrest and detain suspected immigration law violators—was inconsistent with federal law, and thus invalid because the law was preempted.[11]

Arizona v. United States also significantly limited state and local authority to enforce immigration law *indirectly*, by curtailing access to jobs, housing, and schools (Motomura 2014, 125–31). The thinking behind such state or local cutoffs is that denying jobs, housing, and schools will eliminate the original incentives for the unauthorized to migrate to that state or locality, and convince those already there to leave. They would "self-deport," as former California governor Pete Wilson put it in voicing his support for Proposition 187, a state ballot initiative that California voters approved in 1994, as Colbern analyzes in historical context in Chapter 3.[12] It is important to note, however, that *Arizona v. United States* did not disturb state and local authority to comply with federal requests to assist in federal enforcement.

At the opposite end of the political spectrum, other state and local measures reflect a much more skeptical or oppositional attitude toward immigration enforcement. Sometimes given the collective descriptive label of "sanctuary," these laws and policies try to insulate immigrants from the effects of federal laws on immigration and immigrants (Motomura 2018, 437–39). Some state or local measures limit cooperation with federal immigration enforcement. They might, for example, curtail or eliminate any role in identifying, detaining, transferring noncitizens in state or local custody to federal immigration enforcement personnel, or providing information to any federal agency about the date or time of their anticipated release from custody.

States and localities have ample constitutional authority to decline any involvement in federal immigration enforcement. The basis for declining includes several well-established doctrines that are rooted in the Tenth Amendment to the U.S. Constitution. Prominent is the anti-commandeering doctrine, which bars the federal government from requiring state or local governments to perform tasks or engage in any activities on demand by the federal government.[13] Another Tenth Amendment doctrine bars the federal government from using its power over federal spending to "coerce" state or local activity by threatening to withhold unrelated federal funding.[14]

III. Immigrant Integration in California and Federal Climate

A. Integration, Enforcement, and Discretion

Full evaluation of state and local integration of immigrants must include two layers of analysis. The first is the more obvious—to examine laws and policies that directly allow or deny access to public benefits, higher education, driver's licenses, identity documents, and other vehicles of immigrant integration. The less obvious—but equally important—layer of analysis is the enforcement climate. In this context, noncitizens and their families living in the state or locality must make hard choices about whether or not to access those integration vehicles. The first key point is that just as state or local integration measures can offset or enhance immigration enforcement, so, too, can state or local approaches to immigration enforcement retard or enhance immigrant integration.

Put differently, it is vital to resist the temptation to distinguish sharply between enforcement and integration. Legal scholars often define state and local sanctuary measures as insulating noncitizens from federal immigration enforcement, while excluding from the definition any laws or policies that foster the integration of noncitizens (Lasch et al. 2018, 1707; Villazor and Gulasekaram 2018, 1217–18). But as I have explained, some states and localities have tried to enforce immigration law indirectly by cutting off unauthorized migrants' access to jobs, housing, and schools. These measures typically reflect a view that federal immigration enforcement is insufficient. It is just as accurate, however, to think of them as measures to retard integration of the unauthorized. On the other end of the political spectrum, measures to integrate the unauthorized are often also measures to help insulate the unauthorized from federal immigration enforcement. The driver's license is a good example, for reasons sketched in Part I-B.

The second layer of analysis is understanding that this relationship between enforcement and integration is not just a matter of *state and local* measures that enhance or retard immigrant integration in California by offsetting or enhancing immigration enforcement. Just as important—and probably more important—is the overall *federal* immigration enforcement climate. In considering how the federal climate may affect immigrant integration in any state, a core if regrettable feature of federal immigration law is the large gap between the law on the books and the law in action (Motomura 2014, 41–52). One reflection of this gap is the presence of over ten million unauthorized migrants in the United States, contributing their labor to the economy in a system that has long invited and tolerated their presence as an exploitable and disposable workforce, vulnerable to the fluctuating intensity of immigration law enforcement (Motomura 2014, 107–10). As a result, the immigration system depends heavily on the exercise of vast discretion, which determines which noncitizens are arrested and deported (Motomura 2014, 128–31).

In this setting, suppose a state or local government tries to foster the integration of unauthorized migrants by providing them with more access to health care than federal law alone would give them (see Chapter 4). That state or local effort will be undercut if the unauthorized are unwilling to come forward and access health care in any way that might call attention to themselves in a federal enforcement climate that they perceive to be unforgiving or even hostile. The same integration-retarding effects will emerge in an even broader way if unauthorized migrants are afraid to participate in the mainstream economy because they fear detection that could lead to their arrest and deportation. In this scenario, driver's licenses or municipal ID cards will not matter much, even if they might significantly enhance integration in a very different enforcement climate, in which the higher levels of the federal enforcement bureaucracy might better monitor and constrain the exercise of enforcement discretion by federal personnel in the field (Motomura 2014, 204–05).[15]

In general, then, many of the open questions about the effects of actual or proposed state or local measures addressing immigrant integration cannot be answered by examining only what they provide as written. What also matters is the federal enforcement climate in which noncitizens may decide to apply—or not apply—for benefits or programs, or for immigration and citizenship statuses for which they are likely eligible. It is well worth testing the hypothesis that the federal enforcement climate influences the effectiveness of state and local integration measures.

B. Beyond Federal Enforcement and the Unauthorized

So far, almost all of my analysis has focused on unauthorized migrants. For them, the influence of enforcement climate on integration and enforcement may be the most intuitive—though subject to empirical examination. But the same hypothesis applies to the integration of all immigrants. I have explained how the combined federal climate for immigration *enforcement* can undercut state and local integration measures. But recall from Part I-B that enforcement and integration are flip sides of each other. Thus the federal climate for immigrant *integration* can similarly undercut state and local integration measures.

Consider a federal regulation proposed by the Trump administration in late 2018, and published in final form in August 2019.[16] As this afterword goes to press, this regulation has not gone into effect, blocked by federal court orders pending full litigation.[17] If adopted, it would change the interpretation of the public charge ground of inadmissibility set out in the federal Immigration and Nationality Act. The new regulation would expand the types of public benefits that could lead to a finding of inadmissibility—and thus bar a noncitizen from lawful permanent resident status—that is, from acquiring a green card. The regulation would also explicitly expand the discretion of individual government employees to decide that a given noncitizen is "likely to become a public charge" and thus barred.[18] In turn, the mere threat of strict or harsh interpretation may deter noncitizens—and their U.S. citizen family members—from taking advantage of state and local programs intended to foster their integration (Chapter 4). This is an example of the federal climate for immigration and immigrants undercutting state and local integration efforts. Again, these effects are subject to empirical testing.

A distinct but related question is whether the *intent* of the public charge regulation is not just to expand the inadmissibility ground but to have the *threat* of an expanded inadmissibility ground deter noncitizens and their citizen family members from applying for benefits for which they are eligible. For example, this public charge regulation directly affects the H-1B temporary workers who are employed in significant numbers in California's technology sector. They may understand that any hopes of becoming lawful permanent residents are subject to the uncertainties of whether and how the new regulation is actually implemented. In this way, the federal climate may heavily influence the integration of immigrants in California. This is not just the federal climate for immigration enforcement against the unauthorized; it includes the broader federal climate that generated the public charge regulation as part of efforts to limit lawful immigration to the United States. The federal decision to shift the mission of the U.S. Citizenship and Immigration Services agency away from its traditional emphasis on securing "America's promise as a nation of immigrants" is a related sign of a major change in priorities beyond the enforcement sphere (Jordan 2018).

Similar to the new public charge regulation are the significant delays in the processing of naturalization applications. These delays may become a major factor retarding naturalization rates (Jordan 2019). The intensified effort in the current administration to undo the naturalization of citizens adds to this climate (Wessler 2018). Any deterrent effects on naturalizing may disproportionately affect Latino immigrants, who already have low naturalization rates, as Waldinger discusses earlier in this volume (Chapter 5). They may feel most vulnerable to fear—based on the president's own statements (Leonhardt and Philbrick 2018)—that naturalization will expose applicants to risks, delays, or indignities that are not worth any protections that citizenship might offer.

If this federal climate prompts skilled workers to seek better opportunities in other destination countries or in their countries of origin, the immigrant innovation in locales like Silicon Valley—analyzed by Novick and Skrentny in Chapter 6 of this volume—will decline and even disappear. At the same time, the consequences inside the United States of this interplay between integration in California and the federal climate are unclear. If support for immigrant integration is weak in other states, or if attitudes there are closer to the skepticism or hostility elsewhere in the United States, some immigrants may be inclined to stay in California in spite of rising housing costs, rather than move to other states in the patterns explained by Bean, Brown, and Pullés earlier in this volume (Chapter 2). Or at least they may be more inclined to stay in California than they would be if they perceived the federal climate as less threatening.

C. Pushing Back

At the state level, California has adopted several laws that try to insulate its residents from federal immigration law enforcement. SB 54, the California Values Act, limits cooperation by state and local law enforcement with federal immigration enforcement agencies.[19] AB 450 limits the ability of public and private employers in California to cooperate with federal immigration enforcement agencies that want to conduct enforcement activities in the workplace.[20] AB 103 requires the attorney general of California to inspect federal immigration detention facilities located in the state.[21] The federal government sued California to block the implementation of these three laws. A federal district judge declined to block the implementation of SB 54 or AB 103, but blocked parts of AB 450.[22] On appeal, the federal Court of Appeals for the Ninth Circuit largely affirmed, though with slightly different outcomes and somewhat different reasoning.[23] In roughly the same postelection time period, the federal government threatened several sizeable cities and counties in California—and in other states—with the loss of certain federal grant funding for law enforcement. These localities responded with lawsuits—so far successful—to block any federal efforts to withhold or recover federal funding.[24]

Looking beyond the details, these state and local measures that try to insulate immigrants from federal immigration law enforcement may join in practical effect with state and local laws and policies that foster some aspects of the integration of some immigrants. These state and local measures rest on a public opinion foundation, as Hajnal, Lee, and Pathakis discuss earlier in Chapter 8 of this volume. In these ways, California is pushing back against a federal climate that now intensifies enforcement and retards integration. But the larger point remains: that the federal climate for immigrants, in both enforcement and integration dimensions, establishes the context in which all state and local integration takes place.

IV. What Is at Stake?

Now I shift to another question—a basic one that emerges from exploring the tension between immigrant integration in California and a federal climate that now runs generally in the opposite direction, whether as intense immigration enforcement or as a less welcoming attitude toward immigrants regardless of their immigration status. This question probes what is at stake in this tension. Are states becoming places of belonging—that is, of a state citizenship that is an alternative to national citizenship? Or are states becoming places of struggle over the meaning of national citizenship? Are we making Californians as an alternative to Americans, or are we making Americans in California?

So far, the evidence suggests two closely related phenomena: a contest between two visions of national citizenship, and a view of Californians as *Americans* in waiting. As I have written elsewhere, one foundation for effective immigrant integration is the expectation that immigrants become citizens, especially treating immigrants as if they were citizens even before they are citizens (Motomura 2006, 115–50). This approach turns the expectation of full membership itself into an important vehicle for integration. People treated like full members will be more likely to act like full members. But is the integration fostered by the laws, policies, and practices described in this book the integration of immigrants as Californians, or as Americans?

To be sure, some of the rationales advanced in favor of immigrant integration in California—whether expressed as insulation from enforcement or as affirmative integration—speak of protecting California's prerogatives from federal encroachment. But even when relying on Tenth Amendment doctrines, these arguments are rooted in the U.S. Constitution. This national grounding is even more evident in arguments for integration and for insulation from enforcement that express concepts associated with the civil rights movement in the United States (Motomura 2018, 451–57). In this spirit, the heads of the California Senate and Assembly issued a joint statement on November 9, 2016, the day after the presidential election, that was decidedly not presecessionist. Instead, the statement invoked the founding national document in vowing that California "would lead the resistance to any effort that would shred our social fabric or our Constitution" (Greenberg 2019).

The integration of immigrants occurs in fundamentally local ways, in small-scale communities such as neighborhoods, schools, workplaces, and similar venues for interaction with others. But local integration does not mean that citizenship itself is local. In other words, local integration is consistent with national citizenship (Motomura 2014, 165–68). The values driving immigrant integration in California include due process, the rule of law, antidiscrimination, and antisubordination—all values that seek to affirm national constitutional values, not to separate from them. There is a certain symmetry here: It is fitting that the federal climate for immigrants, in both enforcement and integration dimensions, establishes the context in which all state and local integration takes place, because what is at stake in that state and local integration is whether immigrants are Americans in waiting.

Notes

I presented a draft version of Part I's analytical framework for the role of law in immigrant integration at the Conference on Immigrant Integration in Law and Policy: The Role of Public Entities and Private Enterprise, organized by the Transoceanic Integration Rules and Private Enterprises Network (TIGRE) and the Centre for Enterprise Liability at the University of Copenhagen, June 8, 2018. This published version benefited from many helpful suggestions and comments from the conference participants.

1. See 8 U.S.C. § 1621(d).
2. See Driver's Licenses: Eligibility: Required Documentation, AB 60, Chap. 524, 2013–2014 Leg., Reg. Sess. (Cal. 2013).
3. See 8 U.S.C. § 1612(a)(2)(A) (eligibility rules for certain federal public benefits).
4. See 8 U.S.C. § 1612(a)(2)(C) (eligibility rules for certain federal public benefits).
5. See, for example, *Chy Lung v. Freeman*, 92 U.S. 275, 279–81 (1876).
6. See *Plyler v. Doe*, 457 U.S. 202 (1982).
7. See Calif. Stats. 2001, c. 814 (A.B. 540), codified at Calif. Educ. Code § 68130.5.
8. See AB 130 (2011) and AB 131 (2011).
9. See Immigration and Nationality Act (INA) § 287(g), 8 U.S.C. § 1357(g).
10. 567 U.S. 387 (2012).
11. 567 U.S. at 400–15.
12. Proposition 187 would have made unauthorized migrants ineligible for many public benefits and services if a federal court had not blocked its implementation on constitutional grounds.
13. See *Murphy v. NCAA*, 138 S. Ct. 1461, 1478 (2018); *Printz v. United States*, 521 U.S. 898, 935 (1997); *New York v. United States*, 505 U.S. 144, 157 (1992).
14. See *Nat'l Fed'n of Indep. Bus. v. Sebelius*, 567 U.S. 519, 580 (2012); *South Dakota v. Dole*, 483 U.S. 203, 211–12 (1987).
15. Exec. Order No. 13,768, 82 Fed. Reg. 8,799 § 5 (Jan. 25, 2017); see also *City of Philadelphia v. Sessions*, 280 F.3d 579, 635 (E.D. Pa. 2017) (calling a clause in the

Executive Order "an apparent delegation of wildly discretionary power to ICE officers to determine their own enforcement protocol"); Memorandum from John Kelly, Sec., Dept. of Homeland Sec., to Kevin McAleenan et al., Acting Comm'r, U.S. Customs and Border Prot., Implementing the President's Border Security and Interior Enforcement Policies (Feb. 20, 2017).

16. See 84 Fed. Reg. 41,292 (Aug. 14, 2019); 83 Fed. Reg. 51,114 (Oct. 10, 2018).

17. See, for example, *New York v. United States Department of Homeland Security*, 408 F. Supp. 3d 334 (S.D.N.Y. 2019).

18. INA § 212(a)(4), 8 U.S.C § 1182(a)(4).

19. See Law Enforcement: Sharing Data, SB 54, 2017–2018 Leg., Reg. Sess. (Cal. 2017), codified at Cal. Gov't Code § 7284.6 (2018).

20. See Employment Regulation: Immigration Worksite Enforcement Actions, AB 450, 2017–2018 Leg., Reg. Sess. (Cal. 2017).

21. See AB 103, 2017–2018 Leg., Reg. Sess. (Cal. 2017), codified at Cal. Gov't Code § 12532.

22. See *United States v. California*, 314 F. Supp. 3d 1077 (E.D. Cal. 2018).

23. See *United States v. California*, 921 F.3d 865 (9th Cir. 2019).

24. See, for example, *City of Philadelphia v. Attorney General*, 916 F.3d 276 (3d Cir. 2019); *City & County of San Francisco v. Trump*, 897 F.3d 1225 (9th Cir. 2018); *City of Chicago v. Sessions*, 888 F.3d 272 (7th Cir. 2018).

References

Abedi, Jamal. 2004. "The No Child Left Behind Act and English Language Learners: Assessment and Accountability Issues." *Educational Researcher* 31 (1): 4–14.

———. 2008. "Classification System for English Language Learners: Issues and Recommendations." *Educational Measurement: Issues and Practice* 27 (3): 17–31.

Abedi, Jamal, and Patricia Gándara. 2006. "Performance of English Language Learners as a Subgroup in Large-Scale Assessment: Interaction of Research and Policy." *Educational Measurement: Issues and Practice* 25 (4): 36–46.

Abrajano, Marisa, and Zoltan Hajnal. 2015. *White Backlash: Immigration, Race, and American Politics*. Princeton, NJ: Princeton University Press.

Abrego, Leisy. 2008. "Legitimacy, Social Identity, and the Mobilization of Law: The Effects of Assembly Bill 540 on Undocumented Students in California." *Law & Social Inquiry* 33 (3): 709–34.

Acs, Zoltan J., Luc Anselin, and Attila Varga. 2002. "Patents and Innovation Counts as Measures of Regional Production of New Knowledge." *Research Policy* 31:1069–85.

Adams, Tracey L., and Erin I. Demaiter. 2010. "Knowledge Workers in the New Economy: Skill, Flexibility and Credentials." In *Aging and Working in the New Economy: Changing Career Structures in Small IT Firms*, edited by J. A. McMullin and V. W. Marshall, 119–43. Cheltenham, UK: Edward Elgar.

Addison, Tony. 2006. *The International Mobility of Cultural Talent*. WIDER Working Paper Series RP2006-108, World Institute for Development Economic Research (UNU-WIDER).

Akcigit, Ufuk, John Grigsby, and Tom Nicholas. 2017. "Immigration and the Rise of American Ingenuity." *American Economic Review* 107 (5): 327–31.

Alba, Richard. 2009. *Blurring the Color Line: The New Chance for a More Integrated America*. Cambridge, MA: Harvard University Press.

Alba, Richard, and Victor Nee. 2003. *Remaking the American Mainstream: Assimilation and Contemporary Immigration.* Cambridge, MA: Harvard University Press.

Aleinikoff, Alexander, David A. Martin, Hiroshi Motomura, Maryellen Fullerton, and Juliet P. Stumpf. 2016. *Immigration and Citizenship: Process and Policy.* Eagan, MN: West Academic.

Alexander, Michelle. 2012. *The New Jim Crow: Mass Incarceration in the Age of Colorblindness.* Revised ed. New York: New Press.

Allison, Paul D. 1995. *Survival Analysis Using SAS: A Practical Guide.* Cary, NC: SAS Institute.

Almond, Douglas, Hilary W. Hoynes, and Diane Whitmore Schanzenbach. 2011. "Inside the War on Poverty: The Impact of Food Stamps on Birth Outcomes." *Review of Economics and Statistics* 93 (2): 387–403.

Alvarez, Robert R. 1987. "A Profile of the Citizenship Process among Hispanics in the United States." *International Migration Review* 21 (2): 327–51.

American Immigration Council. 2017. *Foreign-Born STEM Workers in the United States.* https://www.americanimmigrationcouncil.org/sites/default/files/research/foreign-born_stem_workers_in_the_united_states_final.pdf.

Aptekar, Sofya. 2015. *The Road to Citizenship: What Naturalization Means for Immigrants and the United States.* New Brunswick, NJ: Rutgers University Press.

Artiga, Samantha, Rachel Garfield, and Anthony Damico. 2019. *Estimated Impacts of Final Public Charge Inadmissibility Rule on Immigrants and Medicaid Coverage.* San Francisco: Kaiser Family Foundation. https://www.kff.org/disparities-policy/issue-brief/estimated-impacts-of-final-public-charge-inadmissibility-rule-on-immigrants-and-medicaid-coverage/.

Atkinson, Robert D., Mark Muro, and Jacob Whiton. 2019. *The Case for Growth Centers: How to Spread Tech Innovation across America.* Washington, DC: Brookings.

Ayers, Alan, Kimberly Miller, Jongwon Park, Lawrence Schwartz, and Rich Antcliff. 2016. "The Hollywood Model: Leveraging the Capabilities of Freelance Talent to Advance Innovation and Reduce Risk." *Research-Technology Management* 59 (5): 27–37.

Baicker, Katherine, Sarah L. Taubman, Heidi L. Allen, Mira Bernstein, Jonathan H. Gruber, Joseph P. Newhouse, Eric C. Schneider, Bill J. Wright, Alan M. Zaslavsky, and Amy N. Finkelstein. 2013. "The Oregon Experiment—Effects of Medicaid on Clinical Outcomes." *New England Journal of Medicine* 368 (18): 1713–22. https://doi.org/10.1056/NEJMsa1212321.

Bailey, Alison L., and Kimberly R. Kelly. 2013. "Home Language Survey Practices in the Initial Identification of English Learners in the United States." *Educational Policy* 27 (5): 770–804. https://doi.org/10.1177/0895904811432137.

Baker, Bryan C. 2010. "Naturalization Rates among IRCA Immigrants: A 2009 Update." Fact Sheet, Department of Homeland Security, Office of Immigration Statistics.

Barley, Stephen A., and Gideon Kunda. 2006. *Gurus, Hired Guns, and Warm Bodies:*

Itinerant Experts in a Knowledge Economy. Princeton, NJ: Princeton University Press.

Batalova, Jeanne, Michael Fix, and Mark Greenberg. 2018. *Chilling Effects: The Expected Public Charge Rule and Its Impact on Legal Immigrant Families' Public Benefits Use.* Washington DC: Migration Policy Institute.

Bean, Frank D. 2016. "Ethnoracial Diversity: Toward a New American Narrative." *American Prospect.* https://prospect.org/civil-rights/ethnoracial-diversity-toward-new-american-narrative/.

———. 2019. "Why the United States Must Renew Opportunities to Achieve the American Dream in Order to Reform Immigration Policy." *Journal of Policy Analysis and Management* 39 (1): 274–79.

Bean, Frank D., James D. Bachmeier, and Susan K. Brown. 2014. *A Crucial Piece of the Puzzle: Demographic Change and Why Immigrants Are Needed to Fill America's Less-Skilled Labor Gap.* New York: Partnership for a New American Economy.

Bean, Frank D., Susan K. Brown, and James D. Bachmeier. 2015. *Parents without Papers: The Progress and Pitfalls of Mexican-American Integration.* New York: Russell Sage Foundation.

Bean, Frank D., Susan K. Brown, and Esther Castillo. 2015. "An Unexpected Legacy: The Positive Consequences of LBJ's Immigration-Policy Reforms." In *LBJ's Neglected Legacy: How Lyndon Johnson Reshaped Domestic Policy and Government,* edited by Robert H. Wilson, Norman J. Glickman, and Lawrence E. Lynn Jr., 124–52. Austin: University of Texas Press.

Bean, Frank D., Jennifer Lee, and James D. Bachmeier. 2013. "Immigration and the Color Line at the Beginning of the 21st Century." *Daedalus* 142 (3): 123–40.

Bean, Frank D., and Gillian Stevens. 2003. *America's Newcomers and the Dynamics of Diversity.* New York: Russell Sage Foundation.

Beaumont, Elizabeth. 2011. "Promoting Political Agency, Addressing Political Inequality: A Multilevel Model of Internal Political Efficacy." *Journal of Politics* 73 (1): 216–31. https://doi.org/10.1017/S0022381610000976.

Becerra, Xavier. 2018. "Comments on Proposed Rule: DHS Docket No. US-CIS-2010–0012; Inadmissibility on Public Charge Grounds," 83 Fed. Reg. 51114 (Oct. 10, 2018), RIN 1615-AA22. https://www.regulations.gov/document?D=USCIS-2010-0012-0001.

Beharie, Nisha, Micaela Mercado, and Mary McKay. 2017. "A Protective Association between SNAP Participation and Educational Outcomes among Children of Economically Strained Households." *Journal of Hunger & Environmental Nutrition* 12 (2): 181–92. https://doi.org/10.1080/19320248.2016.1227754.

Bender, Steven W. 2003. *Greasers and Gringos: Latinos, Law, and the American Imagination.* New York: NYU Press.

Benkler, Yochai. 2006. *The Wealth of Networks: How Social Production Transforms Markets and Freedom.* New Haven, CT: Yale University Press.

Benton, Richard A., and Lisa A. Keister. 2017. "The Lasting Effect of Intergenerational

Wealth Transfers: Human Capital, Family Formation, and Wealth." *Social Science Research* 68:1–14. https://doi.org/10.1016/j.ssresearch.2017.09.006.

Berkowitz, Seth A., Hilary K. Seligman, Joseph Rigdon, James B. Meigs, and Sanjay Basu. 2017. "Supplemental Nutrition Assistance Program (SNAP) Participation and Health Care Expenditures among Low-Income Adults." *JAMA Internal Medicine* 177 (11): 1642–49. https://doi.org/10.1001/jamainternmed.2017.4841.

Bertrand, Marianne, and Sendhil Mullainathan. 2004. "Are Emily and Greg More Employable Than Lakisha and Jamal? A Field Experiment on Labor Market Discrimination." *American Economic Review* 94 (4): 991–1013.

Betts, Julian R., and Magnus Lofstrom. 2000. "The Educational Attainment of Immigrants: Trends and Implications." In *Issues in the Economics of Immigration*, edited by George J. Borjas, 51–116. Chicago: University of Chicago Press.

Blau, Francine D., and Christopher Mackie, eds. 2017. *The Economic and Fiscal Consequences of Immigration*. Washington, DC: National Academies Press.

Bleakley, Hoyt, and Aimee Chin. 2004. "Language Skills and Earnings: Evidence from Childhood Immigrants." *Review of Economics and Statistics* 86 (2), 481–96.

———. 2008. "What Holds Back the Second Generation? The Intergenerational Transmission of Language Human Capital among Immigrants." *Journal of Human Resources* 43 (2): 267–98.

Blinder, Scott, Robert Ford, and Elisabeth Ivarsflaten. 2013. "The Better Angels of Our Nature: How the Antiprejudice Norm Affects Policy and Party Preferences in Great Britain and Germany." *American Journal of Political Science* 57:841–57.

Bloemraad, Irene. 2006. *Becoming a Citizen: Incorporating Immigrants and Refugees in the United States and Canada*. Berkeley: University of California Press.

———. 2017. "Does Citizenship Matter?" In *The Oxford Handbook of Citizenship*, edited by Ayelet Schachar, Rainer Bauböck, Irene Bloemraad, and Maarten Vink, 526–52. New York: Oxford University Press.

Bloemraad, Irene, and Els de Graauw. 2011. *Immigrant Integration and Policy in the United States: A Loosely Stitched Patchwork*. Institute for Research on Labor and Employment. http://escholarship.org/uc/item/2ncom8bm.pdf.

Bloemraad, Irene, and Christine Trost. 2008. "It's a Family Affair: Intergenerational Mobilization in the Spring 2006 Protests." American Behavioral Scientist 52 (4): 507–32. https://doi.org/10.1177/0002764208324604.

Borjas, George J. 2002. "Welfare Reform and Immigrant Participation in Welfare Programs." *International Migration Review* 36 (4): 1093–123.

———. 2011. "Poverty and Program Participation among Immigrant Children." *Future of Children* 21 (1): 247–66.

———. 2015. "The Slowdown in the Economic Assimilation of Immigrants: Aging and Cohort Effects Revisited Again." *Journal of Human Capital* 9 (4): 483–517.

Bottazzi, Laura, and Giovanni Peri. 2003. "Innovation and Spillovers in Regions: Evidence from European Patent Data." *European Economic Review* 47 (4): 687–710.

Bound, John, Gaurav Khanna, and Nicolas Morales. 2016. "Understanding the Economic Impact of the H-1B Program on the U.S." Sloan Foundation Economics

Research Paper No. 2883348. *SSRN* (October 15, 2016). https://dx.doi.org/10.2139/ssrn.2883348.

Brader, Ted, Nicholas Valentino, and Elizabeth Suhay. 2008. "What Triggers Public Opposition to Immigration? Anxiety, Group Cues, and Immigration Threat." *American Journal of Political Science* 52:959–78.

Brown, David W., Amanda E. Kowalski, and Ithai Z. Lurie. 2015. "Medicaid as an Investment in Children: What Is the Long-Term Impact on Tax Receipts?" Working Paper 20835. NBER Working Paper Series. Available at http://www.nber.org/papers/w20835.

Brown, Martin, and Peter Philips. 1986. "Competition, Racism, and Hiring Practices among California Manufacturers, 1860–1882." *Industrial and Labor Relations Review* 40 (1): 61–74. https://doi.org/10.2307/2523946.

Brubaker, Rogers. 1992. *Citizenship and Nationhood in France and Germany*. Vol. 21. Cambridge, MA: Harvard University Press.

Calavita, Kitty. 1983. "California's 'Employer Sanctions' Legislation: Now You See It, Now You Don't." *Politics & Society* 12 (2): 205–30. https://doi.org/10.1177/003232928301200204.

———. 1992. *Inside the State: The Bracero Program, Immigration, and the I.N.S.* New York: Routledge.

California Department of Education. 2007. *Technical Report for the California English Language Development Test (CELDT) 2006–07 Edition (Form F)*. cde.ca.gov/re/pr/documents/formftechreport.pdf.

California Department of Food and Agriculture. 2020. "California Agricultural Production Statistics." https://www.cdfa.ca.gov/Statistics/.

California Office of Historic Preservation. "Latinos in Twentieth Century California: National Register of Historic Places Context Statement." 2015. California Office of Historic Preservation. http://www.ohp.parks.ca.gov/pages/1054/files/latinosmpdf_illustrated.pdf.

Callahan, Rebecca M., and Chandra Muller. 2013. *Coming of Political Age: American Schools and the Civic Development of Immigrant Youth*. Russell Sage Foundation. www.jstor.org/stable/10.7758/9781610447942.

Campbell, Angus, Philip E. Converse, Warren E. Miller, and Donald E. Stokes. 1960. *The American Voter*. Hoboken, NJ: Wiley.

Camuti, Paul A. 2006. "Engineering the Future: Staying Competitive in the Global Economy." *Online Journal for Global Engineering Education* 1 (1): 1–6.

Cappelli, Peter. 2012. *Why Good People Can't Get Jobs: The Skills Gap and What Companies Can Do about It*. Philadelphia: Wharton Digital Press.

Case, Steve. 2016. *The Third Wave*. New York: Simon & Schuster.

Castillo, Richard Griswold del. 1992. *The Treaty of Guadalupe Hidalgo: A Legacy of Conflict*. Norman: University of Oklahoma Press.

Cha, Cathy. 2014. "Lessons for Philanthropy from the Success of California's Immigrant Rights Movement." *Responsive Philanthropy* Winter:1, 13–14. https://bjn9t2lhlni2dhd5hvym7llj-wpengine.netdna-ssl.com/wp-content/uploads/2015/01/RP_Winter14-15_Cha.pdf.

Chavez-Garcia, Miroslava. 2004. *Negotiating Conquest: Gender and Power in California, 1770s to 1880s*. Tucson: University of Arizona Press.

Chen, Ming Hsu. 2014. "Immigration and Cooperative Federalism: Toward a Doctrinal Framework." *University of Colorado Law Review* 85 (April): 1087–104.

Cheyre, Cristobal, Jon Kowalski, and Francisco M. Veloso. 2015. "Spinoffs and the Ascension of Silicon Valley." *Industrial and Corporate Change* 24 (4): 837–58.

Chishti, Muzaffar, and Stephen Yale-Loehr. 2016. *The Immigration Act of 1990: Unfinished Business a Quarter-Century Later*. Issue Brief. Washington, DC. Migration Policy Institute.

Chiswick, Barry R., and Paul W. Miller. 2009. "The International Transferability of Immigrants' Human Capital." *Economics of Education Review* 28 (2): 162–69.

Chiu, Ping. 1963. *Chinese Labor in California, 1850–1880: An Economic Study*. Madison: State Historical Society of Wisconsin for the Department of History, University of Wisconsin.

Chokshi, Dave A., Ji E. Chang, and Ross M. Wilson. 2016. "Health Reform and the Changing Safety Net in the United States." *New England Journal of Medicine* 375 (18): 1790–96. https://doi.org/10.1056/NEJMhpr1608578.

Chua, Amy. 2007. *Day of Empire: How Hyperpowers Rise to Global Dominance—and Why They Fall*. New York: Doubleday.

Clark, William A.V. 1998. *The California Cauldron: Immigration and the Fortunes of Local Communities*. New York: Guilford Press.

Cohen, Deborah. 2011. *Braceros: Migrant Citizens and Transnational Subjects in the Postwar United States and Mexico*. Chapel Hill: University of North Carolina Press.

Cohen, Michael S., and William L. Schpero. 2018. "Household Immigration Status Had Differential Impact on Medicaid Enrollment in Expansion and Nonexpansion States." *Health Affairs (Millwood)* 37 (3): 394–402. https://doi.org/10.1377/hlthaff.2017.0978.

Colbern, Allan. 2017. *Today's Runaway Slaves: Unauthorized Immigrants in a Federalist Framework*. PhD dissertation. Riverside: University of California.

Colbern, Allan, Melanie Amoroso-Pohl, and Courtney Gutiérrez. 2019. "Contextualizing Sanctuary Policy Development in the United States: Conceptual and Constitutional Underpinnings, 1979 to 2018." *Fordham Urban Law Journal* 46 (3): 489–547.

Colbern, Allan, and S. Karthick Ramakrishnan. 2016. "State Policies on Immigrant Integration: An Examination of Best Practices and Policy Diffusion." UCR School of Public Policy Working Paper Series, February 2016, 1–20.

———. 2018. "Citizens of California: How the Golden State Went from Worst to First on Immigrant Rights." *New Political Science* 40 (2): 353–67. https://doi.org/10.1080/07393148.2018.1449065.

———. 2020. *Citizenship Reimagined: A New Framework for State Rights in the United States*. Cambridge, MA: Cambridge University Press.

Coll, Kathleen. 2011. "Citizenship Acts and Immigrant Voting Rights Movements in

the US." *Citizenship Studies* 15 (8): 993–1009. https://doi.org/10.1080/13621025.2
011.627766.

Covered California. 2016."California's Proposal to Waive Affordable Care Act Requirements to Expand Access to Undocumented Individuals." August 5, 2016.
https://www.calhospital.org/sites/main/files/file-attachments/application_fi-
nal_draft__8-5-16.pdf.

Daniels, Roger. 1990. *Asian America: Chinese and Japanese in the United States since
1850*. Reprint ed. Seattle: University of Washington Press.

DeGenova, Nicholas. 2006. *Racial Transformations: Latinos and Asians Remaking the
United States*. Raleigh, NC: Duke University Press.

Delli Carpini, Michael X., and Scott Keeter. 1996. *What Americans Know about Politics and Why It Matters*. New Haven, NJ: Yale University Press.

Department of Health Care Services. 2015. *Full Scope Medi-Cal for All Children: Implementation Overview*. October 13, 2015. http://www.dhcs.ca.gov/services/medi-
cal/eligibility/Documents/SB75/ImplementationOverview.pdf.

Deverell, William. 2004. *Whitewashed Adobe: The Rise of Los Angeles and the Remaking of Its Mexican Past*. Berkeley: University of California Press.

Didion, Joan. 2003. *Where I Was From*. New York: Knopf.

Dietz, Miranda, Dave Graham-Squire, Tara Becker, Xiao Chen, Laurel Lucia, and Ken
Jacobs. 2016. *Preliminary CalSIM v 2.0 Regional Remaining Uninsured Projections*.
http://laborcenter.berkeley.edu/pdf/2016/Preliminary-CalSIM-20-Regional-Re-
maining-Uninsured-2017.pdf.

Dillon, Liam. 2018. "Experts Say California Needs to Build a Lot More Housing. But
the Public Disagrees." *Los Angeles Times*, October 21, 2018, B1, B4. https://www.
latimes.com/politics/la-pol-ca-residents-housing-polling-20181021-story.html.

Dreby, Joanna. 2015. "U.S. Immigration Policy and Family Separation: The Consequences for Children's Well-Being." *Social Science & Medicine* 132:245–51. https://
doi.org/10.1016/j.socscimed.2014.08.041.

Elias, Stella Burch. 2013. "The New Immigration Federalism." *Ohio State Law Journal*
74:703–52.

Entwisle, Doris R., and Karl L. Alexander. 1993. "Entry into School: The Beginning
School Transition and Educational Stratification in the United States." *Annual
Review of Sociology* 19:401–23.

Epstein, Ann S., Lawrence J. Schweinhart, Andrea DeBruin-Parecki, and Kenneth B.
Robin. 2004. *Preschool Assessment: A Guide to Developing a Balanced Approach*.
New Brunswick, NJ: National Institute for Early Education Research.

Esses, Victoria M., John F. Dovidio, Lynne M. Jackson, and Tamara L. Armstrong.
2001. "The Immigration Dilemma: The Role of Perceived Group Competition,
Ethnic Prejudice, and National Identity." *Social Issues* 57 (3): 389–412.

Faust, Drew Gilpin. 2015. "John Hope Franklin: Race and the Meaning of America."
New York Review of Books, December 17, 2015, 97–99.

Feliciano, Cynthia. 2006. *Unequal Origins: Immigrant Selection and the Education of
the Second Generation*. New York: LFB Scholarly Publishing.

Fine, Janice. 2006. *Worker Centers: Organizing Communities at the Edge of the Dream.* Ithaca, NY: Cornell University Press.

———. 2015. "Alternative Labour Protection Movements in the United States: Reshaping Industrial Relations?" *International Labour Review* 154 (1): 15–26. https://doi.org/10.1111/j.1564–913X.2015.00222.x.

Finkelstein, Amy, Sarah Taubman, Bill Wright, Mira Bernstein, Jonathan Gruber, Joseph P. Newhouse, Heidi Allen, and Katherine Baicker. 2012. "The Oregon Health Insurance Experiment: Evidence from the First Year." *Quarterly Journal of Economics* 127 (3): 1057–106.

Fiscal Policy Institute. 2018. *"Only Wealthy Immigrants Need Apply." How a Trump Rule's Chilling Effect Will Harm the U.S.* http://fiscalpolicy.org/wp-content/uploads/2018/10/US-Impact-of-Public-Charge.pdf.

Fisk, Catherine L., and Michael J. Wishnie. 2005. "The Story of *Hoffman Plastic Compounds v. NLRB*: Labor Rights without Remedies for Undocumented Immigrants." In *Labor Law Stories*, edited by Laura J. Cooper and Catherine L. Fisk, 399–438. New York: Foundation Press. Chapter available at https://scholarship.law.duke.edu/faculty_scholarship/1243.

FitzGerald, David, and David Cook-Martín. 2014. *Culling the Masses: The Democratic Origins of Racist Immigration Policy in the Americas.* Cambridge, MA: Harvard University Press.

Fix, Michael E., and Jeffrey S. Passel. 1999. *Trends in Noncitizens' and Citizens' Use of Public Benefits Following Welfare Reform, 1994–97.* Washington DC: Urban Institute.

———. 2002. *The Scope and Impact of Welfare Reform's Immigrant Provisions.* Washington DC: Urban Institute.

Flavin, Lila, Leah Zallman, Danny McCormick, and J. Wesley Boyd. 2018. "Medical Expenditures on and by Immigrant Populations in the United States: A Systematic Review." *International Journal of Health Services* 48 (4): 601–21. https://doi.org/10.1177/0020731418791963.

Fox, Cybelle. 2012. *Three Worlds of Relief: Race, Immigration, and the American Welfare State from the Progressive Era to the New Deal.* Princeton, NJ: Princeton University Press.

Fox, Liana. 2019. "The Supplementary Poverty Measure: 2018." *Current Population Reports* P60–268(rv), October 2019. Washington, DC: U.S. Department of Commerce and U.S. Bureau of the Census. https://www.census.gov/content/dam/Census/library/publications/2019/demo/p60-268.pdf.

———. 2016. "Unauthorized Welfare: The Origins of Immigrant Status Restrictions in American Social Policy." *Journal of American History* 102 (4): 1051–74.

Frank, Reanne, Ilana Redstone Akresh, and Bo Lu. 2010. "Latino Immigrants and the U.S. Racial Order: How and Where Do They Fit In?" *American Sociological Review* 75 (3): 378–401.

Frey, William H. 2018. *Diversity Explosion: How New Racial Demographics Are Remaking America.* Washington, DC: Brookings Institution Press.

Frymer, Paul. 2014. "'A Rush and a Push and the Land Is Ours': Territorial Expansion, Land Policy, and U.S. State Formation." *Perspectives on Politics* 12 (1): 119–44.

———. 2017. *Building an American Empire: The Era of Territorial and Political Expansion.* Princeton, NJ: Princeton University Press.

Fujiwara, Lynn. 2008. *Mothers without Citizenship: Asian Immigrant Families and the Consequences of Welfare Reform.* Minneapolis: University of Minnesota Press.

Galston, William. 2001. "Political Knowledge, Political Engagement, and Civic Education." *Annual Review of Political Science* 4:217–34.

García, María Cristina. 2006. *Seeking Refuge.* Berkeley: University of California Press.

García Bedolla, Lisa, and Rosaisela Rodríguez. 2011. *Classifying California's English Learners: Is the CELDT Too Blunt an Instrument?* Berkeley, CA: Center for Latino Policy Research. http://escholarship.org/uc/item/2m74v93d.

García-Pérez, Mónica. 2016. "Converging to American: Healthy Immigrant Effect in Children of Immigrants." *American Economic Review* 106 (5): 461–66. https://doi.org/10.1257/aer.p20161110.

Gerst, Kerstin, and Jeffrey A. Burr. 2011. "Welfare Use among Older Hispanic Immigrants: The Effect of State and Federal Policy." *Population Research and Policy Review* 30 (1): 129–50. https://doi.org/10.1007/s11113-010-9181-2.

Ghosh, Anirban, Anna Maria Mayda, and Francesc Ortega. 2015. "The Impact of Skilled Foreign Workers on Firms: An Investigation of Publicly Traded U.S. Firms." IZA Discussion Papers 8684, Institute of Labor Economics (IZA). Available at https://www.iza.org/publications/dp/8684/the-impact-of-skilled-foreign-workers-on-firms-an-investigation-of-publicly-traded-us-firms.

Gilbertson, Greta, and Audrey Singer. 2003. "The Emergence of Protective Citizenship in the USA: Naturalization among Dominican Immigrants in the Post-1996 Welfare Reform Era." *Ethnic and Racial Studies* 26 (1): 25–51.

Gilson, Ronald J. 1999. "The Legal Infrastructure of High Technology Industrial Districts: Silicon Valley, Route 128, and Covenants Not to Compete." *New York University Law Review* 74:575–629.

Gleeson, Shannon. 2012. *Conflicting Commitments: The Politics of Enforcing Immigrant Worker Rights in San Jose and Houston.* Ithaca, NY: Cornell University Press.

———. 2015. "Brokering Immigrant Worker Rights: An Examination of Local Immigration Control, Administrative Capacity and Civil Society." *Journal of Ethnic and Migration Studies* 41 (3): 470–92. https://doi.org/10.1080/1369183X.2014.921568.

Glick, Jennifer E., Laquitta Walker, and Luciana Luz. 2014. "Linguistic Isolation in the Home and Community: Protection or Risk for Young Children?" *Social Science Research* 42 (1): 140–54.

Goldenberg, Claude, and Sara Rutherford Quach. 2010. *The Arizona Home Language Survey: The Identification of Students for ELL Services.* Los Angeles: Civil Rights Project/Proyecto Derechos Civiles, UCLA.

Gómez, Laura E. 2007. *Manifest Destinies: The Making of the Mexican American Race.* New York: New York University Press.

Gonzalez-Barrera, Anna, and Jens Manuel Krogstad. 2018. "Naturalization Rate among U.S. Immigrants Up since 2005, with India among the Biggest Gainers." Pew Research Center. http://www.pewresearch.org/fact-tank/2018/01/18/naturalization-rate-among-u-s-immigrants-up-since-2005-with-india-among-the-biggest-gainers/.

González-López, Gloria. 2006. "Heterosexual Fronteras: Immigrant Mexicanos, Sexual Vulnerabilities, and Survival." *Sexuality Research & Social Policy* 3 (3): 67–81. https://doi.org/10.1525/srsp.2006.3.3.67.

Graauw, Els de. 2015. "Nonprofits and Cross-Organizational Collaborations to Promote Local Labor Rights Policies." *WorkingUSA* 18 (1): 103–26. https://doi.org/10.1111/wusa.12155.

———. 2016. *Making Immigrant Rights Real: Nonprofits and the Politics of Integration in San Francisco*. Ithaca, NY: Cornell University Press.

Greenberg, Michael. 2019. "California: The State of Resistance." *New York Review of Books*, January 17, 2019. https://www.nybooks.com/articles/2019/01/17/california-the-state-of-resistance/.

Grewal, David Singh. 2008. *Network Power: The Social Dynamics of Globalization*. New Haven, CT: Yale University Press.

Gubernskaya, Zoya, Frank D. Bean, and Jennifer Van Hook. 2013. "(Un)Healthy Immigrant Citizens: Naturalization and Activity Limitations in Older Age." *Journal of Health and Social Behavior* 54 (4): 427–43. https://doi.org/10.1177/0022146513504760.

Gulasekaram, Pratheepan, and S. Karthick Ramakrishnan. 2015. *The New Immigration Federalism*. New York: Cambridge University Press.

Gulbas, Lauren E., Luis H. Zayas, Hyunwoo Yoon, Hannah Szlyk, Sergio Aguilar-Gaxiola, and Guillermina Natera. 2016. "Deportation Experiences and Depression among U.S. Citizen-Children with Undocumented Mexican Parents." *Child: Care, Health and Development* 42 (2): 220–30. https://doi.org/10.1111/cch.12307.

Gundersen, Craig, and James P. Ziliak. 2015. "Food Insecurity and Health Outcomes." *Health Affairs (Millwood)* 34 (11): 1830–39. https://doi.org/10.1377/hlthaff.2015.0645.

Hadden, Sally E. 2001. *Slave Patrols: Law and Violence in Virginia and the Carolinas*. Harvard Historical Studies 138. Cambridge, MA: Harvard University Press.

Hajnal, Zoltan, and Michael Rivera. 2014. "Immigration, Latinos, and White Partisan Politics: The New Democratic Defection." *American Journal of Political Science* 58:773–89.

Hall, Eleanor, and Norma Graciela Cuellar. 2016. "Immigrant Health in the United States: A Trajectory toward Change." *Journal of Transcultural Nursing* 27 (6): 611–26. https://doi.org/10.1177/1043659616672534.

Hamad, Rita, and David H. Rehkopf. 2016. "Poverty and Child Development: A Longitudinal Study of the Impact of the Earned Income Tax Credit." *American Journal of Epidemiology* 183 (9): 775–84. https://doi.org/10.1093/aje/kwv317.

Hamad, Rita, David H. Rehkopf, Kai Y. Kuan, and Mark R. Cullen. 2016. "Predicting Later Life Health Status and Mortality Using State-Level Socioeconomic Characteristics in Early Life." *SSM Population Health* 2:269–76. https://doi.org/10.1016/j.ssmph.2016.04.005.

Hao, Lingxin, and Melissa Bonstead-Bruns. 1998. "Parent-Child Differences in Educational Expectations and the Academic Achievement of Immigrant and Native Students." *Sociology of Education* 71 (3): 175–98.

Haubert, Jeannie, and Elizabeth Fussell. 2006. "Explaining Pro-Immigrant Sentiment in the U.S.: Social Class, Cosmopolitanism, and Perceptions of Immigrants." *International Migration Review* 40 (3): 489–507.

Hayduk, Ron. 2012. *Democracy for All: Restoring Immigrant Voting Rights in the U.S.* New York: Routledge.

Hayes, Joseph, and Laura Hill. 2017. "Undocumented Immigrants in California." Public Policy Institute of California. http://www.ppic.org/publication/undocumented-immigrants-in-california/.

Hayes-Bautista, David E., and Gregory Rodriguez. 1996. "A Tale of Two Migrations, One White, One Brown." *Los Angeles Times*, March 17, 1996. https://www.latimes.com/archives/la-xpm-1996-03-17-op-47974-story.html.

Herring, Cedric. 2009. "Does Diversity Pay? Race, Gender, and the Business Case for Diversity." *American Sociological Review* 74 (2): 208–24.

Hersch, Joni. 2008. "Profiling the New Immigrant Worker: The Effects of Skin Color and Height." *Journal of Labor Economics* 26 (2): 345–86.

———. 2011. "The Persistence of Skin Color Discrimination for Immigrants." *Social Science Research* 40 (5): 1337–49.

Hersch, Matthew H. 2015. *Equitable Growth and Southern California's Aerospace Industry.* Washington, DC: Washington Center for Equitable Growth. https://equitablegrowth.org/research-paper/equitable-growth-and-southern-californias-aerospace-industry/?longform=true.

Hessick, Carissa Byrne, and Gabriel J. Chin, eds. 2014. *Strange Neighbors: The Role of States in Immigration Policy.* New York: NYU Press.

Higginbotham, Stacy. 2015. "Rambus Switches from Licensing to Making Chips (Sort Of)." *Fortune*, August 17, 2015. https://fortune.com/2015/08/17/rambus-switches-model/.

Hinojosa-Ojeda, Raúl. 2012. "The Economic Benefits of Comprehensive Immigration Reform." *Cato Journal* 32 (1): 175–200.

Hira, Ron. 2010. "Bridge to Immigration or Cheap Temporary Labor?" Economic Policy Institute. *EPI Briefing Paper* 257:1–17.

Hoffman, Abraham. 1974. *Unwanted Mexican Americans in the Great Depression: Repatriation Pressures, 1929–1939.* Tucson: University of Arizona Press.

Hoynes, Hilary, Diane Whitmore Schanzenbach, and Douglas Almond. 2012. "Long-Run Impacts of Childhood Access to the Safety Net." *American Economic Review* 106 (4): 903–34.

Humphries, Melissa, Chandra Muller, and Kathryn S. Schiller. 2013. "The Political Socialization of Adolescent Children of Immigrants." *Social Science Quarterly* 94 (5): 1261–82.

Hunt, Jennifer. 2011. "Which Immigrants Are Most Innovative and Entrepreneurial? Distinctions by Entry Visa." *Journal of Labor Economics* 29 (3): 417–57.

———. 2015. "Are Immigrants the Most Skilled US Computer and Engineering Workers?" *Journal of Labor Economics* 33 (S1): S39–S77.

Hunt, Jennifer, and Marjolaine Gauthier-Loiselle. 2010. "How Much Does Immigration Boost Innovation?" *American Economic Journal: Macroeconomics* 2 (2): 31–56.

Hunt, Jennifer, and Bin Xie. 2019. "How Restricted Is the Job Mobility of Skilled Temporary Work Visa Holders?" *Journal of Policy Analysis and Management* 38 (1): 41–64.

Iceland, John, and Melissa Scopilliti. 2008. "Immigrant Residential Segregation in U.S. Metropolitan Areas, 1990–2000." *Demography* 45 (1): 79–94.

International Monetary Fund. 2019. *World Economic Outlook* (October 2019). https://www.imf.org/external/datamapper/datasets/WEO.

Jacobs, Ken, and Laurel Lucia. 2018. "Universal Health Care: Lessons from San Francisco." *Health Affairs (Millwood)* 37 (9): 1375–382. https://doi.org/10.1377/hlthaff.2018.0432.

Jacobson, Robin Dale. 2008. *The New Nativism: Proposition 187 and the Debate over Immigration.* Minneapolis: University of Minnesota Press.

Jennings, M. Kent, and Richard C. Niemi. 1968. "The Transmission of Political Values from Parent to Child." *American Political Science Review* 62 (1): 169–84.

Jennings, M. Kent, Laura Stoker, and Jake Bowers. 2009. "Politics across Generations: Family Transmission Reexamined." *Journal of Politics* 71 (3): 782–99.

Johnson, Hans. 2017. "California Is Still Golden for College Graduates." Public Policy Institute of California. Blog post, June 20, 2017. https://www.ppic.org/blog/california-still-golden-college-graduates/.

Johnson, Hans, and Sergio Sanchez. n.d. "Just the Facts: Immigrants in California." San Francisco: Public Policy Institute of California. http://www.ppic.org/publication/immigrants-in-california/.

Johnston, Allison, and Ann Morse. 2013. "2012 Immigration-Related Laws and Resolutions in the States." National Conference of State Legislatures. https://www.ncsl.org/research/immigration/2012-immigration-related-laws-jan-december-2012.aspx.

Jones, Benjamin F. 2009. "The Burden of Knowledge and the 'Death of the Renaissance Man': Is Innovation Getting Harder?" *Review of Economic Studies* 76 (1): 283–317.

Joo, Myungkook, and Jeounghee Kim. 2013. "Net Effects of Poverty on Welfare Use and Dependency among Children by Family Immigration and Citizenship Statuses." *Children and Youth Services Review* 35 (9): 1556–65. https://doi.org/10.1016/j.childyouth.2013.06.011.

Jordan, Miriam. 2018. "Is America a 'Nation of Immigrants'? Immigration Agency Says No." *New York Times,* February 22, 2018. https://www.nytimes.com/2018/02/22/us/uscis-nation-of-immigrants.html.

————. 2019. "Wait Times for Citizenship Have Doubled in the Last Two Years." *New York Times*, February 21, 2019. https://www.nytimes.com/2019/02/21/us/immigrant-citizenship-naturalization.html.

Junn, Jane. 2004. "Diversity, Immigration, and the Politics of Civic Education." *PS: Political Science & Politics* 37 (2): 253–55.

Kanazawa, Mark. 2005. "Immigration, Exclusion, and Taxation: Anti-Chinese Legislation in Gold Rush California." *Journal of Economic History* 65 (3): 779–805.

Kandula, Namratha R., Colleen M. Grogan, Paul J. Rathouz, and Diane S. Lauderdale. 2004. "The Unintended Impact of Welfare Reform on the Medicaid Enrollment of Eligible Immigrants." *Health Services Research* 39 (5): 1509–26. https://doi.org/10.1111/j.1475–6773.2004.00301.x.

Kang, Hannah S., Eileen Haddad, Chuansheng Chen, and Ellen Greenberger. 2014. "Limited English Proficiency and Socio-Emotional Well-Being among Asian and Hispanic Children from Immigrant Families." *Early Education and Development* 25 (6): 915–31.

Kao, Grace, and Marta Tienda. 1995. "Optimism and Achievement: The Educational Performance of Immigrant Youth." *Social Science Quarterly* 76 (1): 1–19.

Kasinitz, Philip, John H. Mollenkopf, Mary C. Waters, and Jennifer Holdaway. 2008. *Inheriting the City: The Children of Immigrants Come of Age.* New York and Cambridge, MA: Russell Sage Foundation and Harvard University Press.

Katz, Michael B. 1996. *In the Shadow of the Poorhouse: A Social History of Welfare in America, Tenth Anniversary Edition.* 2nd ed. New York: Basic Books.

————. 2002. *The Price of Citizenship: Redefining the American Welfare State.* New York: Holt Paperbacks.

————. 2013. *The Undeserving Poor: America's Enduring Confrontation with Poverty.* 2nd ed. Oxford, NY: Oxford University Press.

Katznelson, Ira. 2006. *When Affirmative Action Was White: An Untold History of Racial Inequality in Twentieth-Century America.* New York: Norton.

Keister, Lisa A., and Brian Aronson. 2017. "Immigrants in the One Percent: The National Origin of Top Wealth Owners." *PLoS One* 12 (2): e0172876. https://doi.org/10.1371/journal.pone.0172876.

Keister, Lisa A., Jody Agius Vallejo, and E. Paige Borelli. 2014. "Mexican American Mobility: Early Life Processes and Adult Wealth Ownership." *Social Forces* 93 (3): 1015–46.

Kelley, A. Taylor, and Renuka Tipirneni. 2018. "Care for Undocumented Immigrants—Rethinking State Flexibility in Medicaid Waivers." *New England Journal of Medicine* 378 (18): 1661–63. https://doi.org/10.1056/NEJMp1801871.

Kerr, Sari Pekkala, Christopher Parsons, William R. Kerr, and Ça lar Özden. 2016. "Global Talent Flows." *Journal of Economic Perspectives* 30 (4): 83–106.

Kerr, William R. 2010. "Breakthrough Inventions and Migrating Clusters of Innovation." *Journal of Urban Economics* 67 (1): 46–60.

————. 2019. *The Gift of Global Talent.* Stanford, CA: Stanford Business Books.

Kerr, William R., and William F. Lincoln. 2010. "The Supply Side of Innovation: H-1B

Visa Reforms and U.S. Ethnic Invention." *Journal of Labor Economics* 28 (3): 473–508.

Keyssar, Alexander. 2009. *The Right to Vote: The Contested History of Democracy in the United States.* New York: Basic Books.

Khouri, Andrew. 2018. "High Cost of Housing Drives Up Homeless Rates, UCLA Study Indicates." *Los Angeles Times,* June 13, 2018. www.latimes.com/business/la-fi-ucla-anderson-forecast-20180613-story.html.

Kieffer, Michael J. 2008. "Catching Up or Falling Behind? Initial English Proficiency, Concentrated Poverty, and the Reading Growth of Language Minority Learners in the United States." *Journal of Educational Psychology* 100 (4): 851–68.

King, Desmond. 2000. *Making Americans: Immigration, Race, and the Origins of the Diverse. Democracy.* Cambridge, MA: Harvard University Press.

Kini, Tara. 2005. "Sharing the Vote: Noncitizen Voting Rights in Local School Board Elections." *California Law Review* 93 (1): 271–321.

Ko, Michelle, Cary Sanders, Sarah de Guia, Riti Shimkhada, and Ninez A. Ponce. 2018. "Managing Diversity to Eliminate Disparities: A Framework for Health." *Health Affairs (Millwood)* 37 (9): 1383–93. https://doi.org/10.1377/hlthaff.2018.0438.

Ku, Leighton. 2019. "New Evidence Demonstrates That the Public Charge Rule Will Harm Immigrant Families and Others." *Health Affairs Blog,* October 9, 2019. https://www.healthaffairs.org/do/10.1377/hblog20191008.70483/full/.

Kuah, Adrian T. H. 2002. "Cluster Theory and Practice: Advantages for the Small Business Locating in a Vibrant Cluster." *Journal of Research in Marketing and Entrepreneurship* 4 (3): 206–28.

Laird, Jennifer, Gregory Kienzl, Matthew DeBell, and Chris Chapman. 2007. *Dropout Rates in the United States: 2005 Compendium Report.* NCES 2007-059. Washington DC: National Center for Education Statistics.

Lancet. 2019. "US Public Charge Rule: Pushing the Door Closed." *Lancet* 393 (10187): 2176. https://doi.org/10.1016/S0140-6736(19)31233-4.

Lasch, Christopher N., R. Linus Chan, Ingrid V. Eagly, Dina Francesca Haynes, Annie Lai, Elizabeth M. McCormick, and Juliet P. Stumpf. 2018. "Understanding 'Sanctuary Cities.'" *Boston College Law Review* 59 (5): 1703–74.

Law, Anna O. 2014. "Lunatics, Idiots, Paupers, and Negro Seamen—Immigration Federalism and the Early American State." *Studies in American Political Development* 28 (2): 107–28.

———. 2015. "The Historical Amnesia of Contemporary Immigration Federalism Debates." *Polity* 47 (3): 302–19.

Lee, Erika. 2003. *At America's Gates: Chinese Immigration during the Exclusion Era, 1882–1943.* Chapel Hill: University of North Carolina Press.

Lee, James. 2011. *U.S. Naturalizations: 2010.* Annual Flow Report. Washington: DHS Office of Immigration Statistics. http://www.dhs.gov/xlibrary/assets/statistics/publications/natz_fr_2010.pdf.

Lee, Jennifer, and Frank D. Bean. 2004. "America's Changing Color Lines: Immigration, Race/Ethnicity, and Multiracial Identification." *Annual Review of Sociology* 30:221–42.

———. 2010. *The Diversity Paradox: Immigration and the Color Line in 21st Century America*. New York: Russell Sage Foundation.

Lee, Jennifer, and Min Zhou. 2015. *The Asian American Achievement Paradox*. New York: Russell Sage Foundation.

Lee, Taeku, and Sunmin Kim. 2018. "The Mechanics of Immigration Polls—A Review." *Public Opinion Quarterly* 82 (1): 148–70.

Leonhardt, David, and Ian Prasad Philbrick. 2018. "Donald Trump's Racism: The Definitive List, Updated." *New York Times*, January 15, 2018. https://www.nytimes.com/interactive/2018/01/15/opinion/leonhardt-trump-racist.html.

Loh, Katherine, and Scott Richardson. 2004. "Foreign-Born Workers: Trends in Fatal Occupational Injuries, 1996–2001." *Monthly Labor Review* 127:42–53.

Lu, Yao, Neeraj Kaushal, Nicole Denier, and Julia Shu-Huah Wang. 2017. "Health of Newly Arrived Immigrants in Canada and the United States: Differential Selection on Health." *Health & Place* 48:1–10. https://doi.org/10.1016/j.healthplace.2017.08.011.

Lupton, Robert, and William Jacoby. 2016. "The Reliability of the ANES Feeling Thermometers." Presented at the Annual Meeting of the Southern Political Science Association. San Juan, Puerto Rico, January 7, 2016.

Luthra, Renee, Thomas Soehl, and Roger Waldinger. 2018. *Origins and Destinations: The Making of the Second Generation*. New York: Russell Sage Foundation.

Lyons, Elizabeth. 2017. "Team Production in International Labor Markets: Experimental Evidence from the Field." *American Economic Journal: Applied Economics* 9 (3): 70–104.

Mann, Ralph. 1982. *After the Gold Rush: Society in Grass Valley and Nevada City, California, 1849–1870*. Stanford, CA: Stanford University Press.

Markowitz, Sara, Kelli A. Komro, Melvin D. Livingston, Otto Lenhart, and Alexander C. Wagenaar. 2017. "Effects of State-Level Earned Income Tax Credit Laws in the U.S. on Maternal Health Behaviors and Infant Health Outcomes." *Social Science & Medicine* 194:67–75. https://doi.org/10.1016/j.socscimed.2017.10.016.

Marks, Paula Mitchell. 1998. *Precious Dust: The Saga of the Western Gold Rushes*. Lincoln: University of Nebraska Press.

Martin, Philip. 2009. *Importing Poverty? Immigration and the Changing Face of Rural America*. New Haven, CT: Yale University Press.

Marx, Matt. 2011. "The Firm Strikes Back: Non-Compete Agreements and the Mobility of Technical Professionals." *American Sociological Review* 76 (5): 695–712.

Massey, Douglas S., Jorge Durand, and Nolan J. Malone. 2003. *Beyond Smoke and Mirrors: Mexican Immigration in an Era of Economic Integration*. New York: Russell Sage Foundation.

McCabe, Brian E., Emma M. Mitchell, Rosa Maria Gonzalez-Guarda, Nilda Peragallo, and Victoria B. Mitrani. 2017. "Transnational Motherhood: Health of Hispanic

Mothers in the United States Who Are Separated from Children." *Journal of Transcultural Nursing* 28 (3): 243–50. https://doi.org/10.1177/1043659616644960.

McClain, Charles J. 1994. *In Search of Equality: The Chinese Struggle against Discrimination in Nineteenth-Century America*. Berkeley: University of California Press.

McMorrow, Stacey, Genevieve M. Kenney, Sharon K. Long, and Dana E. Goin. 2016. "Medicaid Expansions from 1997 to 2009 Increased Coverage and Improved Access and Mental Health Outcomes for Low-Income Parents." *Health Services Research* 51 (4): 1347–67. https://doi.org/10.1111/1475-6773.12432.

McWilliams, Carey, and Matt S. Meier. 1990. *North from Mexico: The Spanish-Speaking People of the United States*. Updated by Matt S. Meier, 2nd ed. New York: Praeger.

Melnick, Glenn A., Katya Fonkych, and Jack Zwanziger. 2018. "The California Competitive Model: How Has It Fared, and What's Next?" *Health Affairs (Millwood)* 37 (9): 1417–24. https://doi.org/10.1377/hlthaff.2018.0418.

Menchaca, Martha. 2010. *The Mexican Outsiders: A Community History of Marginalization and Discrimination in California*. Austin: University of Texas Press.

Migration Policy Institute. 2018. "State Immigration Data Profile: California." https://www.migrationpolicy.org/data/state-profiles/state/demographics/CA.

Milkman, Ruth, ed. 2000. *Organizing Immigrants: The Challenge for Unions in Contemporary California*. Ithaca, NY: Cornell University Press.

———. 2006. *LA Story: Immigrant Workers and the Future of the US Labor Movement*. New York: Russell Sage Foundation.

———. 2011. "Immigrant Workers, Precarious Work, and the US Labor Movement." *Globalizations* 8 (3): 361–72. https://doi.org/10.1080/14747731.2011.576857.

Miller, Stuart Creighton. 1969. *The Unwelcome Immigrant: The American Image of the Chinese, 1785–1882*. Berkeley: University of California Press.

Miller, Warren Edward, and J. Merrill Shanks. 1996. *The New American Voter*. Boston: Harvard University Press.

Molina, Natalia. 2014. *How Race Is Made in America: Immigration, Citizenship, and the Historical Power of Racial Scripts*. Berkeley: University of California Press.

Monroy, Douglas. 1981. "An Essay on Understanding the Work Experience of Mexicans in Southern California, 1900–1939." *Aztlan: A Journal of Chicano Studies* 12 (1): 59–74.

Moretti, Enrico. 2012. *The New Geography of Jobs*. Boston: Houghton Mifflin Harcourt.

———. 2019. "The Effect of High-Tech Clusters on the Productivity of Top Inventors." Working Paper 2620. Cambridge, MA: National Bureau of Economic Research.

Motomura, Hiroshi. 2006. *Americans in Waiting: The Lost Story of Immigration and Citizenship in the United States*. New York: Oxford University Press.

———. 2014. *Immigration Outside the Law*. New York: Oxford University Press.

———. 2018. "Arguing about Sanctuary." *UC Davis Law Review* 52:435–69.

Muennig, Peter A., Babak Mohit, Jinjing Wu, Haomiao Jia, and Zohn Rosen. 2016.

"Cost Effectiveness of the Earned Income Tax Credit as a Health Policy Investment." *American Journal of Preventive Medicine* 51 (6): 874–81. https://doi.org/10.1016/j.amepre.2016.07.001.

Muñoz-Blanco, Sara, Jessica C. Raisanen, Pamela K. Donohue, and Renee D. Boss. 2017. "Enhancing Pediatric Palliative Care for Latino Children and Their Families: A Review of the Literature and Recommendations for Research and Practice in the United States." *Children (Basel)* 5 (1). https://doi.org/10.3390/children5010002.

Myers, Dowell. 2007. *Immigrants and Boomers: Forging a New Social Contract for the Future of America*. New York: Russell Sage Foundation.

Nam, Yunju, and Hyo Jin Jung. 2008. "Welfare Reform and Older Immigrants: Food Stamp Program Participation and Food Insecurity." *Gerontologist* 48 (1): 42–50. https://doi.org/10.1093/geront/48.1.42.

National Economic Council. 2011. *A Strategy for American Innovation: Securing Our Economic Growth and Prosperity* (February 2011). Washington, DC: The White House.

National Low Income Housing Coalition. 2018. *Out of Reach 2018*. Washington, DC: National Low Income Housing Coalition. Available for download at https://reports.nlihc.org/oor/2018.

———. 2019. *Out of Reach 2019*. Washington, DC: National Low Income Housing Coalition. https://reports.nlihc.org/sites/default/files/oor/OOR_2019.pdf.

Neuburger, Bruce. 2013. *Lettuce Wars: Ten Years of Work and Struggle in the Fields of California*. New York: Monthly Review Press.

Neuman, Gerald L. 1993. "The Lost Century of American Immigration Law (1776–1875)." *Columbia Law Review* 93 (8): 1833–901.

———. 2010. *Strangers to the Constitution: Immigrants, Borders, and Fundamental Law*. Princeton, NJ: Princeton University Press.

New American Economy. 2016. *The Contributions of New Americans in California*. http://research.newamericaneconomy.org/wp-content/uploads/2017/02/nae-ca-report.pdf.

New York Immigration Coalition. 2017. *Blueprint for Immigrant New York*. http://www.thenyic.org/userfiles/file/nyic_Blueprint_for_ImmigrantNY_v5.pdf.

Newsom, Gavin. 2020. *California Budget 2020–21*. Sacramento: California Department of Finance. http://www.ebudget.ca.gov.

Ngai, Mae M. 2004. *Impossible Subjects: Illegal Aliens and the Making of Modern America*. Princeton, NJ: Princeton University Press.

Nissen, Bruce, Alejandro Angee, and Marc Weinstein. 2008. "Immigrant Construction Workers and Health and Safety: The South Florida Experience." *Labor Studies Journal* 33 (1): 48–62. https://doi.org/10.1177/0160449X07312075.

North, David S. 1987. "The Long Grey Welcome: A Study of the American Naturalization Program." *International Migration Review* 21 (2): 311–26.

Nunn, Ryan. 2016. "Non-Compete Contracts: Economic Effects and Policy Implications." U.S. Department of the Treasury, Office of Economic Policy.

Obama, Barack. 2016. "United States Health Care Reform: Progress to Date and Next Steps." *JAMA* 316 (5): 525–32. https://doi.org/10.1001/jama.2016.9797.

Ozgen, Ceren, Cornelius Peters, Annekatrin Niebuhr, Peter Nijkamp, and Jacques Poot. 2014. "Does Cultural Diversity of Migrant Employees Affect Innovation?" *International Migration Review* 48:S377–S416.

Page, Kathleen R., and Sarah Polk. 2017. "Chilling Effect? Post-Election Health Care Use by Undocumented and Mixed-Status Families." *New England Journal of Medicine* 376 (12): e20. https://doi.org/10.1056/NEJMp1700829.

Page, Scott E. 2007. *The Difference—How the Power of Diversity Creates Better Groups, Firms, Schools, and Societies.* Princeton, NJ: Princeton University Press.

Panzar, Javier. 2015. "It's Official: Latinos Now Outnumber Whites in California." *Los Angeles Times*, July 8, 2015. http://www.latimes.com/local/california/la-me-census-latinos-20150708-story.html.

Parker, Kunal M. 2015. *Making Foreigners: Immigration and Citizenship Law in America, 1600–2000.* New York: Cambridge University Press.

Parrotta, Pierpaolo, Dario Pozzoli, and Mariola Pytlikova. 2014. "The Nexus between Labor Diversity and Firm's Innovation." *Journal of Population Economics* 27 (2): 303–64.

Passel, Jeffrey S., and Paul Taylor. 2010. *Unauthorized Immigrants and Their U.S.-Born Children.* Pew Research Center Report, August 11, 2010. Washington, DC: Pew Research Center.

Pastor, Manuel. 2018. *State of Resistance: What California's Dizzying Descent and Remarkable Resurgence Mean for America's Future.* New York: New Press.

Pastor, Manuel, and Justin Scoggins. 2012 "Citizen Gain: The Economic Benefits of Naturalization for Immigrants and the Economy." Los Angeles: USC Center for the Study of Immigrant Integration.

Pawel, Miriam. 2010. *The Union of Their Dreams: Power, Hope, and Struggle in Cesar Chavez's Farm Worker Movement.* New York: Bloomsbury Press.

———. 2015. *The Crusades of Cesar Chavez: A Biography.* Reprint ed. New York: Bloomsbury Press.

Pérez, Efrén. 2016. *Unspoken: Implicit Attitudes and Political Thinking.* New York: Cambridge University Press.

Peri, Giovanni. 2007. *How Immigrants Affect California Employment and Wages.* Public Policy Institute of California. https://www.ppic.org/content/pubs/cacounts/CC_207GPCC.pdf.

———. 2019. "Should the U.S. Expand Immigration?" *Journal of Policy Analysis and Management* 39 (1): 266–81.

Perreira, Krista M, Robert Crosnoe, Karina Fortuny, Juan Pedroza, Kjersti Ulvestad, Christina Weiland, Hirokazu Yoshikawa, and Ajay Chaudry. 2012. "Barriers to Immigrants' Access to Health and Human Services Programs." ASPE Research Brief. Washington, DC: Office of the Assistant Secretary for Planning and Evaluation.

Perreira, Krista M., Kathleen Mullan Harris, and Dohoon Lee. 2006. "Making It in America: High School Completion by Immigrant and Native Youth." *Demography* 43 (3): 511–36.

Pew Research Center. 2016. "U.S. Unauthorized Immigration Population Estimates." http://www.pewhispanic.org/interactives/unauthorized-immigrants/.

———. 2019. "How Americans See Illegal Immigration, the Border Wall, and Political Compromise." https://www.pewresearch.org/fact-tank/2019/01/16/how-americans-see-illegal-immigration-the-border-wall-and-political-compromise/.

Plascencia, Luis F., Gary P. Freeman, and Mark Setzler. 2003. "The Decline of Barriers to Immigrant Economic and Political Rights in the American States: 1977–2001." *International Migration Review* 37 (1): 5–23.

Ponce, Ninez A., Susan D. Cochran, Vickie M. Mays, Jenny Chia, and E. Richard Brown. 2008. "Health Coverage of Low-Income Citizen and Noncitizen Wage Earners: Sources and Disparities." *Journal of Immigrant and Minority Health* 10 (2): 167–76. https://doi.org/10.1007/s10903–007–9059–5.

Ponce, Ninez A., Laurel Lucia, and Tia Shimada. 2018. "Proposed Changes to Immigraton Rules Could Cost California Jobs, Harm Public Health." https://healthpolicy.ucla.edu/publications/Documents/PDF/2018/publiccharge-factsheet-dec2018.pdf.

Ponce, Ninez A., Thu Quach, Ignatius Bau, Dong Suh, Riti Shimkhada, Dahai Yue, and Sherry Hirota. 2018. "Immigrants, US Values, and the Golden State." *Health Affairs Blog*, August 22, 2018. https://www.healthaffairs.org/do/10.1377/hblog20180817.59208/full/.

Pong, Suet-ling, and Lingxin Hao. 2007. "Neighborhood and School Factors in the School Performance of Immigrants' Children." *International Migration Review* 41 (1): 206–41.

Popkin, Samuel L., and Michael A. Dimock. 1999. "Political Knowledge and Citizen Competence." In *Citizen Competence and Democratic Institutions*, edited by Stephen L. Elkin and Karol Edward Soltan, 117–46. University Park: Pennsylvania State University Press.

Porter, Michael E. 1998. "Clusters and the New Economics of Competition." *Harvard Business Review* 76 (November-December): 77–90.

———. 2000. "Location, Competition, and Economic Development: Local Clusters in a Global Economy." *Economic Development Quarterly* 14 (1): 15–34.

Portes, Alejandro. 1977. "Labor Functions of Illegal Aliens." *Society* 14 (6): 31–37. https://doi.org/10.1007/BF02712515.

Portes, Alejandro, and Patricia Fernández-Kelly. 2008. "No Margin for Error: Educational and Occupational Achievement among Disadvantaged Children of Immigrants." *ANNALS of the American Academy of Political and Social Science* 620 (1): 12–36.

Portes, Alejandro, and Lingxin Hao. 2004. "The Schooling of Children of Immigrants: Contextual Effects on the Educational Attainment of the Second Generation." *PNAS* 101 (33): 11920–27.

Portes, Alejandro, and Erik Vickstrom. 2011. "Diversity, Social Capital, and Cohesion." *Annual Review of Sociology* 37:461–79.

Pourat, Nadereh, Steven P. Wallace, Max W. Hadler, and Ninez Ponce. 2014. "Assessing Health Care Services Used by California's Undocumented Immigrant Population in 2010." *Health Affairs (Millwood)* 33 (5): 840–7. https://doi.org/10.1377/hlthaff.2013.0615.

Purnell, Thomas, William Idsardi, and John Baugh 1999. "Perceptual and Phonetic Experiments on American English Dialect Identification." *Journal of Language and Social Psychology* 18 (1): 10–30.

Putnam, Robert D. 2007. "*E Pluribus Unum*: Diversity and Community in the Twenty-First Century: The 2006 Johan Skytte Prize Lecture." *Scandinavian Political Studies* 30 (2): 137–74.

Ramakrishnan, S. Karthick. 2005. *Democracy in Immigrant America.* Stanford, CA: Stanford University Press.

Ramakrishnan, S. Karthick, and Mark Baldassare. 2004. *The Ties That Bind: Changing Demographics and Civic Engagement in California.* San Francisco: Public Policy Institute of California.

Ramírez, Ricardo. 2013. *Mobilizing Opportunities: The Evolving Latino Electorate and the Future of American Politics.* Charlottesville: University of Virginia Press.

Raskin, Jamin B. 1993. "Legal Aliens, Local Citizens: The Historical, Constitutional and Theoretical Meanings of Alien Suffrage." *University of Pennsylvania Law Review* 141 (4): 1391–470. https://doi.org/10.2307/3312345.

Rehkopf, David H., Kate W. Strully, and William H. Dow. 2014. "The Short-Term Impacts of Earned Income Tax Credit Disbursement on Health." *International Journal of Epidemiology* 43 (6): 1884–94. https://doi.org/10.1093/ije/dyu172.

Reisler, Mark. 1976. *By the Sweat of Their Brow: Mexican Immigrant Labor in the United States, 1900–1940.* Westport, CT: Praeger.

Rhode, Paul Webb. 2001. *The Evolution of California Manufacturing.* San Francisco: Public Policy Institute of California. www.ppic.org/content/pubs/report/R_1001PRR.pdf.

Rodriguez, Cristina M. 2008. "The Significance of the Local in Immigration Regulation." *Michigan Law Review* 106 (4): 567–642.

Ruggles, Steven J., Sarah Flood, Katie Genadek, Ronald Goeken, Josiah Grover, Jose Pacas, and Matthew Sobek. 2019. IPUMS USA: Version 9.0. Minneapolis, MN: IPUMS, 2019. https://doi.org/10.18128/D010.V9.0.

Ruiz Soto, Ariel G., Sarah Hooker, and Jeanne Batalova. 2015. "States and Districts with the Highest Number and Share of English Language Learners." ELL Information and Fact Sheet Series. Washington, DC: Migration Policy Institute. http://www.migrationpolicy.org/research/states-and-districts-highest-number-and-share-english-language-learners.

Rumberger, Russell W., and Patricia Gándara. 2004. "Seeking Equity in the Education of California's English Learners." *Teachers College Record* 106 (10): 2032–56.

———. 2014. *Handbook of Research in Education Finance.* New York, NY: Routledge.

Ryan, Camille. 2013. *Language Use in the United States: 2011.* American Community Survey Reports. https://www2.census.gov/library/publications/2013/acs/acs-22/acs-22.pdf.

Rytina, Nancy. 2005. "Estimates of the Legal Permanent Resident Population and Population Eligible to Naturalize in 2003." Washington: Office of Immigration Statistics, U.S. Department of Homeland Security. https://www.dhs.gov/sites/default/files/publications/LPR%20Population%20Estimates Population%20Eligible%20to%20Naturalize%20in%202003.pdf.

———. 2011. "Estimates of the Legal Permanent Resident Population in 2010." Washington: Office of Immigration Statistics, Policy Directorate, U.S. Department of Homeland Security. https://www.dhs.gov/xlibrary/assets/statistics/publications/ois_lpr_pe_2010.pdf.

Salyer, Lucy E. 1995. *Laws Harsh as Tigers: Chinese Immigrants and the Shaping of Modern Immigration Law*. Chapel Hill: University of North Carolina Press.

Salzman, Hal. 2016. "The Impact of High-Skill Guestworker Programs and the STEM Workforce." Statement submitted to the Senate Committee on the Judiciary, U.S. Senate, February 25, 2016. https://doi.org/10.7282/T3474CXX.

Salzman, Hal, Daniel Kuehn, and B. Lindsay Lowell. 2013. "Guestworkers in the High-Skill U.S. Labor Market." Economic Policy Institute. *EPI Briefing Paper* 359:1–35.

Sassen, Saskia. 1996. *Losing Control? Sovereignty in an Age of Globalization*. New York: Columbia University Press.

Saxenian, AnnaLee. 1996. *Regional Advantage: Culture and Competition in Silicon Valley and Route 128*. Cambridge, MA: Harvard University Press.

———. 2002. *Local and Global Networks of Immigrant Professionals in Silicon Valley*. San Francisco: Public Policy Institute of California.

———. 2006. *The New Argonauts*. Cambridge, MA: Harvard University Press.

Saxton, Alexander. 1971. *The Indispensable Enemy: Labor and the Anti-Chinese Movement in California*. Berkeley: University of California Press.

Scellato, Giuseppe, and Paula Stephan. 2012. "Mobile Scientists and International Networks." NBER Working Paper No. 18613. Cambridge, MA: National Bureau of Economic Research.

Schevitz, Tanya. 2000. "California Minorities Become Majority." *SFGate*, August 30, 2000. https://www.sfgate.com/news/article/California-Minorities-Become-Majority-Census-3238512.php.

Schildkraut, Deborah J. 2010. *Americanism in the Twenty-First Century: Public Opinion in the Age of Immigration*. New York: Cambridge University Press.

Schmidt, Ronald, Sr. 2000. *Language Policy and Identity Politics in the United States*. Philadelphia: Temple University Press.

Schneider, Dorothee. 2001. "Naturalization and United States Citizenship in Two Periods of Mass Migration: 1894–1930, 1965–2000." *Journal of American Ethnic History* 21(1): 50–82.

Schuman, Howard, Charlotte Steeh, Lawrence D. Bobo, and Maria Krysan. 1998. *Racial Attitudes in America*. Rev. ed. Cambridge, MA: Harvard University Press.

Shih, Johanna. 2006. "Circumventing Discrimination: Gender and Ethnic Strategies in Silicon Valley." *Gender & Society* 20 (2): 177–206.

Siegel, Paul, Elizabeth Martin, and Rosalind Bruno. 2001. "Language Use and Linguistic Isolation: Historical Data and Methodological Issues" U.S. Census Bureau. https://www.census.gov/hhes/socdemo/language/data/census/li-final.pdf.

Silicon Valley Institute for Regional Studies. 2016. *2016 Silicon Valley Index*. San Jose, CA: Joint Venture Silicon Valley.

Smith, Stacey L. 2013. *Freedom's Frontier: California and the Struggle over Unfree Labor, Emancipation, and Reconstruction*. Chapel Hill: University of North Carolina Press.

Sommers, Benjamin D., Katherine Baicker, and Arnold M. Epstein. 2012. "Mortality and Access to Care among Adults after State Medicaid Expansions." *New England Journal of Medicine* 367 (11): 1025–34. https://doi.org/10.1056/NEJMsa1202099.

Spencer, Rachael A., and Kelli A. Komro. 2017. "Family Economic Security Policies and Child and Family Health." *Clinical Child and Family Psychology Review* 20 (1): 45–63. https://doi.org/10.1007/s10567-017-0225-6.

Starr, Kevin. 2005. *California: A History*. New York: Random House.

———. 2009a. *Embattled Dreams: California in War and Peace, 1940–1950: Americans and the California Dream*. New York: Oxford University Press.

———. 2009b. *Golden Dreams: California in an Age of Abundance, 1950–1963*. New York: Oxford University Press.

State of California Office of Historic Preservation, ed. 1988. *Five Views: An Ethnic Sites Survey of California*. Sacramento: State of California, the Resources Agency, Department of Parks and Recreation, Office of Historic Preservation.

Stiglitz, Joseph E. 2018. "The American Economy Is Rigged." *Scientific American*, October 18, 2018. https://www.scientificamerican.com/article/the-american-economy-is-rigged/.

Stoll, Michael A., and Janelle S. Wong. 2007. "Immigration and Civic Participation in a Multiracial and Multiethnic Context." *International Migration Review* 41 (4): 880–908.

Stringer, Scott M. 2016. "Opening the Golden Door: Lowering the Cost of Citizenship in the Immigrant Capital of the World." New York: Office of the New York City Comptroller, Bureau of Policy and Research. https://comptroller.nyc.gov/wp-content/uploads/documents/Citizenship_Report.pdf.

Takaki, Ronald. 1998. *Strangers from a Different Shore: A History of Asian Americans, Updated and Revised Edition*. Boston: Little, Brown.

Teke, John, and Waleed Navarro. 2018. "Nonimmigrant Admissions and Estimated Nonimmigrant Individuals: 2016." Fact Sheet, Office of Immigration Statistics, U.S. Department of Homeland Security. https://www.dhs.gov/sites/default/files/publications/Nonimmigrant%20Admissions%20and%20Estimated%20Nonimmigrant%20Individuals%20Fact%20Sheet%202016.pdf.

Terriquez, Veronica. 2012. "Civic Inequalities? Immigrant Incorporation and Latino Mothers' Participation in Their Children's Schools." *Sociological Perspectives* 55 (4): 663–82.

Tichenor, Daniel. 2002. *Dividing Lines: The Politics of Immigration Control in America*. Princeton Studies in American Politics. Princeton, NJ: Princeton University Press.

Tichenor, Daniel, and Alexandra Filindra. 2012. "Raising Arizona v. United States: Historical Patterns of American Immigration Federalism." *Lewis & Clark Law Review* 16:1215–47.

Torres, Jacqueline M., and Maria-Elena D. Young. 2016. "A Life-Course Perspective on Legal Status Stratification and Health." *SSM—Population Health* 2:141–48. http://dx.doi.org/10.1016/j.ssmph.2016.02.011.

Tourangeau, Roger, Lance J. Rips, and Kenneth Rasinski. 2000. *The Psychology of Survey Response*. Cambridge, UK: Cambridge University Press.

Toussaint-Comeau, Maude, and Sherrie L.W. Rhine. 2004. "The Relationship between Hispanic Residential Location and Homeownership." *Economic Perspectives* 28 (3): 2–12.

Tseng, Vivian. 2004. "Family Interdependence and Academic Adjustment in College: Youth from Immigrant and U.S.-Born Families." *Child Development* 75 (3): 966–83.

U.S. Bureau of Economic Analysis. 2019. *Gross Domestic Product (GDP) by State*. https://www.bea.gov/data/gdp/gdp-state.

U.S. Bureau of Labor Statistics. 2017. "Trends among Native- and Foreign-Origin Workers in U.S. Computer Industries." *Monthly Labor Review* (December 2017). https://www.bls.gov/opub/mlr/2017/article/trends-among-native-and-foreign-origin-workers-in-us-computer-industries.htm.

U.S. Bureau of Labor Statistics. 2019. *Employment Projections: 2018–2028*. https://www.bls.gov/news.release/pdf/ecopro.pdf.

U.S. Bureau of the Census. 2019. *Annual Population Estimates, Estimated Components of Resident Population Change, and Rates of the Components of Resident Population Change for the United States, and Puerto Rico: April 1, 2010 to July 1, 2019*. https://www.census.gov/data/tables/time-series/demo/popest/2010s-state-total.html.

———. 2020. *Population, Population Change, and Estimated Components of Population Change: April 1, 2010 to July 1, 2019* (NST-EST2019-alldata). https://www.census.gov/data/tables/time-series/demo/popest/2010s-national-total.html.

U.S. Department of Homeland Security. 2019a. *Green Card Processes and Procedures: Public Charge*. https://www.uscis.gov/greencard/public-charge.

———. 2019b. *Inadmissibility on Public Charge Grounds*. https://www.federalregister.gov/documents/2019/08/14/2019-17142/inadmissibility-on-public-charge-grounds.

U.S. District Court for the Northern District of California. 2019. *State of California, District of Columbia, State of Maine, Commonwealth of Pennsylvania, and State of Oregon v. US Department of Homeland Security, Kevin McAleenan, US Citizenship and Immigration Services, and Kenneth T. Cuccinelli*. https://oag.ca.gov/system/files/attachments/press-docs/Public%20Charge%20Complaint.pdf.

Ueda, Reed. 1980. "Naturalization and Citizenship." In *Harvard Encyclopedia of American Ethnic Groups*, edited by Stephan Thernstrom, Ann Orlov, and Oscar Handlin, 734–48. Cambridge, MA: Belknap Press.

Valentino, Nicholas, Ted Brader, and A. E. Jardina. 2013. "Immigration Opposition among U.S. Whites: General Ethnocentrism or Media Priming of Attitudes about Latinos?" *Political Psychology* 34:149–66.

Valenzuela, Abel. 1999. "Gender Roles and Settlement Activities among Children and Their Immigrant Families." *American Behavioral Scientist* 42 (4): 702–42.

van der Meer, Tom, and Jochem Tolsma. 2014. "Ethnic Diversity and Its Effects on Social Cohesion." *Annual Review of Sociology* 40:459–78.

Vara, Vauhini. 2015. "How California Bested Texas." *New Yorker,* January 9, 2015. https://www.newyorker.com/business/currency/california-bested-texas.

Varsanyi, Monica, ed. 2010. *Taking Local Control: Immigration Policy Activism in U.S. Cities and States.* Stanford, CA: Stanford University Press.

Vellos, Diana. 1996. "Immigrant Latina Domestic Workers and Sexual Harassment." *American University Journal of Gender and the Law* 5:407–32.

Viladrich, Anahí. 2012. "Beyond Welfare Reform: Reframing Undocumented Immigrants' Entitlement to Health Care in the United States, a Critical Review." *Social Science & Medicine* 74 (6): 822–29. https://doi.org/10.1016/j.socscimed.2011.05.050.

Villazor, Rose Cuison, and Pratheepan Gulasekaram. 2018. "Sanctuary Networks." *Minnesota Law Review* 103:1209–83.

Wadhwa, Vivek. 2009. "A Reverse Brain Drain." *Issues in Science and Technology* 25 (3): 45–52.

Wadhwa, Vivek, Ben Rissing, AnnaLee Saxenian, and Gary Gereffi. 2007. "Education, Entrepreneurship and Immigration: America's New Immigrant Entrepreneurs, Part II." *SSRN* (June 11, 2007). Available for download at https://dx.doi.org/10.2139/ssrn.991327.

Wallace, Steven P., and Maria Elena de Trinidad Young. 2018. "Immigration versus Immigrant: The Cycle of Anti-Immigrant Policies." *American Journal of Public Health* 108 (4): 436–37. https://doi.org/10.2105/ajph.2018.304328.

Walsh, Diana. 1996. "Bold Plan to Let Noncitizens Vote on School Items." *SFGate,* February 6, 1996. http://www.sfgate.com/news/article/Bold-plan-to-let-noncitizens-vote-on-school-items-3159327.php.

Walsh, Jess. 1999. "Laboring at the Margins: Welfare and the Regulation of Mexican Workers in Southern California." *Antipode* 31 (4): 398–420. https://doi.org/10.1111/1467-8330.00111.

Walshok, Mary Lindenstein, and Abraham Shragge. 2013. *Invention and Reinvention: The Evolution of San Diego's Innovation Economy.* Stanford, CA: Stanford Business Books.

Waters, Mary C., and Tomás Jiménez. 2005. "Assessing Immigrant Assimilation: New Empirical and Theoretical Challenges." *Annual Review of Sociology* 31:105–25.

Waters, Mary C., and Marisa Gerstein Pineau, eds. 2015. *The Integration of Immigrants into American Society.* Washington, DC: National Academies Press. Available for download at https://doi.org/10.17226/21746.

Weil, Alan R. 2018. "California: Leading the Way?" *Health Affairs (Millwood)* 37 (9): 1351. https://doi.org/10.1377/hlthaff.2018.1047.

Weil, David. 2012. "'Broken Windows,' Vulnerable Workers, and the Future of Worker Representation." *Forum* 10 (1). https://doi.org/10.1515/1540–8884.1493.

Wessler, Seth Freed. 2018. "Is Denaturalization the Next Front in the Trump Administration's War on Immigration?" *New York Times Magazine*, December 19, 2018. https://www.nytimes.com/2018/12/19/magazine/naturalized-citizenship-immigration-trump.html.

Wherry, Laura R., Genevieve M. Kenney, and Benjamin D. Sommers. 2016. "The Role of Public Health Insurance in Reducing Child Poverty." *Academic Pediatrics* 16 (3 Suppl): S98–S104. https://doi.org/10.1016/j.acap.2015.12.011.

White, Michael J., and Gayle Kaufman. 1997. "Language Usage, Social Capital, and School Completion among Immigrants and Native-Born Ethnic Groups." *Social Science Quarterly* 78 (2): 385–98.

Whitley, Richard. 2006. "Project-Based Firms: New Organizational Form or Variations on a Theme?" *Industrial and Corporate Change* 15 (1): 77–99.

Wilcox, Clyde, Lee Sigelman, and Elizabeth Cook. 1989. "Some Like It Hot: Individual Differences in Responses to Group Feeling Thermometers." *Public Opinion Quarterly* 53:246–57.

Williams, Wendy. 2005. "Model Enforcement of Wage and Hour Laws for Undocumented Workers: One Step Closer to Equal Protection under the Law." *Columbia Human Rights Law Review* 37:755–86.

Wlezien, Christopher. 2005. "On the Salience of Political Issues: The Problem with 'Most Important Problem.'" *Electoral Studies* 24:555–79.

Woetzel, Jonathan, Jan Mischke, Shannon Peloquin, and Daniel Weisfield. 2016. *A Tool Kit to Close California's Housing Gap: 3.5 Million Homes by 2025*. Los Angeles: McKinsey Global Institute. https://www.mckinsey.com/featured-insights/urbanization/closing-californias-housing-gap.

Wong, Janelle, S. Karthick Ramakrishnan, Taeku Lee, and Jane Junn. 2011. *Asian American Political Participation: Emerging Constituents and Their Political Identities*. New York: Russell Sage Foundation.

Wong, Janelle, and Vivian Tseng. 2007. "Political Socialisation in Immigrant Families: Challenging Top-Down Parental Socialisation Models." *Journal of Ethnic and Migration Studies* 34 (1): 151–68.

Wong, Tom K. 2012. "287(g) and the Politics of Interior Immigration Control in the United States: Explaining Local Cooperation with Federal Immigration Authorities." *Journal of Ethnic and Migration Studies* 38 (5): 737–56.

———. 2016. *The Politics of Immigration: Partisanship, Demographic Change, and American National Identity*. New York: Oxford University Press.

Wright, Lawrence. 2017. "America's Future Is Texas." *New Yorker*, July 10, 2017. https://www.newyorker.com/magazine/2017/07/10/americas-future-is-texas.

———. 2018. *God Save Texas: A Journey into the Soul of the Lone Star State*. New York: Knopf.

Wright, Robert J. 2010. *Multifaceted Assessment for Early Childhood Education*. Thousand Oaks, CA: SAGE.

Yoo, Chol, Gilbert C. Gee, and David Takeuchi. 2009. "Discrimination and Health among Asian American Immigrants: Disentangling Racial from Language Discrimination." *Social Science and Medicine* 68 (4): 726–32.

Yoo, Grace J. 2008. "Immigrants and Welfare: Policy Constructions of Deservingness." *Journal of Immigrant & Refugee Studies* 6 (4): 490–507.

Youniss, James, Jeffrey A. McLellan, Miranda Yates. 1997. "What We Know about Engendering Civic Identity." *American Behavioral Scientist* 40 (50): 620–31.

Yu, Stella M., Zhihuan J. Huang, Renee H. Schwalberg, Mary Overpeck, and Michael D. Kogan. 2003. "Acculturation and the Health and Well-Being of U.S. Immigrant Adolescents." *Journal of Adolescent Health* 33 (6): 479–88.

Zaller, John R. 1992. *The Nature and Origins of Mass Opinion*. New York: Cambridge University Press.

Zallman, Leah, Karen E. Finnegan, David U. Himmelstein, Sharon Touw, and Steffie Woolhandler. 2019a. "Care for America's Elderly and Disabled People Relies on Immigrant Labor." *Health Affairs (Millwood)* 38 (6): 919–26. https://doi.org/10.1377/hlthaff.2018.05514.

———. 2019b. "Implications of Changing Public Charge Immigration Rules for Children Who Need Medical Care." *JAMA Pediatrics* 173 (9): e191744. https://doi.org/10.1001/jamapediatrics.2019.1744.

Zallman, Leah, Steffie Woolhandler, Sharon Touw, David U. Himmelstein, and Karen E. Finnegan. 2018. "Immigrants Pay More in Private Insurance Premiums Than They Receive in Benefits." *Health Affairs (Millwood)* 37 (10): 1663–68. https://doi.org/10.1377/hlthaff.2018.0309.

Zhang, Wei, Seunghye Hong, David T. Takeuchi, and Krysia N. Mossakowski. 2012. "Limited English Proficiency and Psychological Distress among Latinos and Asian Americans." *Social Science and Medicine* 75 (6): 1006–14.

Zhou, Min, Jennifer Lee, Jody Agius Vallejo, Rosaura Tafoya-Estrada, and Xiong Yang Sao. 2008. "Success Attained, Deterred, and Denied: Divergent Pathways to Social Mobility in Los Angeles's New Second Generation." *ANNALS of the American Academy of Political and Social Science* 620 (1): 37–61. https://doi.org/10.1177/0002716208322586.

Ziol-Guest, Kathleen M., and Ariel Kalil. 2012. "Health and Medical Care among the Children of Immigrants." *Child Development* 83 (5): 1494–500. https://doi.org/10.1111/j.1467–8624.2012.01795.x.

Zolberg, Aristide R. 2006. *A Nation by Design: Immigration Policy in the Fashioning of America*. Cambridge, MA: Harvard University Press.

Zuk, Miriam, and Karen Chapple. 2016. *Housing Production, Filtering and Displacement: Untangling the Relationships*. Institute of Governmental Studies, University of California, Berkeley.

Index

The authorized representative in the EU for product safety and compliance is:
Mare Nostrum Group
B.V Doelen 72
4831 GR Breda
The Netherlands

www.ingramcontent.com/pod-product-compliance
Lightning Source LLC
Chambersburg PA
CBHW030730280326
41926CB00086B/1024